THE BLACK MEGACHURCH

THE BLACK MEGACHURCH

Theology, Gender, and the Politics of Public Engagement

Tamelyn N. Tucker-Worgs

BAYLOR UNIVERSITY PRESS

Cover Design by Cynthia Dunne, Blue Farm Graphics
Cover Image © iStockphoto.com / Richard Goerg

Library of Congress Cataloging-in-Publication Data

Tucker-Worgs, Tamelyn, 1971–
The Black megachurch : theology, gender, and the politics of public
engagement / Tamelyn Tucker-Worgs
275 p. cm.
Includes bibliographical references (p. 223) and index.
ISBN 978-1-932792-74-4 (hardback : alk. paper)
1. African American churches. 2. Big churches--United States. I. Title.
BR563.N4T83 2011
277.3'08996073--dc22
                    2010053039

Printed in the United States of America on acid-free paper with a minimum of
30% pcw recycled content.

This book is dedicated to
"Nana" Georgia Patterson Conner
and in loving memory of
"Papa" Hugh Lee Conner (1912–2006)

TABLE OF CONTENTS

LIST OF TABLES

LIST OF FIGURES

ACKNOWLEDGMENTS

When I arrived in Prince George's County, Maryland, ready to start my graduate career, I began the process of looking for a church home away from home. This entailed visiting a different church each week, or "church hopping" as some call it. A couple of my fellow graduate students and I would go from church to church, "shopping," trying to see what was the best fit. I had engaged in church hopping before when I first went away to college, but this time it was different. This time I became addicted to the church hopping experience. I was simply amazed by the numbers of extremely large black churches that dotted D.C. and its surrounding suburbs. These churches were different from those I had attended back home. First of all, they seemed to be open twenty-four hours a day, seven days a week, and they seemed to have "ministries" that fulfilled every need one could possibly imagine. Furthermore, the ministers did not shy away from preaching about thisworldly and relevant topics that covered anything from one's love life to one's pocketbook. And there were so many people who attended them each week. I was surprised to find that the congregations primarily consisted of young people—young families and single people—not older women with a sprinkling of men (which was what I was used to). Some friends and I used to say, "Black people in Prince Georges County sure do love church!"

These black megachurches were exciting, and attending them was like going to a show or an event. After a while, though, the excitement about the spectacle of the megachurch began to wear off. Yet I remained intrigued by the phenomenon and began to think about a series of questions. I began to ask myself, is this right? Should churches be so entertaining? Should they be housed in such grand edifices? Should they display such opulence and wealth? They seemed to be engaged in the community, but how much? And was it in proportion to the resources that they had amassed? As a political scientist I began to question the political implications of the phenomenon, particularly the implication for black politics. It was here that my journey to understand the black megachurch phenomenon's impact on black public life began.

There are so many people to thank for this project. At the top of the list is the late Linda Faye Williams, my teacher, mentor, and dissertation advisor who was there from the beginning of this project and who undoubtedly had a major impact on the final product. When I approached her with my topic—which was a bit out of the ordinary for a political scientist—she assured me that it was an important phenomenon that needed to be studied and that I was the one to do it. It really meant a lot to me that someone of her stature, intellect, and integrity displayed so much confidence in my work. Dr. Williams was the "academic mother" to many of us graduate students at the University of Maryland, College Park in the late 1990s. She nurtured, reprimanded, protected, defended, and loved us. Beyond that, she provided a model for how to be a scholar. Her ethic about her own scholarship, which was not merely to perform intellectual gymnastics but to engage in important scholarship in an attempt to "make a better world," presented to me a model for the kind of scholar, teacher, and mentor that I want to be. I cannot help but to hope that she is proud of this work.

When I started this project as a dissertation I was fortunate to be surrounded by a community of graduate students who started as colleagues and professional acquaintances but became like family. I would like to express my deepest gratitude to Wendy Smooth, Yusifu Bangura, Erika Gordon, Cedric Johnson, Sekile Nzinga Johnson, Avis Jones-DeWeever, Guy DeWeever, Donn Worgs, Adolphus Belk, Bill Hennif, Guichard Cadet, Circe Stumbo, Lorrie Frasure, Chris Whitt, C. Nicole Mason, and Gloria Anglon for the community that we created. I truly appreciate the late-night work sessions, mock presentations, and deep discussions that helped me to iron out my ideas and forced me to clarify my questions and eventually my conclusions.

Many people at the University of Maryland were integral to the formation of this project. I would like to thank Ronald Walters, Clarence Stone, Ollie

Johnson, Lynn Bolles, and Wayne MacIntosh, who all served on my dissertation committee and provided suggestions that assisted in transitioning the manuscript from a dissertation to a book. I would also like to thank Johnetta Davis and the Office of Graduate Minority Education, the Committee on Africa and the Americas, and the African American Leadership Institute for financial support of this project in its early stages.

I want to especially express my deepest gratitude to the late Ronald Walters for the guidance he provided to me in my study of the black church and black politics. Our work together on black churches in D.C. was a wonderful learning experience that I truly appreciate. Even at the end of my writing of the book, Dr. Walters was still opening doors for me. Ministers who respected him and his work gave me access because I was his student. His generous spirit and legacy of good works reverberate more than we will ever know.

I wish to thank R. Drew Smith for the opportunity to collaborate and the opportunity to work on the Public Influences of the African American Church Project (PIAACP). The PIAACP experience especially provided me with the wonderful chance to interact with others studying comparable issues, which helped me to put my work into a broader context. I would also like to thank Lawrence Mamiya who encouraged my participation in the Project 2000 survey and was there periodically to support my work and to give advice.

I am grateful to those others who read portions of the manuscript, shared their work, and gave me feedback that helped to sharpen my thinking about the topic. For this I want to thank Michael Leo Owens, Allison Calhoun-Brown, Cheryl Sanders, Frederick Harris, Shayne Lee, Scott Thumma and Dorith Grant-Wisdom. I also wish to express my deep gratitude to Hoda Zaki, my professor at Hampton University, who is now my colleague at Hood College.

I would like to thank Carey Newman and Baylor University Press for supporting the project and seeing it through. I wish to thank the anonymous reviewers for reading the manuscript and providing insight that helped a great deal when revising the manuscript.

I also wish to thank my colleagues, friends, and students at Hood College. I especially thank my colleagues in the Political Science Department and the Hood students who took my courses, "Politics of the Black Church" and "Black Theology," where a number of my arguments were worked out. I also want to acknowledge the research assistance of three undergraduate students, Brittany Owens, John Love, and Aziza Jones, in addition to Susan Day in Faculty Services. I would like to thank the Hood College Board of Associates for financial support of this project through a number of summer research grants.

I want to express my deepest gratitude to those whom I interviewed for this project including church members, pastors and assistant ministers, church administrators, executive directors of megachurch-affiliated community-based organizations, as well as all of the lay critics and supporters of black megachurches. I would especially like to thank Rev. Alice Davis, Rev. H. Beecher Hicks, Rev. Harold Carter Sr., and Rev. Willie Wilson who all talked to me at length about their own churches and the black church in general, which gave me better insight. I would also like to thank Rev. Jerome Stephens for sharing his sagacious wisdom on black churches and politics and also for facilitating several interviews with black megachurch pastors.

There were many friends and family who helped to facilitate my research in various ways including giving advice and encouragement, listening to my ideas, sharing their black megachurch experiences, providing critiques, and welcoming me as a house guest while I was in town to visit a local black megachurch. For this I would like to thank Donald Conner, Nelda Conner Lewis, Leon and Celika Caldwell, Elaine Bonner-Tompkins, Sterling Ashby, Renel Lewis Jenkins, Bryan Jenkins, Harold Mitchell, Ronda Lewis, Taneka Shehee, Chante' Merritt, Donita Conner Bessard, Ronald Lewis, Nicole Jackson, Alfreda Bell, Glenn and Shaundra Myers, and Shandra Cushingberry.

This project could not have been completed without the support and encouragement of my family. I would like to express my deepest gratitude to my aunt, the late Callie McPherson, as well as to the McPherson family, the Conner family, and the Worgs family. I would like to especially thank my mother-in-law Una Worgs for the child care that gave me time to write.

I wish to thank my brilliant and talented sisters, Kaylen Tucker and Leslie Perkins. Leslie and her husband Michael have provided constant support and encouragement, and spending time with them and their family has been a great joy.

I want to express my deepest gratitude to my sister Kaylen for all the help that she gave me while writing this book. I appreciate her for always being supportive in so many ways including sharing her considerable editing skills, listening to ideas, visiting churches with me, babysitting my children, and reading and commenting on a great portion of the manuscript.

My mother, Sandra Conner Tucker, and father, Henry Edward Tucker Jr., have been a constant source of support throughout this process, and I truly appreciate it. They watched children, provided financial aid, gave counsel, and provided us with a summer vacation spot and me with a writing retreat location. I am deeply grateful to my mother (who for the past several years has been a revolutionary Sunday school teacher) for instilling in me concerns about social justice and what the role of the church *ought* to be. I am grateful to my father for his unwavering confidence in me.

I would also like to thank my children, Kamel and Kamaria, who were patient as I engaged in what I'm sure to them seemed a never-ending project. But not only were they patient, they really became involved in this quest to understand black megachurches—making it clear that it was "our" book. They asked a million brilliant questions about the churches and the book writing process and cheered for me when I was done.

Finally, this book about black megachurches would not have been written if not for the help and support of Donn Worgs, and truly this book may as well have been coauthored. I want to thank Donn for being my best friend, most loving critic, and partner in life for over ten years. I am truly grateful to Donn for reading and commenting on the book in its entirety, encouraging me and pushing me when I needed it, and taking over my share of family work and duties to give me time to work on the book.

As I acknowledge here, many have contributed to the conceptualizing and writing of this book. I, however, of course take total responsibility for any omissions or mistakes. If there are those whom I have failed to thank, please charge it to my head and not my heart.

This book is dedicated to my grandparents Georgia Patterson Conner and Hugh Lee Conner. Through most of the writing of this book Nana and Papa were both there cheering me, bragging about me, and supporting me. Papa did not live to see the end of this book but nonetheless always had faith that there would be an end. The lessons that they shared about how to live a long fruitful life while loving your friends, family, and community helped me to keep everything in perspective, and for these lessons I am forever grateful.

Chapter 1

INTRODUCTION
Answering the Knock at Midnight

The church must be reminded that it is not the master or the servant of the state, but rather the conscience of the state. It must be the guide and the critic of the state, and never its tool. If the church does not recapture its prophetic zeal, it will become an irrelevant social club without moral or spiritual authority. If the church does not participate actively in the struggle for peace and for economic and racial justice, it will forfeit the loyalty of millions and cause men everywhere to say that it has atrophied its will. But if the church will free itself from the shackles of a deadening status quo, and recovering its great historic mission, will speak and act fearlessly and insistently in terms of justice and peace, it will enkindle the imagination of mankind and fire the souls of men, imbuing them with a glowing and ardent love for truth, justice and peace. Men far and near will know the church as a great fellowship of love that provides light and bread for lonely travelers at midnight.

—Martin Luther King Jr., "A Knock at Midnight" (1963)

In his 1963 sermon "A Knock at Midnight," Martin Luther King Jr. delivered one of his most concise yet complex statements about the role of the church in public life. The sermon provided both a critique of the role churches were

1

playing and a normative statement about the role they should play. Referring to Jesus' parable, King pondered how the church should respond when a man knocks on the door of the church asking for bread at midnight. The "man" of course refers to people in need. The midnight hour—the deepest, darkest hour of the night—symbolizes the time of most urgent need. Delivering this sermon in 1963, in the midst of the civil rights revolution, King described many different "midnights," both collective and individual: the midnight of racial oppression, the midnight of war, the midnight of economic deprivation, the midnight of the moral order, and the midnight of despair.

It is clear from his sermon that King viewed most churches as failing to respond to human need. White churches in the United States resistant to civil rights advances answered the knock with "cold indifference or blatant hypocrisy" instead of the bread of justice and freedom. And black churches did not escape King's critique. He noted that "many so-called Negro churches also failed to feed the lonely traveler." He said that there were two kinds of black churches that failed to answer the knock—the type that "burns with emotionalism" and the type that "freezes with classism." These churches had "neither the vitality nor the relevant gospel to feed hungry souls."[1]

"A Knock at Midnight" was a call to action for the church—a normative statement about the role the church should play in public life. Churches should be activist and not apolitical. They should engage in public life to meet human need, but they should do so not as "master or servant of the state" but as the state's "guide and critic." The church should also provide hope and assurance that things will eventually get better. King noted that the churches themselves should be reminded of the Negro spiritual "I'm So Glad Trouble Don't Last Always."[2]

In the more than forty years since Martin Luther King Jr. challenged the church to progressively engage public life, American society has changed. For African Americans the positive impact of the civil rights revolution is undeniable. The opening of the electoral system resulted in the drastically increased number of black elected officials—including the election of Barack Obama as the first African American president of the United States. The number of blacks who graduate high school and finish college has also drastically increased, and the fruits of the Civil Rights Movement include an expanded black middle class.

Related to this expanded middle class there is also a change in the landscape of black churches—the development of the black megachurch. These black megachurches, some of which feature seating for ten to twenty thousand people, multi-million-dollar business enterprises, and opulence, display wealth and luxury that surprise even the most ardent critics.

But even with all these signs of progress it is clear it is still midnight for many African Americans. Persistent racial disparities in health, housing, education, employment, incarceration, household income, and mortality indicate what the disproportionately black victims of Hurricane Katrina made obviously clear. While parts of black America are doing better, much of black America is doing worse.

In assessing the current state of affairs, King would likely judge the megachurch phenomenon by the same standards that he judged the church of his day. He would be concerned about whether the black megachurch is answering the knock at midnight. Certainly these new black megachurches present the potential to engage in politics and public life even more so than the average church. These churches have large membership bases that potentially give them a greater number of volunteers and access to greater amounts of financial and other resources. But writing at a time in which globally the Christian church was increasing in membership, King expressed a note of skepticism about large congregations, claiming that "[a]n increase in quantity does not automatically bring an increase in quality. A larger membership does not necessarily represent a correspondingly increased commitment to Christ." He added that "Jumboism . . . is an utterly fallacious standard for measuring positive power."[3]

Yet despite this skepticism, King also expressed hope in the possibility that the church could make things better. He noted,

> Although a numerical growth in membership does not necessarily reflect a concomitant increase in ethical commitment, millions of people do feel that the church provides an answer to the deep confusion that encompasses their lives. It is still the one familiar landmark where the weary traveler by midnight comes. It is the one house which stands where it has always stood, the house to which the man travelling at midnight either comes or refuses to come. Some decide not to come. But the many who come and knock are desperately seeking a little bread to tide them over.[4]

Are black megachurches answering the knock at midnight? Are they attempting to provide the social and political bread that black communities need? Are they trying to provide the "bread of freedom" or economic justice that King spoke of? I attempt to answer these questions and others as I explore the black megachurch phenomenon and the role that black megachurches are playing in African American public life.

In this introductory chapter I first lay out the book's argument and then contextualize the study—historically and theoretically. I end the introduction with a description of the chapters to follow and a discussion of how they fit into the book's overall argument.

Black Megachurches in Public Life

There has been much said and written about the black megachurch but surprisingly little that has been informed by intensive empirical research on the phenomenon. Some important and significant insights have been presented based upon case studies or small studies of a handful of churches but none thus far that have captured a picture of the phenomenon in its entirety. This book is the culmination of the only comprehensive study of the black megachurch to date. Utilizing surveys of church leaders, dozens of interviews, site visits, analyses of sermons, church documents, mission statements, and other records, I have garnered a wealth of information from which to both paint a picture of the black megachurch phenomenon in the United States and address the question of whether black megachurches are trying to meet the challenges facing black communities in the post–civil rights era.

This book argues that, like the storefront churches of the early twentieth century fulfilled the socioreligious needs of black migrants from the South, black megachurches fulfill the needs of the new black middle-class suburbanites. Black megachurches are "thisworldly" churches, are relevant to the "here and now," and generally participate in public life. But their participation cannot be painted with one broad brushstroke—as there is considerable variation. Some black megachurches are engaged in extensive public activities that one might consider "answering the knock at midnight"—others make little if any attempt to meet the most urgent challenges. The megachurches' theological orientations or underlying theological tenets provide the motives for their public engagement, and distinct strands are noticeable and related to how they participate in public life. Furthermore, among the "activist" churches (those aggressively engaged in trying to solve the problems facing black communities) we see that their strategies for trying to address these problems reflect the emergence of an expanded repertoire of political behavior that emphasizes a community development approach. Their public engagement activities are also influenced by the gendered division of labor in black churches and women's overparticipation in church work.

The evolution of the black megachurch is a distinct post-1980 phenomenon. These churches fulfill a religious niche created by the 1980s–1990s black suburban migrants. The megachurches offer this transplanted population a religious experience that is accessible, professional, and relevant to their everyday lives. Through their various ministries and programs black megachurches also cater to the consumer-like needs of the expanded black middle class. These churches also give their members an opportunity to engage in civil society.

While the churches have the above characteristics in common, they vary in terms of their founding dates, sizes, denominations, and public engagement activities. They also vary in terms of their theological orientations—or the basic tenets about the identity of God and what the role of the church in the world should be. The theological orientations of the churches actually serve as the motive for their public engagement, so that the varied theological orientations result in varied public engagement activities.

The activist black megachurches are not engaging public life primarily through electoral or protest politics—which is the way activist black churches distinguished themselves in the civil rights and pre–civil rights era. Instead, the community development approach—providing actual goods and services and measurable physical improvements to revitalize communities (and often collaborating with government to do so) has become a very important part of the expanded repertoire for how black megachurches engage in public life. This is reflected in the high frequency of black-megachurch-affiliated community development organizations (CDOs), which the majority of black megachurches have formed.

The public engagement activities of black megachurches are also influenced by the gendered division of labor in black megachurches. Traditionally black women have been responsible for the "outreach" or "public arm" of the black church, and black megachurch public engagement reflects this. Women disproportionately lead black megachurch CDOs (when compared to CDOs in general). Furthermore, black megachurch CDOs most resemble women-led CDOs in their approaches toward community development and the programs that they establish.

There are political implications of the "activist" black megachurch's increasing focus on the community development strategy. The black megachurch that engages in electoral politics and the occasional black megachurch that participates in protest politics are also the ones most likely to do community development. These churches have to make important decisions about where to best use their resources and sometimes have to make important trade-offs. This is complicated by the fact that churches have limited political capital—so that engaging in one type of activity limits how much a church can engage in another.

This can become particularly problematic when it comes to making decisions about whether to challenge the status quo. When black megachurches engage in community development projects that entail collaboration with government and therefore compete for municipal and federal grants, this may limit their ability to carry out Martin Luther King Jr.'s charge to be the "guide and critic" of government and not the "tool" of government.

Martin Luther King Jr.'s vision of the publically involved black church, one that is not stifled by "classism" or "emotionalism," one that is not an "agent of the state," and one that works for social and economic justice, is difficult to achieve. This is the case even for the several black megachurches that are "activist" churches—those that believe that it is a part of their mission to engage the political world and to do so on behalf of the most vulnerable of society. The challenge is to determine the best strategy that will allow these churches to work progressively to increase social, political, and economic justice.

Contextualizing the Study

Since 1980 at least 149 black megachurches have developed across the United States. These churches are physical marvels with their enormous campuses and sanctuaries that seat several thousand worshipers. Some of them boast of recording studios, fitness centers, and helicopters to transport their ministers from one side of town to the other. Beyond the edifice, megachurches offer a wide range of activities and ministries for their flocks to participate in. These black churches that have from two thousand to as many as seventeen thousand people attending Sunday services have emerged all across the nation wherever African Americans (especially suburbanites) are found in high population density. Despite the size of the sanctuaries, come late to a megachurch Sunday morning service and you just might not get a seat. These churches usually have several "overflow rooms" to accommodate those who do not get a seat in the main sanctuary and utilize closed-circuit televisions and video screens that broadcast the activities in their main sanctuaries. Despite arguments that Americans have decreased their civic affiliations, black megachurch growth patterns indicate that there are signs of further expansion, not decline.

The black megachurch phenomenon has not gone unnoticed. Lay observers and academics alike have vehemently debated the significance of the black megachurch's role in public life, but with few exceptions this debate has been without the benefit of much empirical data. One exception is the work of Sociologist Shayne Lee, who has written a book about probably the most famous of black megachurch ministers—Bishop T. D. Jakes. Lee calls Jakes "America's new

preacher" and argues that Jakes is at the forefront of a movement in the black
church and American Protestantism that is characterized by the production of
"spiritual commodities" and the mass appeal that they create.[5] One other exception is the work of Jonathan Walton, who writes about black televangelism and
focuses on three black televangelists who also pastor black megachurches. He
teases out the differences among the theological orientations, political orientations, and social thought of these "religious broadcasters" and shows that they
are not monolithic.[6]

A few other examinations have produced case studies of black megachurches in the context of larger black church studies (Lincoln and Mamiya;
Gilkes; Billingsley; Mamiya; and Owens). Others have theorized about the
impact on African American politics of black megachurches preaching the
prosperity gospel (a theological orientation that God will reward the faithful materially) and the impact of the prosperity gospel on African American
politics (Harris; Pinn; Harris-Lacewell). Very few have looked at black megachurches specifically and tried to shed some light on their role in public life
(Smith and Tucker-Worgs; Tucker-Worgs; and Hall-Russell). The new black
megachurch has not been studied comprehensively, however, and therefore is
frequently misunderstood.[7]

Journalistic sources have been more plentiful in addressing the significance
of the black megachurch phenomenon. In 1997 journalist Hamil Harris wrote
one of the first articles about the black megachurch phenomenon. It was pub-
lished in *Emerge Magazine* and included a list of churches. Since then there
have been a number of articles in national papers as well as in magazines like
Ebony and *Black Enterprise* that have featured black megachurches and black
megachurch ministers.[8]

From these accounts black megachurches are pointed to as both the best
and the worst of the "new" black churches in America. For example, advocates
of greater church-based participation in social service provision point to examples of "best practices" in faith-based community revitalization, often to black
megachurches like First African Methodist Episcopal Church in Los Angeles or
Abyssinian Baptist Church in New York, both of which have engaged in extensive community revitalization projects like developing affordable housing.[9]

While black megachurches are sometimes pointed to for their efforts in
community revitalization and civic engagement they are more often held up as
evidence that the black church has *lost* its prophetic voice. Critics argue that the
post–civil rights black church has lost the will to facilitate civic engagement or
community revitalization and thus has lost its relevance to black communities.

The black megachurch is at the center of this indictment. The jets, mansions, expensive cars, and high-profile celebrity statuses of several megachurch pastors cause some to accuse these church leaders of fleecing their many congregants for their own benefit. To many observers, the megachurch appears as the bastion for capitalist exploitation and the center of the controversial "prosperity gospel" theology. Political activist Rev. Al Sharpton summed up the critique of prosperity gospel ministers when he said, "They make people feel good but don't have people doing better. People that are in shackles don't need people to anoint their shackles. Many of us treat church like a Sunday jackpot, hoping you get some material blessing from God, like some wheel in Las Vegas."[10]

Black megachurches are accused of using space and resources in black communities that could be used for legitimate community revitalization, while not really engaging in any worthwhile community revitalization or community advocacy efforts, bringing to question their relevance to communities that face a number of social, political, and economic challenges. Perhaps the comments of Rev. Freddie Haynes, a megachurch minister who is critical of other megachurches, sums up this sentiment best. He claims that "[t]he message of many churches has been co-opted by American capitalism" and asserts that "[a] megachurch should not just be known for the traffic jam it creates on Sunday, but for doing something more in the community."[11] Many have concluded that most black megachurches have adopted the gospel of prosperity and have strayed from the social gospel tradition of the black church.

Students of the black religious experience in America will not be surprised that there are these divergent opinions about the black megachurch. Scholars of the black church have historically debated the role that these churches play in public life. This begs a historical perspective. What has been the public tradition of the black church? Next I turn to a historical perspective of the role of black churches in public life, which helps to put the current situation in context.

The Black Church in Public Life, a Historical and Theoretical Perspective

Religion, specifically Christianity, has been found to have served a number of functions during the period of American slavery. On one hand it was used by slaveholders to justify the institution of slavery and support this institution by pacifying the enslaved Africans, helping in the "deculturation process" that they were subjected to and helping to "create uniformity among peoples of diverse cultural backgrounds."[12] Those who used the Bible to justify slavery would often quote the Pauline letters. A favorite of course was Ephesians 6:5, which reads, "Slaves, obey your earthly masters with fear and trembling, in singleness of heart, as you obey Christ."[13]

On the other hand Christianity was also used by abolitionists to argue that slavery was wrong. For example, Maria Stewart, the free black woman abolitionist, argued in her "Address to Friends in Boston" that her religious faith implored her to speak against slavery. Even among whites, religious groups like the Methodists and Quakers were known to have opposed slavery, and the Methodist conferences in the late 1700s "condemned slavery as contrary to the Christian gospel."[14]

It has also been argued that religion was mainly used as a refuge and for purposes of survival for the enslaved Africans themselves. For example, the religious songs that the enslaved people created—the spirituals or "sorrow songs," as Du Bois called them—often contained themes that promoted black humanity. This was in spite of the inhumane way that they were treated. The spirituals promoted the idea that everyone is equal according to God.[15]

Finally, religion also served to motivate people to revolt against the system of slavery. Major slave revolt leaders Nat Turner, Denmark Vesey, and Gabriel Prosser were all motivated by their religious beliefs.[16] Furthermore, several black ministers recruited for and fought in the Civil War. Henry McNeal Turner best exemplifies this—comingling religious and political aims. Turner was a black nationalist, an activist, and an African Methodist Episcopal (AME) bishop and he recruited black soldiers for the Union Army and also served as a chaplain in the Union Army. After the Civil War Turner actively promoted emigration to Africa for black people in America and also seriously raised the issue of reparations. Religious beliefs motivated these freedom fighters in their political activism against the system of slavery and the discrimination that followed.[17]

At the same time, the independent black church movement that was instigated in the northern United States in the late 1700s was yet another early illustration of the important role that black churches played in public life. This movement is said to have been sparked when Richard Allen and Absalom Jones led other blacks out of the integrated St. George's Methodist Episcopal Church in Philadelphia in protest to their maltreatment based on their race in the church. They had been "pulled from their knees during worship in a gallery they did not know was closed to black Christians."[18] In a context where black people were losing privileges and facing segregation during worship services and in which the Methodist church had softened its stance against slavery, the AME church was founded. By sparking the independent black church movement this "walkout" had very important political implications. The independence of black

churches is what made them so politically significant and unique. This political importance was probably understood by the Methodist power structure,
which actively discouraged Allen from forming a completely separate institution. The political importance was also attested to by the fact that even after the
Civil War ministers had trouble bringing the AME church to the South. Those
interested in maintaining the slavocracy were intent on limiting independent
black institutions.[19]

After the Civil War, during the period of Reconstruction, African American men exhibited a considerable amount of political freedom in comparison
to the previous period of enslavement. Black political participation resulted in
several black elected officials and their white Republican allies, a number not to
be seen again until after the Civil Rights Movement. The black church played a
key role. In the *History of the Negro Church*, Carter G. Woodson describes the
post–Civil War black church as not only the most independent black institution but also one in which the minister could not escape the lure of a political
life. Black ministers were often the most well prepared to accept political leadership roles and were in fact the ones to most often do so.[20]

The post-Reconstruction era brought the retraction of the newly gained
rights of black freedmen. With the removal of Union troops, white southerners
used strategies of terror, violence, and intimidation to take back state governments and put into law formal restrictions on black male and female citizenship that were not returned until after the Civil Rights Movement. During this
period black-church-based self-help initiatives were quite visible—particularly
due to the development of black women's auxiliaries, missionary groups, and
clubs that took on these functions.[21] Yet while many black churches were building schools and engaged in social welfare and self-help, most were not engaging in confrontational politics that challenged the status quo. Although the
self-help initiatives illustrated that many black churches were concerned about
everyday social issues, arguably they were "deradicalized."[22]

The post-Reconstruction, pre–civil rights movement black churches,
however, maintained an institutional centrality that led Carter G. Woodson
to describe the black church as the "all comprehending institution."[23] Mays and
Nicholson, despite being quite critical of the "Negro church" of the 1920s and
1930s, concluded that although black churches of this era were "static," "nonpro-
gressive," and not overwhelmingly protest centered, they had a certain "genius."
These churches were independent of white control, and their ministers were
relatively free to be politically and socially active on behalf of the "underprivi-
leged." According to Mays and Nicholson, the black minister was free to

condemn from his pulpit practices with respect to low wages, long hours, the working of children in industry, the unfair treatment of women in factories, the denying to the worker the right to organize and the injustices of an economic system built on competition, self interests, and profit—he is more likely not to be censured.[24]

The independence of the black church was essential to their potential to better the plight of black people in the United States.

The public role of the black church during the Civil Rights Movement is of course one of the clearest examples of the close relationship between the black church and politics. The politics of the *progressive* black church can, with some exceptions, be equated with the black politics of the day. Black churches provided leadership, resources, and motivation for participating in civil rights activity. The mass base of this movement is attributed to the black church.[25]

It is important to note, however, that even during the civil rights years, while black churches and black church leadership were at the forefront of the movement, *most black churches did not participate* in the movement. Charles Payne, for example, found that in the Mississippi Delta in some of the most repressive conditions, black women participated in civil rights activity *despite* the discouragement of their ministerial leaders, who warned them severely against letting the civil rights workers in their homes or participating in civil rights activities in any way.[26]

These contrasting observations of the black church during the Civil Rights Movement, either inspiring or discouraging civil rights activity, are excellent examples of the historical theoretical debate about the black church in public life—the liberator/opiate debate. Scholars have debated whether the black church served as a tool for the liberation of black people in the United States or, to the contrary, operated as a deterrent from liberation politics. In much of the scholarship about the black church's public role it has been characterized as either a liberator or, in Marxist terminology, an "opiate" used to pacify people and discourage them from activism.[27]

In the context of the Civil Rights Movement, Gary Marx authored the seminal work from the "opiate" perspective. He argued that religion deterred black people from civil rights militancy. He claimed that for black people religion promoted the idea that African Americans should not concern themselves with their situation here on earth and instead should wait for the "sweet by and by" where they would "get a crown" and "walk all over Heaven" with it.[28]

Malcolm X gave one of the most compelling explanations of the "opiate" sentiment in his autobiography. He said,

Christianity is the white man's religion. The Holy Bible in the white man's hands and his interpretations of it have been the greatest single ideological weapon for enslaving millions of non-white human beings. . . . The greatest miracle Christianity has achieved in America is that the black man in white Christian hands has not grown violent. It is a miracle that 22 million black people have not *risen up* against their oppressors—in which they would have been justified by all moral criteria, and even by the democratic tradition.[29]

The black church liberator/opiate debate did not begin with the Civil Rights Movement. E. Franklin Frazier gave probably one of the most stinging indictments against the black church before the modern Civil Rights Movement. In his work, *The Negro Church in America*, Frazier argued that the "Negro church" served to undermine intellectual thought and was the primary cause for the "so-called backwardness of the American Negro."[30] Frazier claimed that the organizational style of the "Negro church" was mimicked by other black organizations such as fraternities, educational institutions, and mutual aid societies. He saw the organizational structure of the black church as authoritarian, antidemocratic and led by various "petty tyrants." Therefore, it was precisely because the black church had been intimately involved in black life and because the black church was the most important institution in the black community that it was so dangerous. Frazier concluded that only through integration, which would allow blacks to be influenced by other organizational structures, could their organizations improve.[31]

After the Civil Rights Movement, the opiate critique resurfaced. For example, in *The Jesse Jackson Phenomenon*, Adolph Reed argued that the historical reference to the black church as a political mobilizer and a source of political leadership is an inaccurate reading of history. The church actually has served as an alternative to political participation and engagement. Reed claimed that the black church is by nature anticonfrontational and antipolitical and has served as a mechanism for social control more often than it has served in a political mobilizing role.[32]

Those writing after the Civil Rights Movement, however, have been more likely to describe the black church as an instrument for liberation.[33] Some have argued that the black church had been misjudged.[34] Others have argued that the Civil Rights Movement in fact changed the black church from an obstacle to the primary resource for black liberation.[35]

Black liberation theologians like James Cone have been at the forefront of those who have suggested that liberation is the major theme in black religion. After tracing the evolution of the black church from the "invisible institution" of the American slavery period to today's "African-American church," he concluded that "[l]iberation is the central core of the gospel as found in the scriptures and in the religious history of black Americans."[36]

Those who have looked at black religion as liberation oriented have argued that themes of protest and liberation in black religion can be found even as early as the "Negro spirituals" sung during slavery.[37] They have pointed to the "invisible institution" (gatherings of worship among the enslaved Africans that took place out of the view of the slave owners and overseers) as places where the enslaved Africans reaffirmed their humanity and worshiped in freedom and repeated and reinforced the liberation themes of Exodus in the Bible.[38] They have argued that these examples point to the vital role that black churches have traditionally played in public life.[39]

Beyond the Liberator/Opiate Dichotomy

Most of the recent studies about the role of black churches in public life go beyond the liberator/opiate dichotomy. Generally, these take the perspective that the interpretation of the black church as either liberator or opiate is much too simplistic, and instead of providing more insight they ignore the intricacies of the black church. Lincoln and Mamiya, for example, describe the black church in terms of six dialectical tensions that evolve but never synthesize (in the Hegelian sense).[40] Instead, these dialectical tensions can all exist to a various extent in any given church. They conclude that this perspective of the black church allows for the interpretation of the dynamic nature of the black church. It facilitates an examination of the black church as it responds to social conditions.[41]

Similarly, Baer and Singer conclude that black religion is "contradictory by nature."[42] They agree that it had been used to justify slavery, but at the same time it has been the inspiration for many black revolutionaries as African Americans "reworked Christianity" and used it to serve a number of needs.[43] They further show that the relationship between opiate and liberator is complicated. For example, although generally one would consider community outreach activities as being a part of a "liberation" tradition, Baer and Singer argue that they can sometimes serve an "accommodation" role. "In pursuing these activities, African American religion often exhibited an accommodative dimension by attempting to create an acquiescent space for blacks in a racist society, whether it was in the rural areas of the South or the cities of the North."[44]

Gayle Tate describes this apparent contradiction as the "duality of the black church" and argues that the black church attempts to both maintain aspects of the status quo and advocate for political change. However, these dual functions are not necessarily contradictory and may complement one another. She writes,

> By merging the quest for political emancipation with its otherworldly prom-
> ise the black church sustained its duality by serving the spiritual and earthly
> needs of an oppressed people. This dichotomy is not as great as it may appear.
> Heaven may be interpreted as the ultimate state of freedom, an extension
> of the earthly freedom quest. African Americans then could protest against
> their earthly oppression at the same time they soothed their souls.[45]

Evelyn Brooks Higginbotham (whom we will revisit in chapter 5) said that the relationship between black churches and public life is not "dialectical" (like Lincoln and Mamiya's claim) but "dialogic." For example, using a gender lens to examine the early black Baptist movement she shows that at the same time that women were being denied access to positions in the ministerial hierarchy, they were forming auxiliary groups and missionary societies where they developed leadership skills and had a profound impact on their communities. In other words, *at the same time* that they were accommodating the status quo they were also resisting it.[46]

Despite the various conclusions that scholars have come to about the nature of the black church in public life (e.g., that the essence of the church is as a liberator or an opiate or its duality and multiplicity), it is clear that the black church has been a central social, political, and cultural institution for African Americans. Recall that even E. Franklin Frazier, the fierce critic of the "Negro church," thought that it was precisely because of its unparalleled influence that the black church was so detrimental to the black community. More recently, several black church scholars have moved beyond the liberator/opiate debate by placing the public role of black religion squarely within the civic engagement and civil society discourse.[47] Next I examine the black church in this theoretical context.

Civic Engagement and the Multidimensional Black Church

Since Putnam drew attention to the connections among social capital, civic engagement, and democracy scholars have passionately debated the state of civic engagement and the ramifications for American democracy. These schol-ars have debated the importance of associations and networks for a thriving democracy. Generally they have argued that when people engage, join asso-ciations, and so on democracy is usually enhanced. On the other hand, when people do not engage, do not form organizations, and do not interact socially, democracy often suffers.[48]

One of the concerns in the civic engagement literature is the role of organizations of civil society like churches in enhancing or detracting from civic engagement. This is important because in the United States more time is spent in churches than in any other type of voluntary association or organization.[49] Studies of churches and civic engagement have concluded that churches generally facilitate civic engagement and enhance civil society.[50] Robert Wuthnow has identified several ways that religious involvement can enhance civic engagement. First, religious organizations can build social capital, "connections among individuals—social networks and the norms of reciprocity and trustworthiness that arise from them."[51] Second, religious organizations also define community by requiring affiliation and connection with other people. Third, religious organizations provide for the possibility of a "spillover effect" of volunteerism to other civic organizations from the religious organizations. Fourth, religious organizations teach transferable civic skills. Church members learn and develop skills like leadership, how to run a meeting, or how to embark upon and complete a project that they use when they participate in other organizations. Finally, religious organizations provide normative values of appropriate actions, for example whether or not one ought to participate in civic engagement.[52]

While much of the literature finds that religious organizations enhance civic engagement, some argue that instead of facilitating civic engagement there are some religious organizations that actually detract from it. For example, Kraig Beyerlein and John Hipp argue that religious organizations may promote normative values that counter civic participation. Furthermore, the social capital that religious organizations cultivate is not "necessarily advantageous for communities as a whole."[53] Beyerlein and Hipp make a distinction between developing "bridging social capital," which transfers skills from one organization to another, and "bonding social capital," which strengthens the social capital "within homogenous groups in communities."[54] They point to denominational affiliation as an important factor in determining whether a church will cultivate bridging or bonding capital.[55] They argue that participation in some religious organizations like black Protestant, mainline Protestant, and Catholic organizations builds "bridging social capital" while participation in evangelical Protestant organizations builds "bonding" social capital.[56]

Accordingly, Wuthnow argued that a decline in mainline denominational churches and rise of evangelical denominational churches may lead to the "depletion of the society's wider stock of social capital" because members of evangelical Protestant churches are less likely to hold membership in nonreligious organizations where they can transfer the civic skills learned in church.[57]

Participation in African American churches has been shown to build social capital, enhance electoral participation, and help to define community—especially "black group identification and black group consciousness."[58] Of course, not all black churches enhance civic engagement and promote political participation. Three factors, especially important for this study, (1) size of the church, (2) education level of the pastor, and (3) the church's theological orientation, have all been found to contribute to the level of black church civic engagement. Larger black churches are more likely to be involved in civic activities than smaller black churches. Wealthier black churches are more likely to be involved than less wealthy churches. Theologically conservative black churches are less likely than theologically liberal to be involved in civic activities. Black churches whose pastors have higher levels of education are likely to be more active in civic involvements than those whose pastors are less educated.[59]

In a national study of black church civic engagement, Smith and Smidt ranked various independent variables that influence black church civic involvement. They found that the minister's educational attainment was the most influential variable on black-church-based civic involvement, followed by congregational resources, social theology, and finally congregation size.[60]

A Frame for Understanding Black Churches in Public Life

While the civic engagement frame is helpful to understanding black churches in public life by helping us to understand why churches might or might not facilitate civic engagement, both Harris and Calhoun-Brown point out the challenges of applying the debates and concerns of the civic engagement literature to the black church. Calhoun-Brown writes, "Embedded in a large part of this literature is the assumption that participation in voluntary associations such as churches serves to reinforce the social order. Yet African American churches have been bases for challenging this order."[61] Black churches have on occasion served as spaces, resources, and motivation for revolutionary politics. Likewise, Harris emphasizes what he calls the "multidimensionality" of black religion and of black political activism.[62] He argues that for African Americans, churches generate "material resources and oppositional consciousness and culture." His theory of "oppositional civic culture" maintains that black churches affect black civic culture in two contradictory ways.

> They serve as a source of civic culture by giving African Americans the opportunities to practice organizing and civic skills and to develop positive orientations toward the civic order. The same institutions, however, also provide African Americans with material resources and oppositional dispositions to

challenge their marginality through modes of action and thought that call for inclusion in the political system instead of exclusion from the polity.[63]

Struggles for liberation for African Americans do not necessarily equate to struggles for African American democratic participation through the electoral system. Electoral participation can lead to liberation, equality, justice, and a change in material conditions, but this participation has been a *means* to equality, liberation, and justice, not the *end* in itself. When observing American democracy play itself out, Malcolm X reminded us that blacks in America have not been the beneficiaries of U.S. democracy but in fact the "victim[s] of America's so-called democracy."[64] For African Americans in U.S. politics, democracy has not been enough.

Christian Smith describes the religion that challenges instead of reinforces the status quo as "disruptive religion." Smith claims that religion has a natural tendency to be conservative and reinforce the status quo because religion primarily seeks to explain why the world exists the way that it does. Yet religion also "contains within it the seeds of radical social criticism and disruption." Through what he calls "sacred transcendence," religious justification and authority are placed higher than the authority of the keepers of the status quo. This allows religion to sometimes subvert the status quo by using motivational assets (e.g., legitimating protest), organizational resources (e.g., leadership, financial resources, and participants), shared identity, and social and geographical positioning.[65]

Michael Owens points out that collaboration among activist black churches, the state, and other private actors to better communities is an important aspect of the black church's role in public life that should also be explored and that political scientists should include these activities in the study of civic engagement activities in which black churches participate. He argues that this collaboration is overlooked in most studies about black churches and public life, which tend to focus on the protest and electoral activities of the churches. He asks, "But what of the political involvement of African American clergy and congregants after voters cast their ballots? What of the political activities of African American churches after protests die down?" The churches engaging in community development activities are in fact trying to influence public policy, and as such attempts to understand the role of black churches in politics must take these activities into consideration.[66]

Owens argues that some activist churches "coproduce" public goods and services in collaboration with government. However, not only do black churches collaborate with government and engage in coproduction, but also they produce goods and services without government. Such independent activity is just as important (and just as neglected in studies of black politics) as collaboration. Many black churches choose to do what they perceive the state as not doing. In a sense they step in for government when electoral politics has not been sufficient to fulfill the needs of black communities. So while black churches are more likely than other churches to take advantage of government funds to help provide social services, a number of black churches have also taken on projects that they feel fill community needs without collaborating with government— like developing independent private schools, child care centers, food co-ops, and substance abuse counseling.[67]

In sum, early theoretical debates about the public role of black churches revolved around the liberator/opiate debate. Scholars contended that black churches either inspired black communities to liberation through political activism or discouraged them from the same. As scholars moved beyond the liberator/opiate dichotomy they began to argue that black religion was multidimensional, and contemporary discourses on the role of black churches in public life wrestle with this complexity. Sometimes the black church has served as an opiate, other times a liberator, and there have been other theological orientations besides liberator or opiate that have characterized black churches. The role of black churches in public life has more recently been explored by looking at the black church in terms of how it enhances or detracts from civic engagement and the "multidimensionality" of the black church.

Black Megachurches and the Multifaceted Repertoire of Public Actions

This study fits well with these recent works and also wrestles with the complexity of the black church's public role. I take the position that the public role of the black church is best understood from the perspective that the black church is multidimensional and has a multifaceted repertoire of public actions that can be used strategically depending on the context. This repertoire includes three categories of public action: (1) electoral politics, (2) protest politics, and (3) community development. Obviously these categories overlap and are not mutually exclusive. Furthermore, a church can participate in the different categories at once or participate in none of them at all.

Since black churches choose from a multifaceted repertoire of public actions, the important questions concerning black megachurches and public life become the following: What activities do black megachurches choose to participate in? Why do the various black megachurches choose to participate in some activities and not others? What are the motivational aspects that explain a particular megachurch's participation portfolio? What about the structural aspects? What resources are available for black megachurches to actively engage in public life?

In the preface to their seminal work, *The Black Church in the African American Experience*, Lincoln and Mamiya write, "[A] critical observer with an open mind can gain invaluable insight into the *structural* and *motivational* cosmos out of which particular behaviors emerge as distinctive earmarks particularizing a given population."[68] This study examines both motivational (theological orientation) and structural aspects of these black megachurches to help us understand the choices that black megachurches make from a repertoire of public actions. Key characteristics of a particular megachurch along with key aspects of the church's social and political context determine the extent to which black megachurches engage in public life and the nature of their involvement.

I began this book with Martin Luther King Jr.'s challenge to the black church to "answer the knock at midnight," actively participate in public life, and try to make the world a better place. In the chapters that follow I argue that black megachurches, like black churches in general, are not monolithic and in fact post–civil rights black megachurches are varied in terms of whether or not they try to answer the "knock at midnight" and in terms of how they choose to engage in public life if they choose to answer the knock. For example, there are some black megachurches that are inwardly focused on the individual prosperity of their members, and the ministries and activities of these churches reflect this theological orientation. On the other end there are black megachurches that are focused on black communities at large, particularly the "least of these"—those African American communities and individuals who have not benefitted from the civil rights revolution—and the ministries of these churches reflect this theological orientation. Black megachurches choose from a repertoire of public action that ranges from inaction to protest politics, electoral politics, and community development activities, and the choices of action are based on their theological orientations and reflect the structural contexts of the megachurches themselves.

The Chapters

The six chapters of this book support this general argument about the black megachurch phenomenon and the participation of these churches in black public life. Chapter 2 describes the megachurch phenomenon, why it developed, and its key characteristics. I show that black megachurches are a post–civil rights phenomenon that developed in part due to the 1980s–1990s black suburbanization. I also illustrate how the black megachurch phenomenon is similar to but distinct from other nonblack megachurches. Chapter 3 examines the "motivational" aspects of the public role of black megachurches. I focus on the dominant theological orientations of black megachurches (neo-Pentecostal theology, prophetic theology, black liberation theology, nondenominational-ism, and the prosperity gospel) and explore the relationship between the basic underlying theological tenets of a church and its public/political activities.

Chapters 4 and 5 look at the structural contexts of megachurch public action. They both examine the churches' choices of strategies for public engage-ment given the social, political, and economic contexts. Chapter 4 explores the community development approach that a disproportionate number of black megachurches are taking to public engagement. The majority of black mega-churches have created CDOs that help them to harness resources for their public engagement projects. I show that there are both benefits and challenges to using the community development approach.

Chapter 5 examines the impact of gender on black megachurch public engagement. In this chapter I explain the dual gendered spheres of leadership, labor, and authority in black megachurches in which men operate in one sphere and women operate in another. Women are largely barred from taking formal lay and ministerial leadership positions, and they are primarily responsible for the community outreach function of the churches. This is reflected in the black megachurch CDOs, which strongly resemble women-led CDOs.

The conclusion, chapter 6, summarizes the major arguments and find-ings in the book and then applies these findings to contemporary debates in black politics by examining the participation of select black megachurches in the 2000, 2004, and 2008 U.S. presidential elections. In each of these elec-tions black megachurches participated in public discourses about strategies and philosophies concerning how the church and larger community should go about meeting post–civil rights challenges. In the 2000 U.S. presidential elec-tion black megachurch leaders participated in debates about cooperation with government and faith-based initiatives. In 2004 black megachurches engaged in the "culture wars," some of them arguing what I call a black moral pathol-ogy thesis, which says that moral slippage in black communities is the cause for black/white disparities. But 2008 was most exciting. Black megachurches participated in the campaign and election of Barack Obama by contributing to his political legitimacy, his political persona, and his political campaign strat-egy of deracialization. These three elections show the relevance of black mega-churches for ongoing debates in black politics.

CHAPTER 2

"GET ON BOARD LITTLE CHILDREN, THERE'S ROOM FOR MANY MORE"
The Black Megachurch Phenomenon

In 2000 Pastor Jamal Harrison Bryant, at twenty-nine years old, convened a group of forty-three people for Bible study in his living room. By 2007 that group of forty-three had grown to over six thousand. Bryant was the founding pastor of the Empowerment Temple African Methodist Episcopal (AME) Church, a megachurch whose members presently worship in a former industrial warehouse in northwest Baltimore. When asked about this phenomenal growth Pastor Bryant said that Empowerment Temple fills an important niche that had been neglected in many other churches—what he calls "the hip-hop community."[1]

In contrast to this newly established megachurch, New Shiloh Baptist Church, also in Baltimore, was founded over a century earlier in 1902. According to New Shiloh's pastor, Dr. Harold Carter Sr., New Shiloh first developed in response to the needs of the southern black migrants to Baltimore who came north looking for work and a better life. When Dr. Carter Sr. first arrived at New Shiloh in 1965 it already had a large congregation of eight hundred members. In 1990 New Shiloh built a new sanctuary to accommodate the growing numbers, and by 2007 there were over six thousand members.[2]

These two churches, about five miles apart, illustrate the growing black megachurch phenomenon. Including Empowerment Temple and New Shiloh, there are 23 black megachurches in the Baltimore/Washington, D.C. corridor alone. These churches, as well as the other 147 black megachurches identified in this study, have increasingly gained attention as their massive structures dot the landscapes of metropolitan areas across the country. The edifices range from domed buildings (like New Shiloh), to the warehouse "big-box" churches (like Empowerment Temple), to the very large "traditional" church complete with a church steeple and stained-glass windows. Often they consist of multiple building complexes—with different buildings housing different activities. For example, in 2000 Faithful Central Bible Church, a black megachurch in Los Angeles, California, purchased the 17,500-seat Los Angeles Forum, the former home of the Los Angeles Lakers basketball team. The Forum was added to three other large-capacity buildings that the church had purchased since 1982 (when the current pastor, Kenneth Ulmer, came to the church) to accommodate rapidly increasing membership numbers.[3] Though most megachurches do not have facilities as expansive as Faithful Central, their sheer sizes and the fact that so many of them have developed in a relatively short time period demand our attention.

The churches in this study have a variety of "ministries" that organize the many different (spiritual and worldly) functions of the church. They have parking, transportation, and security ministries that help churchgoers get in and out of the building on Sunday morning. They have ministries strictly focused on evangelizing and proselytizing. They have ministries that encourage spiritual growth such as Bible study classes, Sunday school classes, and Christian education. They have ministries for singles, married couples, children, and seniors. They go skiing, have mixers and retreats, and hold golf benefits, choral concerts, and dramatic productions. Some have black cultural enrichment ministries, and many have social and political outreach ministries, which are of particular importance to this study.

Black megachurches utilize technology in their outreach and worship functions more so than the average church. During church services most utilize sophisticated media technology such as PowerPoint presentations and streaming video. Many have televised church services shown in local markets or nationwide (especially on Black Entertainment Television [BET] and Trinity Broadcasting Network [TBN]). Black megachurches have tapped into the latest technology and developments in communication to reach even larger audiences than the several thousand in their church pews on Sunday mornings. Many of them broadcast church services live on the Internet.[4] Even if they are not podcasting services, almost all black megachurches have sophisticated websites with extensive information like service times, the history of the church, vision statements, mission statements, biographies, resumes and speaking schedules of the pastor, and contact information.

These interactive websites allow the virtual visitor to purchase CDs, audio-cassettes, DVDs, videotapes, and books. Some even allow the virtual visitor to donate money, request a prayer, join the church, and accept Jesus as his or her personal savior online by reading a confessional prayer aloud. This is definitely a new way of doing church! Sometimes these churches have virtual members—people who affiliate with black megachurch ministries but rarely if ever visit the physical church building. In a sense virtual membership is not an altogether new phenomenon given the fact that we have had television ministry for decades. But the megachurches' use of the Internet has taken virtual membership to a new level.

While, as mentioned in the previous chapter, there are some case studies and studies of sets of black megachurches, there has not been a serious attempt to understand or describe the universe of these churches, which is of course is the aim of this book. The task of this chapter is to give an overview of the black megachurch phenomenon. I offer an explanation for its growth and development and a description of key characteristics of black megachurches like their denominational affiliations, their leadership structures, and the public engagement activities in which they participate.

The data come from two surveys of black megachurches conducted in 2000 as well as updated information about the founding dates, locations, and denominations. For this study, "black megachurch" refers to a black church that averages at least two thousand attendees each week and either owned a church facility or was purchasing a facility. Congregations renting schools and other facilities for church use were not counted and are not included in this study.[5] Black megachurches are a part of Lincoln and Mamiya's "greater black church," which means that they include not only the seven major historically black Protestant denominations (National Baptist Convention (USA), National Baptist Convention of America, Progressive National Baptist Convention, African Methodist Episcopal, African Methodist Episcopal Zion, Christian Methodist Episcopal, and Church of God in Christ) but also smaller historically black denominations and African American congregations (majority parishioners and leadership) that are a part of majority-white denominations like the United Methodist Church or the United Church of Christ.[6] Because of the growth of nondenominationalism, particularly within megachurches, nondenominational Protestant churches with African

American leadership and parishioners are also included in my definition of "black megachurch."

As of September 2007 I had identified 149 black megachurches. This number reflects a dynamic phenomenon. In 2000 I had identified 66 black megachurches and estimated that there were at most 5 to 10 that were not identified. The current list of 149 includes a number of churches like Empowerment that have grown rapidly since 2000. It also includes a number of churches that were already large but had not yet reached the threshold of 2000 average weekly attendance. As with all studies of churches, this study is constrained by the fact that there is no comprehensive list of churches and most have membership rolls that fluctuate.

I begin by addressing some basic descriptive questions. What are the characteristics of black megachurches? What kinds of public engagement activities do they participate in? How do black megachurches compare to other black churches and nonblack megachurches? I then move to offer an explanation for why these churches are developing now, at this historical juncture. Black megachurches are distinct from both the traditional black church and megachurches in general. Yet they are an integral part of understanding both the larger megachurch phenomenon and the evolution of the black church—especially as they respond to demographic shifts and changes in African American communities.

The Megachurch Phenomenon

Academic explorations of either the black megachurch phenomenon or the larger megachurch phenomenon are few and far between. Scott Thumma and Dave Travis, who have done the major research on the general megachurch phenomenon, claim that in 2005 there were about 1,250 megachurches across the United States (up from approximately 50 in 1970). As I previously stated, I have identified 149 black megachurches. That means that black megachurches compose approximately 12 percent of the megachurch population—interestingly consistent with the African American percentage of the general population of the United States. These 149 black megachurches, however, do not represent the total African American experience with the contemporary megachurch. Thumma and Travis also found that many megachurches are multiracial—strikingly more so than other church forms in America. The saying that "11:00 a.m. on Sunday morning is the most segregated hour of the week" is less true of megachurches than any other church form.[7] Perhaps then African Americans are "overmegachurched," just as social scientists have sometimes suggested they were overchurched.

Thumma and Travis also explain that the megachurch phenomenon is not entirely a new church organizational style. There were churches that existed before the megachurch boom that exhibited many of the characteristics that we attribute to contemporary megachurches in terms of "size, charismatic leadership, multiple programs, or the use of small group ministries."[8] Anne C. Loveland and Otis B. Wheeler, writing about megachurch architecture, argue that contemporary megachurches are an evolution of earlier Protestant churches such as the "sumptuous auditorium churches" (built between the nineteenth and twentieth centuries), the "gospel tents and tabernacles" (built by the Pentecostals in the late 1800s), and the open air campgrounds and nonreligious structures (used by eighteenth-century evangelists).[9]

Some argue that the large church form was historically more prevalent among black churches than white churches. In "Plenty Good Room" Cheryl Gilkes listed several large churches in the early nineteenth century and suggested that the uniqueness of the contemporary black megachurch form is more apparent than real.[10] Drake and Cayton, in their important study, *Black Metropolis*, wrote about a handful of black Protestant churches in the 1930s that seated more than twenty-five hundred people, where a large number of young people attended.[11] Likewise, in an examination of black churches in Brooklyn, New York, Clarence Taylor discussed several churches that had over one thousand members as early as the 1920s.[12] Although we do not know the average weekly attendance of these churches, it stands to reason that it was probably a sizeable number, especially those churches that he identified as having extremely large memberships such as Antioch Baptist Church, which reported ten thousand members in the early 1950s.[13]

The Founding and Expansion of Black Megachurches

While there have been large churches in the past, what is new about the twenty-first-century megachurch phenomenon in general and the black megachurch phenomenon in particular is the number of churches that fit into this category and the quickness with which they have grown. Although their founding dates span across the nineteenth, twentieth, and twenty-first centuries, the vast majority of the black megachurches became megachurches in the late twentieth century.

As illustrated by Empowerment Temple AME Church and New Shiloh Baptist Church, the founding dates of contemporary black megachurches vary. Of all black megachurches that existed in 2007, 19 percent were founded before the turn of the twentieth century; 49 percent were founded before 1955. On the average, black megachurches then are a little older than megachurches in general (see table 2.1). Among megachurches in general, 36 percent were founded before 1955.

Older black megachurches tend to be located in inner cities and belong to mainline denominations. Three of the older black megachurches in the study, Abyssinian Baptist Church in Harlem, New York (est. 1808), Bethel African Methodist Episcopal Church in Baltimore, Maryland (est. 1785), and Shiloh Baptist Church in Washington, D.C. (est. 1863) fit this description well. Although Abyssinian and Shiloh report to have reached megachurch attendance numbers before the 1980s, contemporary megachurches that reached "megachurch" attendance numbers before the 1980s are exceptions rather than the rule. Almost 90 percent of contemporary African American megachurches became megachurches (reached 2000 in weekly attendance) after 1980, although they may have been established earlier. Figure 2.1 illustrates the explosion of black megachurches in the 1980s. This is consistent with Thumma and Travis' portrayal of megachurches in general. They show that even churches founded before 1965 grew into megachurches only after the mid-1970s.[14]

In addition to the growing number of churches that have megacongregations, the megachurch phenomenon refers to the quickness with which they reached the size requirement. Several black megachurches exemplify this rapid growth pattern. For example, New Birth Missionary Baptist Church in Atlanta, Georgia, grew from three hundred members in 1987 to twenty-two

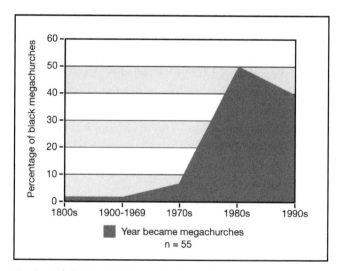

Figure 2.1—Date Black Megachurches Reached Two Thousand Average Weekly Attendance

TABLE 2.1

FOUNDING YEAR: BLACK MEGACHURCHES COMPARED TO ALL MEGACHURCHES

Year of Founding	Share of All Black Megachurches (%)[a]	Share of All Megachurches (%)[b]
Before 1945	45	29
1945–1954	4	7
1955–1964	12	12
1965–1974	8	8
1975–1984	15	20
1985–1994	11	16
1995–2007	5	8[c]

[a] Data from the author, N = 143.
[b] Data from Thumma and Travis, Beyond Megachurch Myths, 25.
[c] Thumma and Travis data stop in 2005 instead of 2007.

Shiloh Baptist Church, Washington, D.C.

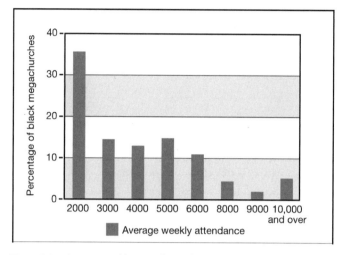

Figure 2.2—Average Weekly Attendance of Black Megachurches in Thousands

thousand members in 2001. Similarly, Windsor Village United Methodist Church went from twenty-five members in 1982 to ten thousand two hundred members in 2001. In fifteen years, St. Paul Community Baptist Church grew from eighty-four to five thousand members. This rapid growth is often accelerated by churches moving to larger facilities either attached to the old ones or in a different location to accommodate the growing numbers. Even with the movement to larger facilities, most black megachurches have multiple Sunday services to accommodate continually growing demand and the schedules of parishioners. Furthermore, the churches in this study gave no indication that this rapid growth would stagnate. In fact, 60 percent of those surveyed reported that they experienced significant growth from 1995 to 2000.[15]

In 2000 black megachurches ranged in attendance size from 2,000 to 18,000 at regular Sunday services. The mean average weekly attendance was 4,832, and the most common average weekly attendance was 2,000. Over 50 percent averaged fewer than 4,000 people per week, and only 6 percent averaged over 10,000 people per week (see figure 2.2).

In their 2005 survey of all megachurches, Thumma and Travis found a similar pattern. The majority of all megachurches (53 percent) averaged from 2,000 to 3,000 attendees each week, and 19 percent averaged 3,000 to 4,000 each week. Only 4 percent averaged 10,000 or more. The overall average attendance of all megachurches was 3,585 people each week.

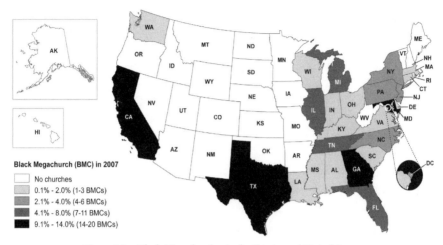

Figure 2.3—Black Megachurches in the Continental United States.
Image courtesy of Paporn Thebpanya.

Location of Black Megachurches

Black megachurches are distinct in their regional locations as well as their locations within metropolitan areas. The majority, 55 percent, are located in Sunbelt cities such as Houston, Dallas, Los Angeles, and Atlanta, while only 25 percent of black megachurches are in the older metropolitan areas of the Northeast and Midwest. The remaining 20 percent are located in the Mid-Atlantic. The largest megachurches, those with over five thousand in average weekly attendance, are typically located in the Sunbelt regions, particularly in the suburban areas of Georgia, Texas, and California (see figure 2.3).

Compared to all megachurches, black megachurches are geographically less spread out. Obviously this is because they are located where there are concentrated black populations. There are megachurches in all but six states. There are black megachurches in fifteen states and the District of Columbia. Table 2.2 compares the state concentrations of black megachurches and all megachurches.

Neighborhood Location

A great majority of black megachurches are located in neighborhoods that are predominantly black regardless of whether they are in the Sunbelt, Rustbelt, suburbia, or inner city. However, many of these megachurches are located in communities that are experiencing or have recently experienced significant

TABLE 2.2

STATE CONCENTRATION OF BLACK MEGACHURCHES COMPARED TO ALL
MEGACHURCHES

Black Megachurch Top 10[a]	Megachurch Top 10[b]
Texas (13%)	California (15%)
Georgia (11%)	Texas (13%)
Maryland (11%)	Florida (7%)
California (9%)	Georgia (6%)
Illinois (7%)	Illinois (4%)
Florida (7%)	Tennessee (4%)
Tennessee (6%)	Ohio (4%)
Michigan (5%)	Michigan (4%)
D.C. (4%)	North Carolina (3%)
New York, Pennsylvania (4%)	Indiana, Washington, Oklahoma (3%)

[a] Data from author.
[b] Data from Scott Thumma, "Database of Megachurches in the U.S.," http://hirr.hartsem.edu/mega-church/database.html (accessed May 2007).

transition. The types of transition that they are experiencing reflect several demographic shifts that are currently occurring in black communities. Black suburbanization, gentrification, and downtown redevelopment in several inner-city areas are changes that are affecting black megachurches.

While a slight majority of black megachurches are located in inner-city areas, black megachurches are tied to suburbanization. They are located in metropolitan areas such as Washington, D.C., Houston, New York City, Los Angeles, and Atlanta that have high populations of black suburbanites. Later in the chapter I explore this relationship between black suburbanization and black megachurches.

Gentrification, a demographic shift that is occurring in many inner-city areas, is also occurring in some neighborhoods where black megachurches are located. Several megachurches reported that their neighborhoods are faced with gentrification in the form of middle-class, mostly white residents beginning to populate what had been predominantly black working-class or low-income areas. This complicates the space issues that megachurches already face as they try to expand or even maintain their memberships. For example, in Washington, D.C., one of several cities experiencing an out-migration of middle- and working-class blacks and an in-migration of upper-class whites, one of the city's black megachurches, Metropolitan Baptist Church, had to reckon with the gentrification of the historically black Shaw neighborhood. Most of the incoming residents had no connection to and thus no appreciation of or tolerance for the very large and ever-expanding institution, so issues such as parking on Sunday morning became irreconcilable. The pastor of Metropolitan, Dr. H. Beecher Hicks, warned against the racial tension that gentrification was causing throughout the city. Meanwhile, the church decided to relocate to Prince George's County, Maryland, where the majority of the members live.[16]

Denominational Affiliation of Black Megachurches

Although the denominational affiliations of black megachurches generally resemble the national trend of black churches, there are a few notable exceptions. Like black churches in general, a majority of black megachurches belong to one of the historically black denominations or conventions and a majority of black megachurches are Baptist (see table 2.3). Black megachurches, however, are much more likely to be nondenominational (though not to the extent of megachurches in general, which are 34 percent nondenominational) and to be a part of the Sanctified (Holiness, Pentecostal, or Apostolic) tradition than black churches in general.[17] Of black megachurches, 10 percent are Sanctified—compared to the less than 2 percent of all black churches—and 21 percent of black megachurches are nondenominational.[18]

As one would expect, when compared to all megachurches, black megachurches are more likely to belong to a historically black denomination. As table

TABLE 2.3
BLACK MEGACHURCH AFFILIATION BY DENOMINATIONAL FAMILY

Denominational Affiliation	% of Black Megachurches
All Baptist	57
Nondenominational	21
Sanctified church (Church of God in Christ, Pentecostal Assemblies of the World, Bible Way Church, Apostolic)	10
Black churches in White denominations (United Methodist, Disciples of Christ, United Church of Christ, Southern Baptist)	9
African Methodist Episcopal	6
Historically Black denominations	70

N = 149

2.4 shows, all megachurches are more likely to be nondenominational (36 percent), compared to 21 percent of black megachurches. Of black megachurches, 57 percent are Baptist, while 23 percent of all megachurches are Baptist.[19]

One of the more interesting findings of this research is the relatively large percentage of black megachurches that are nondenominational. Some scholars suggest that the significance of denominationalism is declining, and black megachurches seem to be on the forefront of a move away from denominationalism.[20] A few of the black megachurches in this study were once affiliated with denominations but have broken away from them in recent years and become independent.

Many megachurches, if affiliated with a denomination, are in fact, as Thumma and Travis have noted, "functionally nondenominational."[21] They have characteristics that are more in common with each other than with other

TABLE 2.4
THE DENOMINATIONAL AFFILIATION OF BLACK MEGACHURCHES
COMPARED TO NONBLACK MEGACHURCHES

Denominational Affiliation	% of Black Megachurches[a]	% of all Megachurches[c]
African Methodist Episcopal	6	—[b]
Apostolic	3	—
Baptist	57	23
Church of God	1	—
Church of God in Christ	4	—
Disciples of Christ	1	—
Nondenominational	21	36
Pentecostal	3	—
United Church of Christ	1	—
United Methodist	3	9
Assemblies of God	—	5
Christian Church	—	4
Evangelical Free Church	—	3
Four Square	—	2

[a] Data compiled by author (2007), N = 149.
[b] Not counted (number too small).
[c] Data from Thumma, Travis, and Bird, "Megachurches Today," http://hirr.hartsem.edu/megachurch/megastoday2005detaileddata.pdf.

churches in their respective denominations. One characteristic is that there is a neo-Pentecostal movement that seems to span black megachurches regardless of their denomination. However, there are characteristics that vary by denomination. Whether churches have community development organizations, where they are located, and their approval of women as pastors of churches are all significantly related to their denominational affiliation. The relationships among these variables are explored further in subsequent chapters.

Black Megachurch Leadership

Almost all of the black megachurches in 2000 were led by charismatic men whose average age was forty-nine years old. They were a highly educated group of ministers, many having doctoral degrees or some postgraduate education. For most of these churches, the leadership has not changed since they reached megachurch numbers. Furthermore, many of the pastors also founded the churches.

According to Thumma, the development of megachurches depends on "nontraditional," charismatic, spiritual, entrepreneurial, ministerial leadership.[22] The charismatic leadership that Thumma points out as "nontraditional" and "different" is quite traditional in black churches. In fact, Gilkes argues that it is this longing for traditional charismatic leadership, as opposed to a longing for change, that in part attracts young black professionals to black megachurches.[23] The nature of charismatic leadership however dictates that it is focused on the leader himself. And as of yet, very few black megachurches have experienced a leadership transition since they have reached megachurch numbers. In fact, in 2000, 45 percent of the black megachurch ministers (virtually all of the nondenominational megachurches) were also the founders of the church. And more than 90 percent of them were ministers when the church reached megachurch numbers. This is consistent with Thumma and Travis' findings about all megachurches. Of all megachurches, 83 percent grew into megachurches under the leadership of their current pastors.[24] It remains to be seen if leadership transition will be a problem for the majority of these megachurches and if we will see a demise of megachurches when these charismatic leaders reach retirement age or have to change leadership for whatever reason.

Another interesting characteristic is the high level of education of the ministers of black megachurches. As previously stated, a disproportionate number of these ministers have advanced degrees, and in 2000 over 90 percent of black megachurch ministers had some seminary education. Of them, 43 percent had earned doctorates (the vast majority in ministry), and an

additional 27 percent had master's degrees. This is interesting when comparing their education to that of black ministers and megachurch ministers in
general. Lawrence Mamiya found that about 20 percent of black clergy were
seminary educated.[25] According to Cheryl Gilkes, the higher levels of education are partially explained by the churchgoers' higher levels of education. As
the laity in black megachurches is becoming increasingly highly educated the
parishioners demand a more professional and educated clergy.[26] Black megachurch pastors' relatively high level of education is comparable to that of the
pastors of all megachurches. Among all megachurches ministers, 72 percent
claimed to have a master's degree or higher.[27]

   An interesting way that black megachurch leadership both is distinct from
and mimics black churches is in terms of gender. Women make up the vast
majority of members in black churches, and scholars have found that they serve
as organizers of church activities and volunteers in the church ministries and
auxiliaries. However, women have generally been confined to lay membership
and are restricted from several aspects of lay and ministerial leadership. In some
denominations like the Church of God in Christ, women are not even ordained
as ministers. In some churches, women do not serve on boards of trustees or as
deacons. In keeping with this, Lincoln and Mamiya found that over 50 percent
of black church ministers disapproved of women pastors.[28]

   In contrast to this finding, 78 percent of black megachurch ministers agreed
that women should be allowed to be pastors of a church. However, less than
1 percent of black megachurches actually had a woman as the senior pastor.
Although many of the black megachurches have women copastors, assistant
pastors, and associate pastors, women members of trustee boards, and women
members of deacons' boards, just as the senior pastor positions are reserved
for men, these other leadership positions are also male dominated. So while
there seem to be more opportunities for leadership for women in black megachurches, there is still a "stained-glass ceiling."[29]

Black Megachurches and Public Engagement Activities

By nature of their membership size and subsequent concentration of resources
(e.g., money, volunteers, and space), megachurches have tremendous potential
to participate in what R. Drew Smith and Corwin Smidt call "civic involvements" even more so than the average sized church.[30] These civic involvements
or public engagement activities, which include political engagement, community development, and social service provision, are the vehicles through which
black megachurches participate in public life.

The data suggest that black megachurches engage in various types of public engagement activities. They primarily engage in direct social service provision, especially health initiatives and food distribution. They also engage in political engagement activities (like voter registration), housing, and commercial development to a lesser extent. Their participation, though encouraging, is modest. Still, in most categories they engage at higher rates than black churches, all megachurches, and churches in general.

Political Engagement

Black megachurches engage in public engagement activities that are specifically intended to encourage citizen participation and/or consciousness raising. These activities may be in the forms of voter registration drives, citizen education, political campaigning, rallying, protest activities, community advocacy, and community organizing.

An important finding in this regard is the number of churches that participate in social issue advocacy. In all, 66 percent reported to have participated in some form of organized social issue advocacy. Of the churches surveyed, 44 percent have ministries dedicated to community political and social affairs. These ministries range in their activities. Most of them serve as social and political awareness groups. These groups facilitate the use of the church as a site for public discourse. For example, some black megachurches, like Shiloh Baptist Church in Washington, D.C., hold candidate forums during local elections. This allows candidates access to community residents, but more importantly it allows community residents access to prospective elected officials. Some black megachurches, like Union Temple Baptist Church, also in Washington, hold information forums on community issues.

This political engagement is the type of public engagement that critics suggest black megachurches are the least likely to be involved in. However, table 2.5 shows that black megachurches' participation in political engagement is equal to or surpasses the participation of other black churches, other megachurches, and other churches in general. Particularly interesting is their participation in organized social issue advocacy. In 2000, 68 percent of the black megachurch survey respondents reported that their churches had participated in some type of organized social issue advocacy in the previous year. This is compared to the 45 percent of black churches that reported such participation and the 56 percent of all megachurches.

TABLE 2.5
POLITICAL ENGAGEMENT OF BLACK MEGACHURCHES COMPARED TO BLACK
CHURCHES, ALL MEGACHURCHES, AND ALL CHURCHES IN THE PAST TWELVE
MONTHS (2000)

Political Activity	Black Mega-churches (%)[a]	Black Churches (%)[b]	All Mega-churches (%)[c]	All Churches (%)[d]
Organized social issue advocacy	67.7	45.0	56.0	—[e]
Voter registration and education	77.4	76.0	52.2	12.5
Social/political concerns ministry	44.0	—	—	—

[a] ITC/Faith Communities Today Project 2000 Megachurch Survey.
[b] Mamiya, "River of Struggle."
[c] Scott Thumma, principal investigator, Megachurches Today 2000 Survey, http://hirr
.hartsem.edu/megachurch/research.html.
[d] Mark Chaves, principal investigator, National Congregations Study (1998).
[e] Not available.

Community Development and Housing

Black churches have participated in a range of activities aimed at improving the economic viability of black communities. These include commercial
enterprises such as worker-owned firms, community financial institutions,
church business endeavors, public-private collaborations through community
development corporations, and workforce mobilization through job training
and referrals.[31] A higher proportion of black megachurches reported involvement in these activities than black churches in general. For example, data from
Lincoln and Mamiya on black church involvement in business activities, such
as the operation of bookstores, child care centers, and housing development
projects, showed that only 6.9 percent of black churches participated in these
types of church-operated businesses during the 1980s.[32] On the other hand,
an astounding 95 percent of black megachurches currently participate in some
form of this activity.

Community financial institutions, including community development
banks, credit unions, and revolving loan funds, are also important vehicles for
economic development used by black megachurches. As shown in table 2.6,
28 percent of black megachurches (compared to 6 percent of black churches)
report that they have credit unions. Organized for the benefit of the members
and not to turn a profit, credit unions potentially provide church constituents

with access to capital for personal lending and consumer credit. They may also help to spur economic development and revitalization of communities.

Commercial development, which is the most expensive form of economic development, is the least common form of community development activity among black megachurches. There are, however, some noteworthy examples of large-scale commercial development projects. Windsor Village United Methodist Church in Houston developed a commercial center, which holds several offices, a bank, an elementary school, a cafeteria, a pharmacy, a health clinic, several government and church social service agencies, and a large reception hall. Hartford Memorial Baptist church in Detroit constructed a multi-million-dollar housing project, a commercial center that includes a large auto care facility, and a shopping center that contains a supermarket, drug store, and restaurants. In New York City, there are several churches with major commercial undertakings including Allen AME in Queens and Abyssinian Baptist Church in Harlem. Allen operates a prenatal and postnatal clinic, travel agency, barber shop, and restaurant and constructed a three-hundred-unit senior citizens housing facility. Other examples of large-scale commercial development by megachurches can be identified in other cities across the country.

Black megachurches also participate in housing projects. Black-megachurch-based housing includes affordable housing, transitional housing such as an AIDS hospice, homeless and women's shelters, and housing for the elderly. In 2000, 60 percent provided some kind of housing program; 43 percent had

TABLE 2.6
SELECT COMMUNITY ECONOMIC DEVELOPMENT PARTICIPATION
OF BLACK MEGACHURCHES, BLACK CHURCHES, ALL MEGACHURCHES, AND ALL
CHURCHES IN THE PAST TWELVE MONTHS

Community Development Activity	Black Megachurches (%)[a]	Black Churches (%)[b]	All Megachurches (%)[c]	All Churches (%)[d]
Affordable housing	43.0	36.0	78.3	32.4
Credit union	28.0	6.0	—[e]	—
Job referral/ job training	61.0	46.0	51.6	1.2

[a] ITC/Faith Communities Today Project 2000 Megachurch Survey.
[b] Mamiya, "River of Struggle."
[c] Scott Thumma, principal investigator, Megachurches Today 2000 Survey, http://hirr .hartsem.edu/megachurch/research.html.
[d] Mark Chaves, principal investigator, National Congregations Study (1998).
[e] Not available.

built or renovated affordable housing—and even more planned to do so in the future. Most of this housing is done through community development organizations.

Examples of housing development are perhaps the most impressive of the community development activities in which black megachurches participate. The community development corporation (CDC) affiliated with Abyssinian Baptist Church in New York City manages, sponsors, or has developed at least three hundred units of housing including senior citizen housing and housing for the homeless. Brentwood Baptist Church in Houston has built housing for people who are living with AIDS. Many of the housing projects, however, are much more modest.

According to Thumma's research, in 2000, 78 percent of all megachurches provided some type of housing. It would be interesting to categorize this participation in terms of the type of housing (i.e., permanent or transitional housing or temporary emergency shelter) and the level of participation (large-scale projects or small-scale projects). It would also be interesting to determine if these projects were done by the church alone or in collaboration with other organizations. Unfortunately, those data are not available for comparison.

Social Service Provision

Most black megachurches participate in some form of direct social service provision. In fact all of the churches that were interviewed participated in some type of health care activities such as inoculations, health screenings, or health information seminars. Most of these churches also have some form of benevolence program that provides emergency funds for people needing assistance with rent or utility payments. Many black megachurches also have "clothing ministries" that sponsor clothing drives and clothing distribution seasonally. In some instances, these clothing ministries specialize in specific types of clothing, such as winter coats, children's clothing, or business attire. Black megachurches also frequently offer food distribution and meal services. Over 90 percent of black megachurches have a food bank that distributes meals daily, weekly, or monthly. As shown on the table 2.7, 75 percent of black churches in general reported participating in this activity. In fact, after health care activities, food distribution represents the most common public engagement activity in which black megachurches currently participate.

While direct social service provision, such as food distribution, has sometimes been criticized for not providing long-term solutions to poverty and unemployment, several black megachurches have promoted more long-term

TABLE 2.7

SOCIAL SERVICE INVOLVEMENTS OF BLACK MEGACHURCHES COMPARED TO BLACK
CHURCHES, ALL MEGACHURCHES, AND ALL CHURCHES

Social Service	Black Mega-churches (%)[a]	Black Churches (%)[b]	All Megachurches (%)[c]	All Churches (%)[d]
Food	91.0	75.0	98.7	48.5
Clothing	78.0	52.0	76.4	17.3
Health project	100.0	62.0	62.4	9.1

[a] ITC/Faith Communities Today Project 2000 Megachurch Survey.
[b] Mamiya, "River of Struggle."
[c] Scott Thumma, principal investigator, Megachurches Today 2000 Survey, http://hirr
   .hartsem.edu/megachurch/research.html.
[d] Mark Chaves, principal investigator, National Congregations Study (1998).

approaches to community food needs such as food co-ops or food shares programs. With food shares programs, for example, people pool their money, buy
food at low-cost bulk prices, and then dispense the food according to member
shares. In some instances, the shares of needy families may be paid or sponsored by other members. The goal of these collective buying programs is both
to respond to immediate needs and to contribute to long-term development by
reducing the cost of living for participating families.

One of the most surprising findings of the survey was that 60 percent
of black megachurches established separate community development organizations (CDOs) and more were planning to do so in the future. CDOs are
separately incorporated nonprofit organizations. The National Congress for
Community Economic Development estimated there to be approximately
4,600 CDCs (the most prevalent form of CDO) across the United States
in 2005.[33] CDCs (many of which have been very active in the development
of affordable housing) have generated increasing interest and enthusiasm as
a strategy for church-based community development. Black-megachurch-
affiliated CDOs have participated in the various public engagement activities
discussed including social service provision, health clinics, political organizing,
business support, job training, and commercial development.

Explaining the Megachurch Phenomenon

The rapid growth of megachurches over the past twenty years begs a number
of questions. Why did they develop when they did? How did the megachurch

form become a preferable church model for so many, so quickly? While there has not be a great deal of complex theorizing on this subject as of yet (scholars are still getting a handle on the phenomenon), below I review the theories that have been presented to explain the general megachurch phenomenon. Then I present an explanation for black megachurch growth in particular. Black megachurches differ in some key ways from the general megachurches and thus require a more nuanced explanation.

The theories presented to explain the general megachurch phenomenon can be grouped into three broad categories: the megaconsumerist explanation, the church growth strategy explanation, and the population growth and demographic shifts explanation. These explanations overlap and are not mutually exclusive, but each emphasizes a different primary reason for the megachurch phenomenon.

Megaconsumerist Explanation

The megaconsumerist explanation for megachurch growth rests on the notion that in a consumer-driven society, churchgoers "shop" for the best "deal." It entails both a "push" and a "pull" strain. From the "pull" perspective, megachurches reflect the "mega" phenomenon permeating the consumer market. For example, the "megamall," the "Super Walmart," and "Super Target," which all promote "one-stop shopping," allow a consumer to purchase everything from luggage to furniture, groceries, electronics, fabric, picture developing, clothing, and gasoline. These megamalls and megastores also purport to provide outlet or discount shopping. This indicates that the consumers will get more value for their money in addition to convenience. This logic transfers to churches in the sense that the ministries and activities that church members can participate in and the services that they receive draw people to megachurches.

Mark Chaves argues that it is not really the megaconsumerist pull to megachurches that explains their phenomenal growth but rather that the rising costs of maintaining a church make smaller churches a less feasible church size model.[34] Chaves argues that the average church size has grown since the 1970s and theorizes that it is not that large churches are simply drawing in new converts or the "unchurched" but rather that church membership is shifting and concentrating. Small churches are no longer seen as viable, and so the tendency is for smaller churches to fade away and for those that remain to be larger. This is an economic explanation but from the "push" side. People are pushed out of smaller churches and into larger ones because smaller churches are no longer economically viable.

Church Growth Strategy

Another explanation for the development of the phenomenon is that mega-churches are the product of conscious church growth strategies. The leaders of megachurches build churches and church congregations by aggressively trying to fill a niche that is not being filled by other churches. According to Loveland and Wheeler, advocates of the church growth strategy "called for a new type of church organization that would be relevant to the contemporary American society and culture." The "seeker" churches engage in this "niche" strategy. Seeker churches target the "unchurched"—those who either have never been affiliated with a church or have rejected church because of some negative experience. Churches using the seeker strategy pull the unchurched into their church by catering to them through worship style, architecture, and other religious symbols that are relatively nontraditional. Loveland and Wheeler observed that Robert H. Schuller's Crystal Cathedral in Garden Grove, California, and Bill Hybels' Willow Creek Community Church in Illinois are two of the earliest examples of churches that used this model. Schuller started conducting services for what later became the Crystal Cathedral in a rented drive-in movie theater. Hybels conducted market research in the South Barrington community where Willow Creek is located to see what turned on and what turned off the "unchurched" and developed Willow Creek according to the feedback on what attracted people to church and what kept them away.[35]

Demographic Shift and Population Growth Explanations

The demographic explanation attributes the megachurch phenomenon to key demographic shifts. At its simplest form, the explanation states that mega-churches are connected to population increases. Churches grow larger to accommodate the population growth. As a large proportion of megachurches are found in suburban America, the most common demographic explanation is that megachurch growth is a result of suburbanization. The suburban explanation reasons that these churches develop there because that is where people have migrated to but also because there is room for the churches to physically expand in the suburbs, unlike in the landlocked central cities. Also the automobile and highways make it easier for people to drive to exercise more religious options and travel further distances to attend church.[36]

While all three of these theories help us to understand the phenomenon a bit more clearly, it is critical to address the black megachurch phenomenon as separate and distinct from the general phenomenon. A focus on the particularities of black megachurches reveals key factors that help to explain them.

The development of the black megachurch phenomenon can be attributed to three key factors: the suburbanization of a substantial number of African Americans in the 1980s and 1990s, what Andrew Wiese has called the "next great migration"; a megaconsumerist orientation; and finally the establishment of a "black megachurch model" for how churches can organize and develop that, once in the public sphere, gets duplicated and the phenomenon expands.[37] The development of the black megachurch resembles the growth of storefront churches during the Great Migration in its social, political, and ecclesiastical significance.

Megachurch Is to Suburbanite as Storefront Is to Migrant

While there have been various transformative movements within the black church, the black megachurch phenomenon is most comparable to the explosion of storefront churches during the twentieth century. At the turn of the twentieth century storefront churches proliferated throughout urban America due to the African American Great Migration and resulting demographic shifts in African American northern communities. Storefront churches filled the social and religious needs of the numerous migrants who "voted with their feet" and left the rural South for the urban South, North, and Midwest to work and live a better life. Robert Boyd has argued that the storefront churches made the North a little warmer and filled a niche that the mainline Baptist and Methodist denominations, which were colder and more distant, could not fill.[38] Drake and Cayton observed that in the 1930s, 75 percent of the black churches in Chicago were storefronts.[39]

To many of the black southern migrants, the storefront church brought a sense of home by providing worship services that were "traditional, emotional and intimate." While usually rejecting participation in progressive politics and being both theologically and socially conservative, storefront churches nonetheless provided temporal resources such as social services and information about employment to their members. Boyd argued that the storefront ministry carved out an ethnic niche just like the providers of personal services such as beauty shops, barbershops, and funeral homes.[40]

The storefront church was so named because these churches appropriated "the often discarded or neglected commercial buildings" that were cheap and plentiful for religious purposes. While this was economically pragmatic, the use of a storefront also had theological significance. The storefront itself served as an alternative to the high culture of the northern mainline black churches. It was not grand but "regular" and "everyday," and this validated the idea that God was no respecter of persons.[41]

In some ways the megachurch is the opposite of the storefront. Most obviously, while the storefront is small, megachurches are extremely large physical structures. Moreover, many megachurches are elaborately decorated and ornate. For example, atop World Changers Church in Atlanta, Georgia, there is a gold dome, and inside the lobby of the church are marble and granite. Furthermore, storefront worship services were relatively spontaneous while megachurch services are well planned out professional productions. The storefront consists of a close-knit, small community where everyone knows everyone else, much like the southern rural home churches of the migrants. On the other hand, the large numbers in a megachurch do not allow for one small, close-knit community. In fact it is possible to attend a megachurch in anonymity.

In spite of the differences, black storefront churches and African American megachurches display some crucial similarities. Although some of the megachurches have very ornate edifices, others are remarkably plain. Just like the storefront church, many megachurches have appropriated commercial buildings for church use—a consciously less expensive alternative.[42] These "big-box" African American megachurch edifices, which include former Kmarts, Walmarts, supermarkets, department stores, and warehouses, were not originally intended for church use. Instead of urban blight, many are in inner-ring suburban blighted areas where the retail stores have moved on but the churches remain. For example, Empowerment Temple in Baltimore (discussed at the beginning of this chapter) has converted a former industrial warehouse into a worship space. In suburban D.C., First Baptist Church of Glenarden used a former Hechinger warehouse until September 2007 when they moved into their

Empowerment Temple, an example of a church using a former warehouse for worship

First Baptist Church of Glenarden, a newly built, state of the art, "grandiose" church

newly built, state-of-the-art, four-thousand-seat sanctuary in nearby Kettering, Maryland. These churches use the "big-box" structures not only for their formal services but also to house their ministries. Windsor Village United Methodist Church in Houston, Texas, uses a traditional space for worship services but has also converted a former Kmart into their center for ministries—the Power Center. Windsor Village also conducts some of their Sunday services at the Power Center. Like the storefront churches, the contemporary black megachurch uses these buildings in part because they are cheaper than new construction. But the use of a big box also can serve a more ecclesiastical function of communicating the message that this church is not bound by traditional church symbols and architecture. The nontraditional church structure appeals to those who are turned off by traditional church symbols and architecture—complementing the stated attitude of Windsor Village on their website: "We are not afraid to think and do ministry outside of the box."[43] In some cases megachurches have actually built these "nontraditional" edifices. Reid Temple AME Church in Glendale, Maryland, for example, built a new structure in 2004 that resembles a large office building more than a traditional church.

The more important comparison, however, between black megachurches and storefront churches is that the black megachurches serve a similar function

Reid Temple AME church, which looks more like a business park than traditional church

for shifting African American populations in the post–civil rights era that the storefronts did during the African American migration. Instead of serving urban migrants, black megachurches help the suburban migrant and working- and middle-class transplants acclimate to their living environments and build their communities.

During the 1980s and 1990s the African American population declined in urban areas but increased in suburbia.[44] In that time the African American suburban population doubled to twelve million from six million.[45] This wave of black suburbanization was fueled by the post–civil rights decline in restrictions on housing, increase in opportunities for education, and better paying jobs. Therefore the next great migration (as urban historian Andrew Wiese calls this time period) was not only a geographic migration from urban America to suburbia. It reflects the expanded black middle class that is a result of the gains of the Civil Rights Movement. Suburbanization has been a manifestation of class upward mobility.

Just like the growth of storefront churches coincided with the original Great Migration, black megachurches expanded with this New Great Migration. Although there were some black megachurches in the 1970s, the black megachurch phenomenon really exploded post-1980, which coincided with the most rapid expansion of black suburbanization. Table 2.8 shows that most black megachurches are in metropolitan areas with high numbers of black suburbanites. Metropolitan areas such as Washington, D.C., Houston, New York City, Los Angeles, and Atlanta are all among the ten metropolitan areas with the highest numbers of black suburbanites.[46] They are also the cities with the largest numbers of megachurches. The Washington, D.C., metropolitan area (which includes Prince George's County, Maryland, Montgomery County, Maryland, and northern Virginia) has the largest number of black megachurches and the

TABLE 2.8
THE TOP TEN: METROPOLITAN AREAS WITH THE LARGEST NUMBERS
OF BLACK MEGACHURCHES AND METROPOLITAN AREAS WITH THE HIGHEST
CONCENTRATIONS OF BLACK SUBURBANITES

Black Megachurches[a]	Black Suburbanites[b]
Washington, D.C. (16)	New York
Atlanta (16)	Washington, D.C.
Chicago (11)	Atlanta
Houston (11)	Miami
Los Angeles (9)	Los Angeles
Dallas (9)	Chicago
Memphis (7)	Philadelphia
Baltimore (7)	Baltimore
Detroit (7)	Detroit
New York (7)	Houston

[a] Data from the author.
[b] Data from John Logan, "The New Ethnic Enclaves in America's Suburbs."

second largest number of black suburbanites (after New York City) of any other metropolitan area in the United States. In fact, over 25 percent of black megachurches are located in the Washington, D.C., and Atlanta, Georgia (which has the third largest number of black suburbanites), metropolitan areas.

For the most part, African American suburbanization did not upset racial segregation patterns but only expanded black areas as the new predominantly black suburbs grew adjacent to the older black urban areas.[47] Most African American suburbanites migrated to majority black suburbs in the inner ring. A good number of the older suburban black megachurches experienced a "rebirth" and became "black" in the 1970s and 1980s due to the movement of white populations from what are now black neighborhoods, commonly known as "white flight." For example, Greenforest Community Baptist Church, a black megachurch in Atlanta, calls this historical moment in their church "the Exodus Experience." In the late 1970s, as the neighborhood changed from white to black, the church lost nearly all of its white members, including the pastor. Their "church history" reads, "On one Sunday nearly all white members, including the pastor, moved their membership from Greenforest Baptist Church. This obviously was a sad day in the life of the Christian Church."[48] Two years after the white pastor left the late Rev. George McCalep (a black pastor) was appointed to the church. Under his leadership, the membership grew from twenty-five to four thousand as a predominantly black church.

While the growth of black megachurches has been fueled by black sub-urbanization, as stated previously a slight majority of black megachurches are actually located in the inner city. They are able to sustain their memberships because they are what Omar McRoberts calls "niche churches." They draw members from all over the metropolitan areas, not just from their immediate geographic communities. This means that for an inner-city black megachurch to be sustained, the members need not live in the inner city. In fact, in 50 percent of the black megachurches in the sample, over 60 percent of the members commute at least fifteen minutes to get to the church.[49] Many of those commuting to the city from the suburbs do so in order to maintain a feeling of connection with the city—and thus what they perceive as the "black community."

The 1980s–1990s black suburbanization created transplants from within the cities or from other places to the suburbs of cities like Washington, D.C., and Atlanta, Georgia. Just like the storefront church met the needs of the southern migrants that the established mainline black churches in the North were not meeting, black megachurch growth is driven by the new migrants' demands for a religious experience that is accessible, enthusiastic, professional, and relevant to the here and now. Accordingly, black megachurches provide a plethora of ministries that help their members to make their communities "places of their own."[50] Whether they develop independent Christian schools or sponsor health seminars, financial workshops, or trips to Africa, each of these churches provides bundles of services and opportunities for their members to engage in civil society.

Black megachurches are accessible to these suburban transplants. These churches, because of their size, have high profiles and are easy to find. They have cultures of welcoming in newcomers supported by their active evangelizing and "opening the doors of the church," encouraging people to join, which is usually the most important part of a megachurch service.

Smaller churches are often not as accessible to these new migrants, and they are definitely not as visible. Smaller churches may be dominated by a few families or groups or may simply be perceived that way. One suburban Washington, D.C., black megachurch member put it this way:

> I was invited by current members to attend both Metropolitan and Reid Temple [black megachurches in the Washington, D.C., area]. I think as someone who did not grow up in a church, I find some comfort in being a

part of congregations that are filled with new folks—I perceive them to be less cliquish, although this is probably not true.[51]

Black megachurches help new migrants transition into the community and get a finger on the pulse of what is happening. In the words of Cheryl Townsend Gilkes these churches are the "church of what's happening now."[52]

Black megachurches also have an enthusiastic worship style that attracts members. The choirs and the style of preaching are more like those of the Sanctified churches and the storefronts than the "silk-stocking" churches of the old black middle class that alienated the southern migrants. Gilkes points out that the black megachurch worship style is the "traditional" worship of many of the new black middle class and allows these transplants to feel a sense of connectedness as if they have "come home to church."[53]

But even though the worship style is enthusiastic like that of the storefronts, the worship services are professional productions. The ministerial staffs are usually highly educated, and the theological messages are often "thisworldly."

Lincoln and Mamiya provide us with valuable insight into the "thisworldly," but also neo-Pentecostal church growth trends in the black church that took place in the 1980s. In *The Black Church in the African American Experience* they pointed out several AME churches with rapidly expanding memberships that mixed a neo-Pentecostal worship style with a thisworldly theological orientation and traditional social justice activism. Although they did not use the term "megachurch," all the churches that they highlighted either were megachurches at the time or eventually grew into megachurches.[54]

Black megachurches appeal to a megaconsumerist sentiment with their various ministries, programs, and activities and their focus on the relevance of church to everyday life and a rejection of otherworldliness. They give the members an outlet for their own talents and areas of expertise. But they can also provide anonymity for their members who want to temper their commitment. One megachurch member who had attended different megachurches put it this way,

> I like the activism of both congregations, the diversity of activities sponsored, the choirs, and the service to the community commitment. And because the congregations are so large, there is a certain level of anonymity that I actually like.[55]

The "diversity" of programs that black megachurches sponsor can be likened to Thumma's "shopping mall" analogy. In his analogy, megachurches are

like shopping malls that serve their diverse consumers by offering an assort-
ment of ministries that provide the services or opportunities that they require
or desire. This often includes banking, shopping, and schooling for young children in addition to the more traditional religious functions. The consumers
(church members) can choose in which ministry or ministries they would like
to participate. The megaconsumerist appeal of black megachurches means that
people choose the church because of the services and opportunities it has to
offer as opposed to something more abstract like denominational ties or loyalty to the church. Instead, the worship style, the theological orientation, and
the ministries serve as the hallmarks for the church. Does the church have a
good choir? Good preaching? A children's ministry? Are members active in
the community? These are the factors that draw members. Although black
megachurches share a thisworldly orientation and the fact that their ministries
are multiple and diverse, the churches may offer very different options for the
would-be consumer/churchgoer.

This "consumer-like" diversity means that black megachurches are "particularistic." This means that megachurches are religious communities that differ
by theological orientations, religious traditions, social and political orientations,
cultural practices, and worship styles (among other differences). According to
Omar McRoberts, the particularistic church allows people to "sort themselves
into religious communities according to complex bundles of preferences."[56]

The bundles of services and opportunities that black megachurches provide are like a brand and individual black megachurches have been branded
the "hip-hop church," "Afro-centric church," "political church," and "prosperity
church," among others. For example, Afro-centric churches have ministries
designed to strengthen cultural connections to other African Americans and
to sustain a group identity as well as give back to black communities. These
include missionary trips, vacations, and cultural tours of Africa and the Carib-
bean. They also include outreach ministries focused on community development and ministries that celebrate black culture. Prosperity churches have
ministries that focus on explicit "prosperity gospel" teachings, and the ministries reflect this theological orientation (like "seed ministries" and "millionaires
ministries," in which the member is encouraged to give money to the church,
with the expectation that he or she will become prosperous in accordance with
the gift).

Because megachurches allow for differing levels of commitment and participation, these brands draw people to the churches even if the churchgoers
do not intend to actually participate in the churches' ministries. Many of the

members just want to be affiliated with churches of one brand or another. The "particularistic" black megachurch is explored further in subsequent chapters.

Conclusion

The 1980s and 1990s witnessed the phenomenal growth of black mega-churches, and by the turn of the twenty-first century these churches had evolved into a distinct and recognizable church form. Their growth was fueled by black suburbanization that took place also in the 1980s and 1990s at a phenomenal pace. While a handful of these churches certainly existed prior to this wave of migration, they now number at least 149, and the vast majority have become megachurches since 1980. These churches fill a niche for this new wave of migrants and provide a worship experience that is accessible, enthusiastic, and relevant to their everyday lives.

Black megachurches tend to be located in metropolitan areas like Washington, D.C., Atlanta, Houston, and Los Angeles where there are large numbers of black suburbanites. They have multiple "ministries"—some of them traditional (like usher and missionary boards) and others not so traditional (like singles ministries and economic development ministries). They utilize sophisticated technology in their church services and on the Internet to get their message out and connect to even more people than the thousands who attend their Sunday services.

These churches are generally engaged in public life. As a group they participate in social service provision, political development activities, and community development at higher rates than other black churches, other megachurches, and all churches in general. Over half of them have established separate CDOs.

While many are engaged in community development and politics and participate in public life, clearly not all of them do. Black megachurches are characterized by this kind of diversity. They are particularistic churches and their theological orientations and public engagement efforts vary. The following chapter examines the theological orientations of black megachurches and how their theological orientations affect their public engagement activities.

Chapter 3

THEOLOGICAL ORIENTATION
AS MOTIVE TO BLACK MEGACHURCH
PUBLIC ENGAGEMENT

First AME Church exists to embody Christ both WITHIN THE WALLS and BEYOND THE WALLS by equipping all people regardless of race or origin—spiritually, economically, politically, and morally—making the Word become flesh through tools in education, health, housing, feeding, job procurement, business and incubator loans, venture capital, transportation, adoptions, mentoring and other ministries of outreach.

—Mission statement of First African Methodist
Episcopal Church, Los Angeles

Consider the above mission statement from First African Methodist Episcopal (FAME) Church. It particularly addresses the theological concern about the church's role in the world. The church's very existence is to "embody Christ." What is interesting about this is that the church's public engagement is *how* the church "embod[ies] Christ" or "make[s] the word become flesh." Given their mission, it is no surprise that FAME Church has a very active social justice and community development agenda. They have a business resource center, entrepreneurial training, a free legal clinic, job placement, an equity fund to invest in small minority-owned businesses, and many more ministries pursuant to this mission.

51

While FAME is the prototypical "activist" church, one that participates in a good deal of public engagement activities, other black megachurches have much shorter and narrower lists of activities. This variance leads one to consider why some black megachurches engage extensively while others do so minimally. What motivates churches to engage in public life?

This chapter explores the concept of "theological orientation" as a motive for public engagement and explains the guiding role that theological orientation plays in the public engagement activities of black megachurches. There are five theological orientations that emerge as dominant among black megachurches—neo-Pentecostalism, black theology, prophetic theology, nondenominationalism, and the prosperity gospel. While neo-Pentecostalism has no impact on the public engagement activities of black megachurches (active churches and relatively inactive churches exhibit neo-Pentecostalism), prophetic theology, black theology, nondenominationalism, and the prosperity gospel all drive the public engagement activities of black megachurches in one direction or another. Black theology and prophetic theology encourage public engagement. The prosperity gospel and nondenominationalism depress it.

At the conclusion of this chapter I present a typology of black megachurch politico-theological orientations that vary along a set of four continua: (1) black theology versus color-blind theology, (2) social gospel versus prosperity gospel, (3) denominational versus nondenominational, and (4) communal versus privatistic.[1] Ultimately this set of politico-theological dichotomies helps to explain how the theological orientations of black megachurches guide their public engagement activity.

The theological orientation of a church is the set of basic underlying theological tenets of the church. Categories used to determine a particular church's theological orientation include the way the church as an institution articulates (1) the identity of God, (2) the understanding of human beings as God's creatures, (3) the understanding of right and wrong, (4) the meaning of the church in the world, and (5) the acknowledgment and meaning of passages in life such as birth, marriage, and death.[2] The mission statement of FAME Church is interesting and instructive for this chapter about the influence of theological orientation on public engagement because it tells us about both the theological orientation of FAME Church and the ways in which the church's activities are guided by their theological orientation.

Theological Orientation as Motive for Public Engagement

A number of religion and politics scholars say that religious interests will be mobilized when there is the requisite combination of means, motive, and opportunity.[3] The "opportunity" for religious political mobilization refers to what social movement theorists describe as the historical, political, and social environment that encourages political mobilization or at least alleviates some of the barriers to mobilization.[4] Public engagement takes place within structures of incentives and disincentives that are extraneous to the churches themselves. In the case of contemporary black megachurches, the policy environment, characterized by an increased emphasis on church/state collaboration through faith-based initiatives and welfare reform legislation, contributes to the context, which provides incentives for certain types of public engagement like developing welfare to work programs.[5] This policy environment might also provide disincentives for other types of public engagement like political protest. So even if given the same means and motives, the incentives and disincentives provided by the social and political context affect the political mobilization of religious groups.

The "means" (taken from social movement theorists who have developed the concept of resource mobilization to explain social movements) refer to the actual resources and capacities needed to carry out the objectives of the religious group. According to Wald et al., religious groups have distinctive and unique access to certain resources (culture, leadership, material resources, communication networks, and space) that are used to mobilize social movements.[6] Black churches have historically been in a unique position to nurture black political leadership, provide material resources, communication networks and space, and culture and identity, and promote civic engagement.[7]

Black megachurches, in particular, have exceptional access to resources that could potentially be used for public engagement. Because of their large membership numbers, black megachurches amass significantly more resources than the average church, including potential volunteers, financial resources, and physical space. In chapter 4, I explore the ways that some churches use their resources to create separate nonprofit community development organizations (CDOs), which build their capacity to participate in particular activities.

The "motive" to engage in public life, which is the focus of this chapter, refers to the driving force behind political mobilization. Those who examine motive look at the cultural aspects of religious groups such as rituals, beliefs, symbols, worldviews, and theology as motivating factors. They examine how, in the words of Richard Wood, "religion qua religion might contribute" to political mobilization. For example, in a study of three churches and one faith-based community organization, Wood found that there are certain religious cultural traits that enhance political capacity and other traits that depress political capacity. In another example, Omar McRoberts examined the Four Corners neighborhood in Boston and found that the churches in Four Corners religiously based orientations about "neighbors" (their surrounding local communities) and "the street" (as either "evil other," "recruiting ground" for church membership, or "point of contact for people in need") influenced the activist orientations of these churches. Likewise, in an examination of black activist churches in Washington, D.C., Walters and Tucker-Worgs found that theological orientation (in particular black theology and prophetic theology) influenced black church electoral activism. These scholars examined the relevance of *ideas* to political mobilization.[8]

While social scientists have applied the social movement theory means, motive, opportunity framework for analyzing the political involvement of churches, most have concentrated on the "means" aspect of this theory. So while there are a number of studies that have concentrated on black churches' unique access to resources that are used for political mobilization, Melissa Harris-Lacewell has correctly noted that the literature has somewhat neglected the study of black churches as places that brings "actors in contact with ideas." Theological orientations are embodiments of these ideas.[9]

Examination of "motive" looks at the reasons black megachurches engage in political activities. What is the purpose of their engagement? What is their intention? What do they hope to achieve? Is it important for the group of believers that is the church to engage in public life? Is it important for the church as an organization? In what manner should believers engage in public life?

A church's theological orientation serves as a motive for public engagement by explicating the church's norms and values about public engagement. A church's culture both explains "how . . . individuals should live [and] suggests the nature of a just society."[10] Thus, theological orientations set guidelines for the proper role of the church in public life.

Religious Traditions and Public Engagement

Much of the political science scholarship that examines the impact of theological orientation on the political engagement of faith communities within the United States focuses on the difference between various religious traditions and the respective political attitudes, vote choices, and levels of political participation of people who identify with these religious traditions. Using public opinion data, these scholars compare the religious beliefs and political attitudes of individuals who identify as Jewish, Catholic, Protestant, Muslim, followers of other religions, and followers of no religion.[11]

The examination of Protestants in this literature is particularly interesting for this study since black megachurches are by definition all Protestant churches. Protestants are usually divided into two major traditions: mainline Protestant and evangelical Protestant. These traditions are composed of churches and denominations that share views about the role of religion in society, views about the Bible, and understandings of Jesus. Black Protestants are often separated into a third category, which will be discussed later. Researchers have noticed a mainline/evangelical gap among white Protestants that reflects a divide between "conservative" and "liberal" orientations. These conservative and liberal orientations are found in both theology and political ideology. White mainline Protestants (including Episcopalians, Congregationalists, Methodists, Lutherans, and Presbyterians) tend to be more liberal in both theological orientation and politics, and evangelical Protestants (including Baptists, Southern Methodists, Presbyterians, nondenominational churches, Pentecostals, Holiness churches, Charismatics, Fundamentalists, and Adventists) tend to be more conservative in theology and politics.[12]

Mainline Protestants more likely view the Bible as the "inspired" word of God that has "deep truths that have to be discerned amidst myth and archaic stories" and that has to be interpreted and not taken literally.[13] This faith tradition places emphasis on Jesus as a promoter of social justice and maintains that "ills of society" "reflect social injustice."[14] These theological beliefs influence the political beliefs of mainline Protestants. Mainline Protestants are more likely to be associated with liberal politics that focus on changing the structure of society. Mainline Protestants generally fall to the political ideological left of evangelical Protestants. They are more likely to identify as Democrats and liberals than are evangelical Protestants.[15]

The evangelical religious tradition is more theologically conservative. Subscribers to this faith tradition are more likely to view the Bible as the "inerrant" word of God. The "individual gospel" that evangelical Protestants preach means that instead of transforming the structures of society, evangelical Protestants focus on individual transformation. When engaged in the public sphere they are more likely to focus on promoting issues of personal morality. The conservative theological perspective of evangelical Christians shapes their more conservative political ideology. Evangelical Protestants are more likely to vote for Republican candidates for president of the United States and more likely to identify as political conservatives than are mainline Protestants.[16]

Wald and Calhoun-Brown interject nuance in the evangelical/mainline Protestant debate and warn that the relationship between theology and political activity is complicated. Theological traditions must be contextualized by society, history, and other aspects of group identity.[17] Moreover, the mainline/ evangelical divide is also becoming recognized as more nuanced, as some notable evangelical Protestants have become more involved in "social justice" issues like poverty, health care, and the environment.[18]

Black Protestants

Social scientists have taken the political and historical context into account in studies of religion and politics by categorizing black Protestants as a distinct faith group from both mainline and evangelical Protestants. The explanation is that while most black Protestants would be classified as "evangelical" in terms of their belief in the Bible as the "inerrant" word of God, the vast majority of black Protestants fall to the left of the political ideological spectrum. According to Lincoln and Mamiya, "[B]lack evangelicals tend to be conservative in their religious views but liberal in their political positions."[19] This means that many black Protestants have in fact "managed to combine the evangelical emphasis on salvation with the mainline commitment to social action."[20] Conservative, mostly white evangelical movements like the Christian Right have been largely unsuccessful in mobilizing black evangelicals to join them.[21]

While it is important and appropriate to distinguish black Protestants from white mainline and evangelical Protestants, there is also a related tendency to treat the black Protestant category as if it is monolithic—especially when it comes to examining the impact of religion on politics. One scholar explained a rationale for this by arguing that African Americans in the United States are overwhelmingly Democrats and "there is little or no within-group variance."[22] The implication is that there is a limited payoff to studying the diversity of black religious attitudes and/or politics. But the consequence of treating the black Protestant category as monolithic is that differing religious beliefs and traditions within the larger black Protestant tradition and the different political behavior and views that these different religious orientations may be associated with are ignored.

Scholars specifically concerned with the black church and black religion have shown that there are in fact different theological orientations and religious traditions among African Americans that help to shape their political attitudes and behavior.[23] While these differing religious traditions within the black Protestant category have not been shown to lead to dramatically different individual political decisions in areas of vote choice, support for civil rights policy, and support for liberal economic policy, religious tradition has been shown to affect some attitudes on social issues such as gay rights, views on abortion, and prayer in schools.[24] Some studies show that black evangelicals are more conservative than black mainline Protestants on abortion, are more likely to favor prayer in schools, and are less likely to favor women in the pulpit.[25] Lincoln and Mamiya observe a relationship between black church denominational affiliation and support for political and civil rights, support for women's ordination, civil rights militancy, and levels of black consciousness.[26]

Theological orientation is an important component of the "means, motive, opportunity" formula for the political mobilization of religious communities. It spells out norms, values, and expectations for the churches' participation in public life. The following sections explain how I measured the theological orientation of black megachurches and focus on how the theological orientations particular to black megachurches influence their public engagement.

Measuring Black Megachurch Theological Orientation

Most studies that examine theological orientation and political attitudes and behavior use survey research to determine the impact of an individual's attitudinal and organizational religiosity on his or her political attitudes and behavior.[27] The attitudinal aspect of religiosity refers to the "guiding role" that religion plays in one's life and the particular doctrine and beliefs that one relies upon. The organizational aspect of religiosity refers to the frequency of church attendance and participation in church activities. While examining the individual is a worthy subject of inquiry, much of the religious influence is done at the institutional level, and both approaches are needed to get a more complete picture of the role of black churches in public life.[28] Scholars have somewhat neglected to study the impact of theological orientation on the activities of churches as institutions.

The Data Sources

Evidence of a church's theological orientations can be found in a variety of church documents such as mission statements, vision statements, creeds, anthems, and hymns. It can be found in the sermons preached, Bible lessons emphasized, views and opinions of the ministerial leadership and laity, denominational traditions and doctrine, formal and informal histories about the church itself, and practices and traditions of the church. These expressions may be either explicit or implicit, and of course when looking at a church in totality they may even be conflicting.

This study relies on five data sources for evidence of theological orienta-tion. The sources are the responses to survey questions designed to measure various aspects of theological orientation, the denominational affiliation of the churches, their mission statements, and church visits and church documents (including sermons, articles and books written by megachurch ministers, church bulletins, responses to interviews, and websites).

Survey Responses

The survey data were collected as a part of a large study: the ITC/Faith Com-munities Today Project 2000. The ITC/Faith Communities Today Project 2000 survey included 1,863 black churches across the United States.[29] I sepa-rately administered the ITC/Faith Communities Today Project 2000 survey to 31 randomly selected black megachurches. The respondents were pastors or assistant pastors of the churches.

The Project 2000 survey included questions that directly addressed the theological orientation of the church along with questions about the church's location, denomination, and public engagement activities. In addition to the closed-ended survey responses there were several open-ended responses that allowed the key informants to explain issues in more depth. Specific questions gauged whether the churches had more prophetic orientations (focused on the issues of the world as central to the mission of the church) or exclusively priestly orientations (focused on the spiritual needs of the members of the church). There were also questions focused on black theology and racial consciousness. Consequently, the Project 2000 data revealed three of the five dominant theo-logical orientations: black theology, prophetic theology, and nondenomination-alism. There were not questions on the survey about neo-Pentecostalism or the prosperity gospel, so these two could not be detected by the survey.

The Project 2000 survey also measured the churches' public engagement activities, which include aspects of social service delivery, economic develop-ment, and housing and more explicitly "political" activities like enhancing voter participation, community organizing, and advocacy.[30]

I used logistic regressions to test the relationship between the churches' theological orientations and their public engagement activities.[31] I also intro-duced several control variables to the models: the education level of the minis-ter, the age of the church, the average weekly attendance, whether the church is located in an inner-city or suburban area, and whether the church is located in the South. These variables are all said to have an impact on how much a church participates in public engagement activities.[32]

Denomination

A church's denomination is particularly relevant to an understanding of its theological orientation. Denominations are groups of affiliated congregations. With denominations come particular histories, traditions, practices, and doctrines. Denominations often take official positions on public policy and teach/promote these positions and their doctrine to their members.[33] Scholars have found that the traditions, practices, and doctrines affiliated with denominations are related to their public engagement.[34] Recall the earlier discussion of evangelical Protestant and mainline Protestant theological orientations and public engagement activities. Both evangelical and mainline traditions are associated with particular denominations.

Black churches do not fall exactly along the lines of the white church mainline/evangelical divide. Instead, black churches more often are described as being a part of either the mainline or Sanctified traditions. Black Baptist and black Methodist churches are considered mainline. The Sanctified tradition consists of Holiness, Pentecostal, and Apostolic churches.[35] This is distinct from but overlaps with the white Protestant mainline/evangelical divide. It is distinct because black Baptists are considered to be in the "mainline" in the black Protestant tradition but are considered evangelical in the white Protestant tradition.

Although there are some important differences scholars have noted among the black denominations, nondenominational or independent churches have been ignored in the great majority of studies on the black church. In this study I consciously chose to include these churches.

Mission Statements

Church mission statements are reflective expressions that explicitly describe a church's theology. As exemplified by FAME's mission statement, they may entail the church's articulation of its role in society. They may also show how that role is influenced by their religious beliefs. I conducted a document analysis of the mission statements of forty-two black megachurches to examine reoccurring themes. They vary in their focus. Some are strictly focused on sacred matters, but most display a mixture of sacred and secular concerns.

Although mission statements are actual products of the theological belief system of churches, they cannot be used as reliable quantifiable evidence because the churches' mission statements are not standardized. For example, in some cases the mission statements were written when a church was first founded (sometimes decades ago), and in others the statements were the product of recent revisions as the church came into a new understanding of itself. Of course the absence of an idea from a mission statement does not mean that the idea is not a part of the church's beliefs or goals. However, the mention of a particular theme or idea in the mission statement does help to illustrate the theology of the church. It tells us about the basic tenets of the church's beliefs in the words of its members.

Church Visits and Related Church Documents

To get an even fuller understanding of black megachurch theology, I conducted site visits to thirty-one black megachurches. Church site visits were especially helpful in documenting "black liberation theology" and the "prosperity gospel." This observational technique helped to address questions such as the following: What is the church's perspective of God as represented in the images presented in the church? What functions does the church deem as important as evidenced by the usage of the space (for example, some churches have a "Christian education" building, centers for community development and/or social service provision, community centers, and youth centers)?

In one example, my visit to Shiloh Baptist Church in Washington, D.C., provided a better understanding of the high priority they placed on "community development." Shiloh had a minister for community development and a center for community development and outreach adjacent to the church. In another example, Mt. Ephraim Baptist Church in Atlanta had a newly developed building for Christian education, in which they housed all Sunday school classes, which incidentally were held not only on Sunday but also throughout the week. This indicates a high priority placed on Christian education. Several of the black megachurches have stained-glass windows that depict black biblical characters and other objects that illustrate an emphasis on black theology. Data from the site visits complemented the data gathered by other methods.

In addition to the site visits, I also made virtual visits to the churches and observed several church services on DVD, on television, or via the Internet. Church websites served as a very useful source of information regarding their theological orientation. Also, many black megachurch ministers have written books that outline their own personal theologies as well as the theologies of their respective churches. This type of qualitative research was very important in that it allowed me to measure concepts that the answers to survey questions did not. For example, while Second Baptist Church of New Jersey had no mention of black theology in their mission statement, they had a picture of a black Jesus (which is one important concept of "black theology") on their website.

Taking both a qualitative and quantitative approach, I used a compilation of survey data, church documents, and site visits to conduct an analysis of the relationship between black megachurch theological orientations and their public engagement activities. Now I turn to the dominant theological orientations that the examination of these sources uncovered and explain their significance to a better understanding about the role of black megachurches in public life.

Five Dominant Black Megachurch Theological Orientations

The analysis of the data revealed five theological orientations that emerged as dominant in black megachurches. These are neo-Pentecostalism, black theology, prophetic theology, nondenominationalism, and the prosperity gospel. These theological orientations are multifaceted and speak to all five of the aspects of a church's theological orientation described at the outset of this chapter (the identity of God, the understanding of human beings as God's creatures, right and wrong, the meaning of the church in the world, and passages of life). Particularly relevant to this study is the "meaning of the church in the world" because it illuminates best how the church acts out theological beliefs.

The black megachurches exhibit combinations of these theological orientations—as opposed to only one orientation. They also exhibit the orientations at varying levels of intensity. Three of the dominant orientations, prophetic theology, black theology, and nondenominationalism, are highly correlated (see table 3.1).

The theological orientations vary in the impact they have on public engagement. Neo-Pentecostalism, like I pointed out in the previous chapter, is a common characteristic of black megachurches that virtually all of them exhibit, albeit to varying degrees. This theological orientation does not depress or inspire public engagement. Both nondenominationalism and the prosperity gospel depress public engagement. Black theology and prophetic theology both encourage public engagement.

The remainder of this section describes the dominant black megachurch theological orientations individually and explains their impact on public engagement activities.

Neo-Pentecostalism

Neo-Pentecostalism is the most widespread theological orientation found in black megachurches. As discussed in the previous chapter, the neo-Pentecostal movement is evident in black megachurches of various denominations, regions,

TABLE 3.1

CORRELATION OF "THEOLOGICAL ORIENTATION" INDEPENDENT VARIABLES

		Prophetic	Black Theology	Nondenominational
Pearson correlation	Prophetic	1.00	.682**	−.416*
	Black theology	.682**	1.00	−.604**
	Nondenominational	−.416*	−.604**	1.00
Sig. (two-tailed)	Prophetic	—	.000	.020
	Black theology	.000	—	.001
	Nondenominational	.020	.001	—
N	Prophetic	31	28	31
	Black theology	28	28	28
	Nondenominational	31	28	65

*Correlation is significant at the .05 level (two-tailed).
**Correlation is significant at the .01 level (two-tailed).
SOURCE: ITC/Faith Communities Today Project 2000 Megachurch Survey.

founding dates, and membership sizes. Nondenominational churches, Baptist churches, AME churches, and churches in predominantly white denominations all practice many of the traditions, rituals, and worship styles of the "Sanctified church." These practices include charismatic and enthusiastic worship and acceptance of and appreciation for the "gifts of the spirit."[36]

The recent neo-Pentecostal movement in black churches has been well documented. Gilkes has noted that several black Baptist and black Methodist churches are commonly referred to as "Bapticostal" and "AMEP" (African Methodist Episcopal Pentecostal) because of their embrace of Pentecostal worship styles. According to Gilkes, this Pentecostal movement has, in a sense, revived "dead" churches.[37] Churches that had declining memberships and relatively reserved worship styles have been able to revive their memberships with a change in worship style, especially attracting younger members.

Lincoln and Mamiya point out a neo-Pentecostal movement in AME churches, particularly those whose pastors were protégés of AME Bishop John Bryant. These churches experienced rapid and phenomenal growth, and the majority of the churches they highlight are actually megachurches—including one of the churches that Bryant formerly pastored, Bethel AME in Baltimore. Lincoln and Mamiya note that these churches are not otherworldly or apolitical, nor do they promote a conservative politics. Instead they combine Pentecostal enthusiastic worship and piety with the traditional AME focus on social justice.[38]

Walton claims that there are actually three different categories of what most call the "neo-Pentecostal movement" in the black church that differ by their theological orientations and religious traditions. The first group (which incidentally Walton calls "neo-Pentecostal") comprises churches that have a denominational connection to traditional Pentecostal denominations or the "Sanctified church." These churches are distinct from traditional Sanctified churches because they have begun to blur the previously strict line between the sacred and the secular that the traditional Sanctified church tends to define as a very strict divide. The second category of churches is made up of what he calls "charismatic mainlines." These churches belong to mainline denominations but have begun to worship in the style and engage in some of the practices of the Sanctified church. This group includes the AME churches that Lincoln and Mamiya describe as well as others. Finally there are the "word of faith" churches. Word of faith churches are nondenominational and have no formal connection to either the Sanctified or the black mainline church tradition (the word of faith or prosperity theology is discussed later in the chapter).[39]

Most black megachurches embrace some of the tenets of Pentecostalism, especially "glossolalia, prophecy, healings, words of knowledge and other so-called supernatural gifts of the Spirit" and the "Baptism in the Spirit."[40]

Examples of neo-Pentecostalism in black megachurches are plentiful, and many of these churches express it in their mission statements and church documents. Cathedral Second Baptist Church's (New Jersey) statement of faith is, "We are a Christian church. Baptist by denomination, Pentecostal by experience, Holiness by choice."

Another example is Greater St. Stephens Full Gospel Baptist Church, which was located in New Orleans before Hurricane Katrina but has since moved much of its operation to Atlanta, Georgia. Greater St. Stephens is what Walton would call a "charismatic mainline" church. It is the mother church of the Full Gospel Baptist Church Fellowship, which was started by the pastor of Greater St. Stephens, Bishop Paul Morton.

When asked why he started the full gospel fellowship Bishop Morton stated,

> God led me to begin the Full Gospel Baptist Church Fellowship, which came out of Greater Saint Stephens. We were a traditional Baptist church. We believed the basics of the Bible that you needed to be saved. We believed in the death, burial, and the resurrection of Jesus Christ. But growing up in the Pentecostal church, I knew that God had another level for us as it related to the fullness of the Holy Spirit, as it related to casting out demons, laying

hands on the sick, speaking in a heavenly language. So what God did, He said "to transition the traditional Baptist church I had into the fullness of the Holy Spirit." Whoever wanted to receive the fullness of the Holy Spirit, with the manifestations of the Heavenly language, with the taking of authority over the Devil, could go to that next level. And God began to bless Greater Saint Stephens in such a mighty way. I was so happy. All of a sudden, I had bridged the gap between Pentecostals and Baptists.[41]

Crenshaw Christian Center (Ever Increasing Faith Ministries) in Los Angeles is another neo-Pentecostal church, but it is a nondenominational word of faith church. Crenshaw Christian Center was founded in 1973 by Rev. Fred K. Price and had three hundred members. Since then it has grown to a membership of over eighteen thousand.[42] Price had been a minister at Baptist, AME, and Presbyterian churches before forming Crenshaw Christian Center but had found the theology and worship style of these denominations unsatisfactory. In Price's biography the author explains what led Price to accept a neo-Pentecostal theological orientation.

> While Dr. Price was pastoring for the Christian and Missionary Alliance at West Washington Community Church, he read Kathryn Kuhlman's book, *God Can Do It Again*. "It stirred my soul," he says. "This was the missing dimension—the demonstration of the power of the Spirit of God," or what the Bible terms "the gifts of the Spirit."
> On February 28, 1970, he received the gift of the Holy Spirit with the evidence of "speaking with other tongues"—also known as "glossolalia." That is the event that Dr. Price considers the jumping-off point in his ministry.[43]

These examples clearly show that black megachurches of various denominational families and traditions exhibit a neo-Pentecostal theological orientation. Now the discussion turns to the impact of neo-Pentecostalism (or lack thereof) on public engagement.

Neo-Pentecostalism and public engagement

Traditional Pentecostalism is considered a part of the more theologically conservative Protestant tradition. Recall our earlier discussion of conservative Protestant churches. It is generally argued that more conservative theological views lead to more conservative politics. Theologically conservative churches are less likely to participate in political and social activities. When they do participate, their participation is likely to consist of advocacy around issues of personal morality.

From this we would expect that a neo-Pentecostal theological orientation would make a church more conservative theologically and politically. However, the evidence shows that the neo-Pentecostal theological orientation is evident in churches that engage extensively in public life as well as those that refrain from engagement.

This of course is consistent with Lincoln and Mamiya's observations about the AME churches that were a part of a neo-Pentecostal movement in the 1980s. As opposed to being politically conservative or apolitical, the AME neo-Pentecostal churches were very politically active, and their action was more liberal than conservative on an ideological spectrum. These churches were in *keeping* with an AME tradition of political activism.

Like the AME churches, there are a number of neo-Pentecostal churches that engage extensively in public life. For example, Cathedral Second Baptist in New Jersey is very active in public engagement. It has an affiliated community development corporation (Cathedral International CDC) that houses activities including the Angel Food network, an ex-offender reentry program, and a counseling center. Their mission statement claims that they are "rebuilding the church and the community," indicating a belief that public engagement is an important component of their role in the world.

Not only is there no evidence of neo-Pentecostalism inhibiting the activism of black megachurches, but also churches in this study that are a part of a "Sanctified" denomination were no less likely to participate in public engagement activities than other churches. Two churches in particular are worth noting—Apostolic Church of God in Chicago and Bible Way Temple in Washington, D.C. Each of these churches is a part of the Sanctified tradition, and each has a history of public engagement with past pastors who have been noted for their active participation in movements for social justice.

For example, Apostolic Church of God's mission statement reads,

> In our service to Christ, we are to call sinners to repentance, lift the fallen, visit the sick, uplift and maintain the highest standards, of morality, and urge all believers to seek a Spirit-filled life. It is essential that we nourish and cultivate the Christian lives of our parishioners, that we concern ourselves with giving aid and comfort to the poor, to work for better living conditions in society in general, and in our community in particular.

The former pastor of Apostolic Church of God, the late Bishop Arthur Brazier, was the founding president of the Woodlawn Organization (TWO), a community organization in Chicago. TWO was organized by Saul Alinsky to stop the University of Chicago from expanding and displacing residents of Woodlawn on the South Side of Chicago. TWO was one of several organizations formed around the country to combat the displacement effects of urban renewal programs that some have referred to as "Negro removal" because of the disproportional impact that these programs had on African American neighborhoods. Rev. Brazier and the church he led for forty-eight years place a strong emphasis on church-based public engagement.[44]

The founder of Bible Way Temple in Washington, D.C., another "Sanctified" megachurch, the late Bishop Smallwood Williams, was known for civil rights activism and public engagement. Williams served as the local chapter president of the Southern Christian Leadership Conference (SCLC) in the 1960s and worked to develop affordable housing in D.C. In his autobiography he expressed his belief that religion and politics go hand in hand:

> The black minister, in particular, has an even greater role to be politically involved, I feel, than clergy of other races because of so many unsolved problems left over from 300 years of human slavery and degradation of his people—the exploitation, the injustices and the deprivations. The social sins of racism found in segregation and economic exploitation can be solved through the political process.[45]

The fact that the Sanctified black megachurches are not necessarily disengaged from public life is consistent with Walton's argument about Sanctified churches in the neo-Pentecostal movement. The "neo-Pentecostal" Sanctified churches are distinguished from "traditional" Sanctified churches because they blur the sacred/secular divide. When the sacred/secular divide is blurred, churches are more likely to engage in public life, which explains why a "neo-Pentecostal" Sanctified church would be as likely as any other to be an activist church.

Neo-Pentecostalism is ubiquitous throughout multiple religious traditions. Some have a political orientation like the AME churches that Lincoln and Mamiya describe and focus on social justice, but others have a more conservative political orientation.[46] Therefore, it is clear that neo-Pentecostalism neither inspires nor depresses public engagement.

Black Theology

A second dominant theological orientation in black megachurches is black theology. Black theology (also called black liberation theology) is a systematic theology that at its core relates the Christian experience to black people's experiences in America—especially within the context of racial oppression and in the struggle for civil and human rights. Theologian James Cone, the author of many of black theology's primary works, calls it "a religious explication of black people's need to define the scope and meaning of black existence in a racist society."[47]

There are important aspects of the "word on God" that emerge from black theology. First, Christianity should be interpreted from a "black perspective" that challenges racism and recognizes an African heritage. Second, Christ is depicted as black. This is not only about the skin color of Christ but even more so about Christ's actions and affinities. The physical appearance of Christ as black relates to his affinity to the black freedom struggle.[48] In other words, the black Christ wants black people to be free. Finally, black theology affirms that Christianity is about "liberating the oppressed" and making the world better for "the least of these."

Systematic black theology developed in the late 1960s in the context of the civil rights and black power eras. James Cone called it black power's "religious counterpart."[49] Gayraud Wilmore said that black theology was "the unmistakable sign that God was saying and doing something about Black people in White America."[50]

While the black liberation movements of the 1960s made up the political context for the development of black theology, it did not develop in a theological vacuum. The work of theologian Joseph Washington was one of the important sparks for its development.[51] In his book *Black Religion*, Washington argued that black religion was not authentic Christianity. It was his view that "the Negro is forced to depend upon civil rights, religious feeling, sentiment and color as substitutes for faith" and that their churches were void of theology.[52] Black theologians countered Washington and argued that black religion was indeed authentic Christianity, and some argued it was even more authentic than white/mainstream Christian theology because it had a social justice emphasis.[53]

The theological antecedents to black theology were the scholarly works of theologians like Howard Thurman, who appropriated the Christian story to the "dispossessed and disinherited" in the United States, and Martin Luther King Jr., who applied the social gospel to the racial situation in the United States. Black theology was also influenced by the philosophical thought of Malcolm X and his poignant critique of the black church and mainstream black Christianity, which he saw as aiding and abetting white racial oppression. What ultimately developed was a black theology that provided an internal critique of the black church for the role it had played in black oppression and an external critique of mainstream white Christianity and U.S. society for the oppression of blacks.[54]

While black theology became a systematic theology studied and explicated in academia in the 1960s, examples of a liberating Christianity for black people in the United States can be traced back to the religious views and practices of the earliest Africans in America. Black people challenged the dominant and oppressive interpretations of Christianity, made Christianity relevant to black struggles for liberation in the United States, and depicted a black Christ even before the civil rights and black power movements. As a practical theology black theology dates back to the days of African enslavement. The religious and political thought of Frederick Douglass, Maria Stewart, Bishop Henry McNeal Turner, Sojourner Truth, and David Walker, among others, the development of "invisible institutions" (plantation churches out of reach of the slave masters and overseers), and independent black religious institutions formed by free blacks in the early nineteenth century like the AME church are all examples of a "liberating" black Christianity.[55]

A general perception about black megachurches is that (even more than other black churches) black theology has "failed to penetrate their ministries."[56] In fact a black theology orientation is evident in black megachurches in a number of ways. The survey responses, churches' mission statements, church documents, rituals, sermons, décor, and other cultural items all reveal examples of black theology's influence on a number of black megachurches.

Black theology in the preached word

In their seminal work on black churches in the United States, C. Eric Lincoln and Lawrence Mamiya found that for the most part black theology had failed to penetrate the walls of academia and that the black church by and large was not influenced by black theology. They found that only about one-third of black churches had been influenced by black theology.

I found that a greater percentage of black megachurches than black churches in general have been influenced by black theology. The Project 2000 survey asked two questions relevant to black theology: "How often does the sermon focus on black liberation theology?" and "How often does the sermon focus on the racial situation in America?" The respondents were given five choices: always, often, sometimes, seldom, and never. The percentage of black megachurches that make reference to black theology was higher than the percentage that Lincoln and Mamiya observed among black churches in general. Whereas Lincoln and Mamiya found that most black ministers do not make reference to black theology in their sermons, a slight majority of black megachurches said that they made reference to black theology at least some of the time. One-third of the megachurches in the survey sample reported they made references to black theology often or always, and another 32 percent reported that they did so sometimes. In addition, the vast majority of black megachurches reported that the racial situation in society was the focus of the minister's sermon at least some of the time.

The difference between Lincoln and Mamiya's findings and the megachurch data can probably be explained by the education level of black megachurch pastors when compared to that of pastors of black churches in general. They found a relationship between the education level of pastors and the likelihood that they mentioned black theology. On average, black megachurch pastors had higher education levels and therefore were more likely to have been exposed to black theology in seminaries, which they were then more likely to focus on in their sermons.

The black megachurch data corroborate the finding of a relationship between education and support for black theology. Table 3.2 shows that whether or not black liberation theology is a theme of the sermons in black megachurches correlates with the education level of the minister and the church's denomination. Those churches that are nondenominational were least likely to make references to black theology in their churches. Black churches in both white and black denominations were likely to make references to black theology.

In addition to the survey data, a qualitative analysis illuminated examples of black theology in black megachurches. These data fall among the three ideas in black theological thought mentioned above (interpreting Christianity from a "black perspective," depicting a black Christ, and promoting the liberation of the oppressed). The following section explains these observations in further detail.

Christianity from a "black perspective"

Several black megachurches clearly expressed their interpretation of Christianity from a "black perspective" in their mission statements. This perspective challenges the marginalized status of blacks in America and racism in general. For example, the mission statement of Antioch Baptist Church North in Atlanta states that Antioch is guided by two principles: "six ministries as defined under Matthew 25:35-36" and "our ethnicity as African Americans."[57] Trinity United Church of Christ (UCC), which gained notoriety during the 2008 U.S. presidential election because of their practice of black liberation theology and President Barack Obama's membership in the church, states in their mission statement, "W.E.B. Du Bois indicated that the problem in the twentieth century was going to be the problem of the color line. He was absolutely correct."

TABLE 3.2
BLACK MEGACHURCH MINISTERS' RESPONSES TO THE QUESTION,
"HOW OFTEN DOES YOUR CHURCH DISCUSS 'BLACK THEOLOGY?'"
DENOMINATIONAL GROUPING AND HIGHEST LEVEL OF EDUCATION

	Always Often or Sometimes (%)	Seldom or Never (%)
Denominational grouping		
Black denomination*	81.3	18.8
Predominantly White denomination**	100.0	0
"Sanctified" denomination**	100.0	0
Nondenominational*	0	100.0
Highest level of education attained**		
Less than college or Bible school	0	100.0
Bachelor's degree	66.7	33.3
Master's degree (i.e., M.Div.)	100.0	0
Doctoral degree (i.e., Th.D. or D.Div)	62.5	37.5

*X² significant at the .05 level.
**X² significant at the .01 level.
SOURCE: ITC/Faith Communities Today Project 2000 Megachurch Survey.

For these churches, black consciousness and identity is especially important for interpreting the role of the church in society.

Black theology also "stems from the recognition that black identity must be defined in terms of its African heritage rather than in terms of European enslavement."[58] Many megachurch mission statements, rituals, and traditions reflect a reliance on an "African heritage." For example, in their mission statement, Trinity UCC states that it "does not apologize for its African Roots," emphasizing a reliance on an African-centered perspective. Metropolitan Baptist Church in Washington, D.C., infuses aspects of a west African naming ceremony into its baby blessing ceremonies, and several black megachurches (including Metropolitan) have African drums as a part of the music. Shiloh Baptist Church, also in Washington, D.C., sometimes uses the Sunday school hour to teach "Black and African History." During black history month Bible Way Temple teaches a series of lessons on the black origins of the Pentecostal movement. Union Temple Baptist Church includes the pouring of libations at major ceremonies such as weddings, burials, baby blessings, and the installation of church officers.

The black Christ

The depiction of a black messiah is another aspect of black liberation theology. Kelly Brown Douglas observes three theories of the black Christ. The first is that the black Christ is biologically and genealogically black. The second is that the black Christ is black because a black Christ liberates black people from spiritual, social, political, and economic oppression. But other ethnic groups and people also should see Christ in their likeness and so become thus liberated. She attributes this perspective to theologian J. Deotis Roberts, who argues that Christ is both universal and particularistic. The third explanation for the black Christ is that the black Christ is symbolically black because of Christ's identification with "the least of these"—the oppressed and those who are at the bottom of the societal hierarchy.[59]

James Cone, who champions this perspective of the black Christ, illustrates this point by asserting that "[i]n America, blacks are oppressed because of their blackness. It would seem, then, that emancipation could only be realized by Christ and his Church becoming black. Thinking of Christ as nonblack in the twentieth century is as theologically impossible as thinking of him as non-Jewish in the first century."[60] In all three of these perspectives, the black Christ embraces blackness, which has been denigrated in the United States. Clearly the black Christ is a symbol of both cultural and political nationalism. Political scientists have used identification with the black Christ alone as a measurement of positive sentiment toward black theology.[61]

Mural, Union Temple Baptist Church

Black megachurches depict a Christ of African descent in their documents, representations in church sanctuaries, and dramatic church performances (like the depiction of Christ as black with dreadlocks in an annual Easter play). In a list of twenty-three core values, Greenforest Community Baptist Church in Atlanta states, "We believe, based on scripture genealogy, that when Jesus came in the flesh He chose to come as a Palestinian Jew with African ancestry." Not only Christ but also other biblical personalities are portrayed as being of African descent in church materials such as Sunday school lesson books and in representations in the sanctuaries and other locations throughout the churches. Several black megachurches have extensive murals that depict a black Christ and black biblical figures in their sanctuaries and throughout their church campuses.

Liberation of the oppressed

Another key tenet of black theology is belief that Christianity requires Christians to identify with the oppressed and actively engage in liberating those who are oppressed. Biblical history is used to substantiate this claim. For example, theologians who promote this perspective point to the New Testament and the story of the life of Jesus. James Cone writes,

> Jesus is pictured as the oppressed one who views his own person and work as an identification with the humiliated condition of the poor. The poor were at the heart of his mission.[62]

He goes on to write,

> Jesus had little toleration for the middle- or upper-class religious snob whose attitude attempted to usurp the sovereignty of God and destroy the dignity of the poor. It is not possible to be for Christ and also for the enslavement of men.[63]

There are black megachurches that express this key tenet. For example, one church describes their church family as "agents of liberation." Union Temple Baptist Church in Washington has a mural in the sanctuary that depicts a black Jesus with black disciples sharing the Last Supper. All of the people depicted as disciples (some of whom are Harriet Tubman, Sojourner Truth, Frederick Douglass, Nelson Mandela, Martin Luther King Jr., and Malcolm X) were political activists. These people were not all men, nor were they all Christians, but they were all people of African descent who fought for black liberation. Black theology is obviously a key component of Union Temple's overall theological orientation.

The "liberation of the oppressed" aspect of black theology particularly denounces class divisions within the African American community. Black theology promotes the economic, social, and political liberation of all blacks through collective action. A few black megachurches express this in their mission and vision statements. The mission statement of Trinity UCC of Chicago states,

> We are called out to be "a chosen people" that pays no attention to socio-economic or educational backgrounds. We are made up of the highly educated and the uneducated. Our congregation is a combination of the haves and the have-nots; the economically disadvantaged, the under-class, the unemployed and the employable. The fortunate who are among us combine forces with the less fortunate to become agents of change for God who is not pleased with Americans economic mal-distribution![64]

In another example, St. John's United Methodist Church in Houston, Texas (which has extensive homeless, employment, and health care ministries), echoes these ideas. Their mission statement states that they endeavor "to remove the barriers of classism, sexism and racism from the worship experience."[65]

Racial consciousness

Many black megachurches emphasize a concern for "race in society," although the church may not show evidence of promoting the ideas of "black theology" per se. This perspective calls on an older tradition of racial consciousness that has as its center the universality of the Christian message and racial inclusiveness as opposed to a primary focus on black nationalism. This older tradition emphasizes pragmatism, racial uplift, and self-help.[66] Table 3.3 shows that in general megachurch ministers were much more likely to say that their sermons often focused on references to "the racial situation in society" than on "black liberation theology."

"Black theology" and public engagement

Previous studies have found black theology to be related to public engagement activities and aspects of racial empowerment.[67] We would expect a black theology orientation to encourage public engagement. The tenets of black theology and even older racial consciousness traditions emphasized racial uplift, which may take the form of public involvement.

To determine if black theology is positively related to public engagement activities I performed several logistic regressions using black theology as the independent variable and controlling for whether they were located in an

TABLE 3.3
FREQUENCY OF BLACK MEGACHURCH MINISTERS RESPONSES TO THE QUESTION,
"HOW OFTEN DOES THE SERMON FOCUS ON . . ."

	References to Black Liberation Theology (%)	References to the Racial Situation in Society (%)
Always	17.9	25.8
Often	10.7	25.8
Sometimes	32.1	38.7
Seldom	21.0	6.5
Never	17.9	3.2
n	28.0	31.0

SOURCE: ITC/Faith Communities Today Project 2000 Megachurch Survey.

inner-city or suburban area, whether they were founded after 1960, and the education level of the minister. The black theology variable was created using the two survey questions that measure two different aspects of the concept. The first question concerns the extent to which black megachurch ministers focus on the "racial situation in society" in their sermons. The second question concerns the extent to which black megachurch ministers focus on black theology in their sermons. A black theology index that combined these two questions was created.

Table 3.4 shows that the higher the church scored on the black theology index, the more likely the church was to participate in commercial development and to build affordable housing. All of the beta coefficients are positive, indicating a positive relationship between the various public engagement activities and black theology.

Black megachurches exhibit black theology in their mission statements, décor, and responses to survey questions. This may be counterintuitive, as these churches are so often associated with prosperity preaching and a lack of a prophetic or civil rights focus. As would be expected, the empirical evidence shows that a black theology orientation encourages public engagement, especially in the areas of housing and commercial development.

Prophetic Theology

A third theological orientation that stands out in black megachurches is the "prophetic" theological orientation. Prophetic theology directly speaks to the theological tenet concerning the role of the church in the world. According to a

TABLE 3.4
LOGISTIC REGRESSION SHOWING THE IMPACT OF "BLACK THEOLOGY" ON PUBLIC ENGAGEMENT ACTIVITIES

	Black Consciousness			Inner City			Founded after 1960			Reverend Education			χ^2	−2 Log Likelihood	N
	B	SE	Odds Ratio	B	SE	Odds Ratio	B	SE	Odds Ratio	B	SE	Odds Ratio			
Community development corporation	0.12	0.25	1.13	−0.37	0.94	0.68	−0.69	1.00	0.49	0.38	0.36	1.47	0.28	30.13	28
Affordable housing	0.54*	0.27	1.73	−0.00	0.93	0.99	−0.02	1.00	0.97	0.06	0.39	1.06	0.13	31.58	28
Commercial development	0.98*	0.45	2.66	−3.06 (.09)	1.84	0.04	1.18	1.35	3.27	0.65	0.65	1.91	0.00	19.19	28
Credit union	0.16	0.32	1.17	0.22	1.18	1.25	−1.52	1.33	0.21	1.59	1.14	4.93	0.09	25.53	28
Food pantry	0.02	0.33	1.02	0.75	1.42	2.13	−1.35	1.42	0.25	−0.11	0.49	0.89	0.90	18.04	28
Political ministry	0.52 (.08)	0.30	1.69	−1.79	1.09	0.16	0.66	1.08	1.94	0.41	0.47	1.51	0.03	26.32	27
Voter education	0.33	0.33	1.40	2.44	1.50	11.55	−0.28	1.23	0.74	0.12	0.41	1.13	0.32	24.44	28
Issue advocacy	0.36	0.30	1.44	0.78	1.08	2.18	−0.58	1.09	0.55	0.48	0.40	1.62	0.08	27.06	28

SOURCE: ITC/Faith Communities Today Project 2000 Survey. * indicates P < .05.

prophetic theological orientation, churches should engage the social and political issues of the contemporary world. Not only should they speak on contemporary social and political issues, but also they should engage in the "African
American jeremiad tradition"[68] and critique political leaders and public policies
when they go against what God would want.

There is a well-established prophetic tradition in the black church. Through
their sermons black ministers have spoken out against racism and segregation
and on behalf of social justice. They have also spoken out against what they
deemed as imperialism perpetrated by the U.S. government. Martin Luther
King Jr. is well known for having engaged in "prophetic preaching."[69] More
recently (in 2008), Rev. Jeremiah Wright, retired pastor of Trinity UCC in
Chicago, drew a storm of criticism when he criticized the U.S. government for
its role in slavery and the general mistreatment of African Americans, women,
and Native people in the United States, imperialism, and generally poor relations between the United States and the rest of the world. The sermon that
drew the most criticism, known to many as the "God damn America" sermon
(actually titled "Confusing God and Government"), is a classic example of the
prophetic tradition in the African American church.

Traditionally the prophetic theological orientation has promoted the idea
that the church should work on behalf of social justice in the tradition of the
"social gospel" and advocate on behalf of the poor, the dispossessed, and the
marginalized of society. However, more recently some black church ministers
have also engaged in prophetic speech and advocacy from a more politically
conservative perspective. A good example of this is megachurch minister Eddie
Long and the church he pastors, the New Birth Missionary Baptist Church in
Atlanta. In December 2004 New Birth sponsored a controversial Civil Rights
Movement–like march that sought to call the nation's attention to the "evils"
of same-sex marriage. This is clearly not a "social gospel" message that is consistent with progressive politics, but interestingly Eddie Long sees himself and
New Birth as following in the prophetic black church tradition.[70] I discuss this
more extensively in this book's final chapter and put the trend of select black
churches mobilizing behind politically/socially conservative causes in the context of contemporary debates about black politics.

It would not be correct to say that the prophetic tradition characterizes
all black churches. However, it is a recurring theme in black megachurches.
This is evidenced by the answers of ministers to Project 2000 survey questions
and is exemplified by church documents. Aspects of the prophetic theological
orientation, concentrating on thisworldly issues, advocating on behalf of social

justice issues, and providing a social critique following the jeremiad tradition, are evident in black megachurches, as I explain below.

Black megachurch clergy responses to survey questions

Three Project 2000 survey questions that addressed prophetic theology showed that prophetic theology is a dominant theological orientation. Respondents were asked, "How often do the sermons at your church focus on social justice or social action?" Figure 3.1 shows that of the churches surveyed, 82 percent reported that the sermons in their churches were focused on social justice or social action at least sometimes.

Respondents were also asked, "How well does 'My congregation is working for social justice' describe your congregation?" Figure 3.2 shows that of the churches, 36 percent said that "working for social justice" described their congregations "very well," compared to 13 percent of the churches that said that this statement did not describe them well at all.

Finally the respondents were asked, "Do you approve of churches expressing their views on day-to-day social and political issues?" Of the respondents, 72 percent said that they strongly approved of churches expressing their views on day-to-day issues, while only 10 percent of the churches disapproved of churches speaking out on day-to-day issues (see figure 3.3).

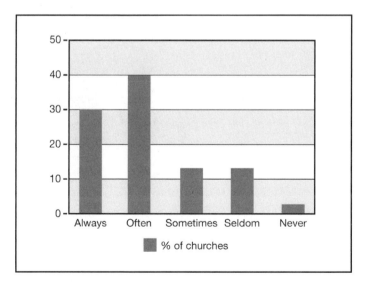

Figure 3.1—How Often Does Your Sermon Focus on "Social Justice or Social Action"?

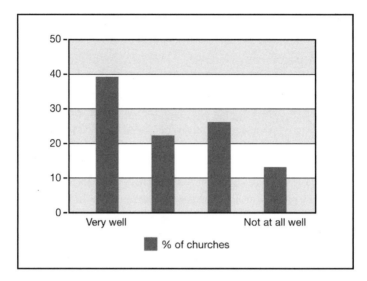

Figure 3.2—*How Well Does the Statement "Our Church Is Working for Social Justice" Describe Your Congregation?*

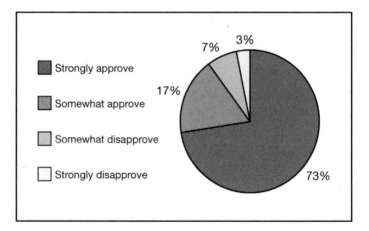

Figure 3.3—*Please Say Whether You Strongly Approve or Strongly Disapprove of "Churches Expressing Their Views on Day-to-Day Social and Political Issues"*

These three survey questions measured different aspects of prophetic theology. The first question looks at the content of sermons. Sermons are important for prophetic theology because they are the vehicles for prophetic preaching. This question asks about social justice or social action (the traditional way black churches have exhibited a prophetic theology)—where ministers as the representatives of their churches might speak out and speak "truth to power." The second question is how the respondents (who were pastors or ministerial leaders of megachurches) view the church. This question also references "social justice." Question 2 is important, as it measures how the respondent views the role of his or her church in the world (from a particularistic perspective). The third question speaks to the meaning of the church in the world from a more universal perspective. This question includes churches that promote the prophetic theology from the evangelical theologically/politically conservative perspective. The survey responses show that most black megachurches churches embrace a prophetic orientation.

Prophetic versus priestly orientations

Lincoln and Mamiya juxtaposed a "prophetic" theological orientation with a "priestly" one. Prophetic-oriented churches are concerned about the social and political issues, while those with a priestly orientation are concerned only with the spiritual life of their members in a strict sense.

In the examination of black megachurches I looked at the tendency to embrace temporal themes *in addition* to "sacred" ones. The tendency to emphasize both is reiterated in black megachurch documents. For example, the vast majority of megachurches (74 percent) include some aspect of secular goals in their mission statements. Tables 3.5 and 3.6 provide lists and frequencies of themes mentioned in the mission statements. The most frequently mentioned themes in the "sacred" category were Christian training and evangelizing/proselytizing. The most frequently mentioned themes in the secular category were community/economic development, social justice, and a holistic approach.

A holistic approach

While tables 3.5 and 3.6 divide mission statements themes into sacred and secular, in reality many black megachurches emphasize the importance of a holistic approach to ministry that combines addressing spiritual and temporal needs. In their mission statement Allen AME Church states, "We are called to address the needs of the total person, as our Savior did." Ben Hill United Methodist Church in Atlanta ministers through "holistic care," and Christian

TABLE 3.5
FREQUENCY OF "SACRED" THEMES IN BLACK MEGACHURCH MISSION STATEMENTS

Sacred Theme	%
Christian training	71
Evangelizing/proselytizing	71
Worship	44
Expressing evangelical beliefs and practices (Bible believing)	27
Spiritual healing	20
Prosperity gospel	20
Expressing Pentecostal beliefs and practices	14
Black theology	10
Removing denominational barriers	5

Data compiled by author, N = 42.

TABLE 3.6
FREQUENCY OF "SECULAR" THEMES IN BLACK MEGACHURCH MISSION
STATEMENTS

Secular Theme	%
Mentions "community"	46
Community development/economic development	39
Social justice	29
Holistic approach	20
Unity across race or class	19
Education	17
Elevating poor people	17
Political empowerment	10
Economic Empowerment	7
Classism	5
Racism	5
Liberation	5
Sexism	2

Data compiled by author, N = 42.

Faith Fellowship Church in Milwaukee seeks to be a church that ministers to "the total man."

These churches emphasize a multiple focus on the local church, the community at large, and the world at large. In another example, Allen AME Church defines as one of their goals to change the "community into a village," and Christian Faith Fellowship states that one of their goals is "To affect the Community." Apostolic Church of God in Chicago states in their mission statement, "It is essential that we nourish and cultivate the Christian lives of our parishioners, that we concern ourselves with giving aid and comfort to the poor, to work for better living conditions in society in general, and in our community in particular." Bethel AME in Baltimore, Maryland, states that as a church it is committed to the "deliverance, development and empowerment of the individual and the community." Finally, Cathedral Baptist states that they are "rebuilding lives and the community in the name of Jesus Christ."

Called to social justice and social action

Other more specific references to a prophetic theology such as social justice and social action are articulated in the mission statements of a few black megachurches. For example, Shiloh Baptist Church in Washington, D.C., says that they are "promoting justice." Wheeler Avenue Baptist Church in Houston says that they are called to "social action," and St. Luke Community United Methodist Church states that they are "combating injustice wherever it may exist; by implementing outreach ministries to meet the needs of the total community." In their vision statement, the People's Community Baptist Church in Silver Spring, Maryland, also articulates a prophetic theological orientation and states,

> The 2121 Vision is our call for concern about salvation and starvation, repentance and racism, faith and family, regeneration and revolution, justification and justice, sanctification and sex, hell and housing, heaven and honesty, and love and law.

Many of these megachurches express that their public engagement activities serve as the vehicle through which they practice their theology. Like FAME Church, which started this chapter, Shiloh Baptist Church also sees public engagement as vital to the practice of their religious beliefs.

> We do this because we are led by the Holy Spirit, and taught by Scriptures to obey the Great Commission: "Go ye therefore, and teach all nations, baptizing them in the name of the Father, and of the Son and the Holy Ghost." (Matt 28:19)

For Shiloh the ultimate goal of obeying the "Great Commission" is clearly related to public engagement. Rev. Alice Davis, the former executive minister of Shiloh Baptist Church, explains, "We try not to draw a strict line between sacred and secular because all of God's creation is sacred. Those aspects of life that are 'secular' may not be controlled by the church but does not mean they are not sacred." She goes on, "During the time that Jesus lived, the church was actively involved in politics therefore ministers should not hesitate to speak of politics from the pulpit. Politics is just how we govern ourselves. It is part of our religious belief to talk about what is wrong in the community."[71]

Prophetic theology and public engagement

One would expect that a prophetic theological orientation would guide a church to participate in public engagement activities. A prophetic theology emphasizes that churches ought to have something to say about the "world." Their role is to be a critic of government on behalf of social justice, and the church or body of believers should work actively for social justice.

In order to determine if the "ought" of prophetic theology leads to *actual* public engagement, the mean of three measures of different aspects of the prophetic theological orientation was used to create a "prophetic" variable. I conducted a logistic regression with "prophetic theology" as the independent variable and the different public engagement activities as the dependent variables. The model controls for the level of the minister's education, whether the church was founded before or after 1960, and whether the church is located in an inner-city or suburban area of town.

As expected, a prophetic theological orientation is related to several types of public involvement activities. The logistic regressions show that churches that scored higher on the prophetic theological orientation index are significantly more likely to participate in commercial development, to have a political or social concerns ministry, and to participate in issue advocacy (see table 3.7). A prophetic theology encourages public engagement.

Nondenominationalism

Some scholars suggest that the significance of denominationalism is declining and that nondenominational churches have become more and more prevalent since the 1960s.[72] Walton even points out that American religion reflects "post-denominational" life.[73] Yet interestingly nondenominational churches are not included in most studies of religion and politics in general—nor black church and politics in particular. Most studies of the black church focus on black Protestant churches that are affiliated with historically black denominations. One

TABLE 3-7

LOGISTIC REGRESSION SHOWING THE IMPACT OF A "PROPHETIC THEOLOGY" ON PUBLIC ENGAGEMENT ACTIVITY

	Prophetic Theology			Inner City			Founded after 1960			Reverend Education			N
	B	SE	Odds Ratio	B	SE	Odds Ratio	B	SE	Odds Ratio	B	SE	Odds Ratio	
CDO	-0.08	0.58	0.91	-0.32	0.89	0.72	-0.24	0.91	1.87	0.62	0.35	1.87	28
Housing development	0.09	0.76	1.10	0.46	1.19	1.58	2.38	1.47	10.86	1.56*	0.59	4.76	28
Affordable housing	1.20	0.64	3.34	-0.30	0.85	0.73	0.02	0.87	1.02	0.12	0.34	1.83	28
Commercial development	5.96*	2.81	391.21	-6.36	3.34	0.0017	2.93	2.13	18.76	0.78	0.92	2.19	28
Credit union	0.70	0.81	2.02	0.64	1.12	1.90	-1.02	1.16	0.35	1.84	1.10	6.33	28
Employment services	0.26	0.62	1.30	1.54	1.14	4.68	0.12	1.04	1.12	0.62	0.40	1.86	28
Food pantry	1.24	0.99	3.47	1.05	1.53	2.88	-0.85	1.48	0.42	-0.29	0.53	0.74	28
Political ministry	2.08*	0.92	8.05	-2.40*	1.22	0.09	1.07	1.14	2.92	0.39	0.46	1.48	28
Voter registration	0.95	0.71	2.59	2.63	1.42	14.00	-0.95	1.09	1.00	0.00	0.40	1.00	28
Issue advocacy	3.18*	1.42	24.13	1.55	1.48	4.71	0.23	1.19	1.26	1.06	0.59	2.90	28

SOURCE: ITC/Faith Communities Today Project 2000 Megachurch Survey. * indicates P < .05.

of the most interesting findings is the rather large percentage (21 percent) of these churches that are nondenominational.

Black megachurches (as noted in the previous chapter) often express a desire to "move beyond denomination." Some of them have actually done so by breaking away from their larger denominational bodies and becoming independent churches. For example in 1999, what was once Full Gospel African Methodist Episcopal Zion (AMEZ) church in suburban Maryland broke away from the AMEZ church and became From the Heart Ministries—an independent church. On their website From the Heart Ministries explains that the now twenty-two-thousand-plus-member church left the AMEZ denomination "[i]n order to maintain our mission and expand our outreach."[74]

More of these churches express a move toward nondenominationalism in their mission statements and other church documents than actually separate from their denominations. As mentioned in the previous chapter, many of the black megachurches in this study can be classified as what Scott Thumma calls "functionally nondenominational." This means that, although they are formally affiliated with denominations, in some ways they operate as if they are independent churches and exhibit characteristics more in line with other megachurches than with other churches affiliated with their denomination. They conference with each other, and the ministers invite each other to speak to their respective congregations.[75]

Despite this "functional nondenominationalism" there are some very important distinctions between actual denominationally affiliated and actual nondenominational black megachurches. As table 3.8 shows, nondenominational black megachurches are usually newer institutions. The vast majority of the nondenominational black megachurches have been founded since the 1980s. Nondenominational black megachurches are more likely to be located in the suburbs (71 percent) compared to denominational churches, which are more likely to be located in inner-city areas. Of all black megachurches that are in the inner city, only 11 percent of them are nondenominational. And while nondenominational pastors are well represented in all of the education categories listed (see table 3.9), the pastors of black megachurches that are a part of denominations are more likely to have a postgraduate education.

Nondenominational theology and public engagement

Although there are very little empirical data about the theological leanings of nondenominational churches, they are generally considered "evangelical" Protestants.[76] This means they have conservative theological views and are more

TABLE 3.8
BLACK MEGACHURCH FOUNDING DATE AND LOCATION
BY DENOMINATIONAL FAMILY

Denominational Family	Founded before 1960 (%)	Founded after 1960 (%)	Located in Urban Area (%)	Located in Suburban Area (%)
Historically Black	67.6	32.4	70.3	29.7
Predominantly White	66.7	33.3	83.3	16.7
Nondenomina-tional	10.5	89.5	31.3	68.8

Data compiled by author.

TABLE 3.9
EDUCATION LEVEL OF BLACK MEGACHURCH SENIOR MINISTER
BY DENOMINATIONAL FAMILY

Denominational Family	Some College/ Bible College (%)	College Graduate (%)	Master's Degree (i.e., M.Div.) (%)	Doctorate (i.e., Th.D. or D.Min.) (%)
Historically Black	3.0	18.2	24.2	54.5
Predominantly White	—	—	40.0	60.0
Nondenomina-tional	21.4	21.4	14.3	28.6
Sanctified	33.0	33.0	33.0	—
Evangelical	9.0	18.2	22.7	43.1

Data compiled by author.

likely to have conservative political views that are manifested in party affiliation, vote choice, and attitudes toward abortion, gay marriage, school prayer, and participation in public life in general.[77] Evangelical Protestants tend to focus more on personal salvation and less on the broader community. Therefore we would expect that a nondenominational orientation, in addition to belonging to more conservative Protestant denominations (like Baptists and Church of God in Christ), would depress black megachurch public engagement activities.

TABLE 3.10

THE PUBLIC ENGAGEMENT ACTIVITIES OF DENOMINATIONAL
AND NONDENOMINATIONAL BLACK MEGACHURCHES

Public Engagement Activity	Denominational Churches (%)	Nondenominational Churches (%)
Issue advocacy*	78.3	37.5
Affordable housing**	58.5	7.7
Community development organization**	72.3	27.8
Commercial development**	32.6	5.9
Credit union**	35.6	6.7
Employment services	78.3	62.5
Housing	73.9	50.0
Political ministry**	46.7	6.3
Voter registration or education	82.6	62.5

*X^2 is significant at the .05 level.
**X^2 is significant at the .01 level.
Data compiled by author.

While there is not a measurable difference in the public engagement activities of evangelical denominational black megachurches (like Baptist, Pentecostal, Holiness, Charismatic) and those that are a part of more "liberal" denominational families (like United Methodists, AME, and UCC), there is a significant difference between nondenominational black megachurches and denominational black megachurches. Black megachurches that are nondenominational are significantly less likely to take part in issue advocacy, housing, and commercial development than churches that are affiliated with denominations (regardless of the strength of their association with a denomination). Nondenominational churches were also less likely to have a political or social concerns ministry or to have developed a CDO than denominationally affiliated churches. Table 3.10 illustrates this by comparing the public engagement activities of nondenominational and denominationally affiliated black megachurches.[78]

Nondenominationalism is an important theological strain among black megachurches. Almost one-fourth of them are nondenominational, and even more express an affinity to nondenominationalism in their church documents. Nondenominationalism tends to depress public engagement.

The Prosperity Gospel

"I have come so that you may have life and have it more abundantly."[79] This scripture (John 10:10) introduces the web page for Abundant Life Cathedral in Houston, which is one of several megachurches that espouse the "prosperity gospel." John 10:10, Deuteronomy 7:12-16 (which explains the blessings that people are awarded for obedience), and Mark 10:29-30 are generally used as the theological basis for this "gospel of prosperity." Mark 10:29-30 reads,

> "I tell you the truth," Jesus replied, "no one who has left home or brothers or sisters or mother or father or children or fields for me and the gospel will fail to receive a hundred times as much in this present age (homes, brothers, sisters, mothers, children and fields—and with them, persecutions) and in the age to come, eternal life."

The prosperity gospel is central to the "word of faith movement," and the terms are often used interchangeably. This theological orientation teaches that God's people are entitled to prosperity—particularly in their finances and their physical health. Furthermore, it teaches that in order to unlock this prosperity, born-again Christians must "know who they are in Christ" and "name and claim" their prosperity.[80] Unlike black theology, which sees poverty as a result of systematic oppression, according to prosperity theology poverty is a curse that afflicts people when they lack the understanding of how to unlock the blessings that God has promised them. Therefore, individuals can prevent or alleviate poverty, ill health, and general suffering once they have unlocked their inner potential.

The contemporary word of faith movement is traced back to the ideas and writings of E. W. Kenyon. Kenyon's *Two Kinds of Faith* described "new thought metaphysics," one of the traditions behind the basic tenets of word of faith theology. New thought metaphysics is the science of "mind over matter." Kenyon claimed that Christians are entitled to good health and material prosperity and that people need to "enjoy their rights in Christ." According to this theology, people can enjoy these "rights" by speaking them aloud through positive confession.[81]

Kenneth Hagin Sr., who is commonly thought of as the father of the word of faith movement, borrowed Kenyon's ideas, and from the 1960s until he died in 2003 Hagin authored a number of books, recorded tapes, and appeared on television and radio where he detailed word of faith theology. Hagin also founded the RHEMA Bible Training Center and mentored several influential word of faith pastors.[82]

One of the ministers whom Hagin mentored was Frederick K. Price of Crenshaw Christian Center (a black megachurch in Los Angeles). In 1975 Price became the first African American to be ordained into Kenneth Hagin Ministries. Price was one of the first African Americans on national television and the first African American word of faith televangelist.[83] He is considered to have introduced "the faith message to the black community."[84] He brought word of faith to black audiences through the teachings at his local church (Crenshaw Christian Center) and his television ministry (Ever Increasing Faith Ministries). Price also spread the prosperity gospel by serving as a mentor to other African American word of faith preachers.[85]

Materialism is not new to black Christian religious communities. In fact, a number of African American religious movements throughout the twentieth century privileged the pursuit of material wealth and prosperity as an important theological tenet. Scholars point to the religious movements of Rev. Ike, Daddy Grace, and Father Divine as examples of ministries that focused on combinations of temporal prosperous living, positive thinking, and charismatic theology.[86]

In addition to these three, Harrison highlights the contributions of Rev. Johnnie Coleman. Coleman predates Price in bringing the contemporary word of faith movement to black audiences. In 1956 Coleman started the first black church that focused on new thought metaphysics, which is the source of the "name it and claim it" tenet of word of faith theology. Coleman's Christ Universal Temple is a megachurch in Chicago.[87]

There are examples of African American versions of health and wealth theology throughout the twentieth century, and there are also long-standing critiques of this theology. Perhaps the most powerful is the "preacher pimp" critique. The "preacher pimp" exploits his flock for his own personal prosperity. Richard Pryor's portrayal of "Daddy Rich" in the 1976 movie *Car Wash* is the archetypal example of the "preacher pimp" character.[88] Aaron McGruder's (author of "The Boondocks") Rev. Rollo Goodlove is another example of the "preacher pimp" character. Both Daddy Rich and Rollo Goodlove exploit the pain and suffering and religious fervor of African Americans for their own personal benefits. The characters drive expensive cars, dress flamboyantly, and are surrounded by objectified women.

The "preacher pimp" critique is also reflected in some of the earliest social science literature on the black church. In Drake and Cayton's 1945 study of black churches, they observed that the critique of the exploiting preacher was prevalent among residents of Chicago's South Side. They found that over and over interviewees called the church "a racket." Some of their quotes included "nobody gets anything out of it but the preachers," "You take some of these preachers, . . . they're living like kings—got great big Packard automobiles and ten or twelve suits," and "The preachers want to line their pockets with gold. They are supposed to be the leaders of the people, but they are fake leaders."[89]

The prosperity gospel is also the subject of critique from a number of theologians from a variety of theological perspectives. From the perspective of black theology, James Cone has been one if its most vocal critics. In the 2003 State of the Black Union Conference in Detroit, Cone explained his perspective on the prosperity gospel. He said the black church is too concerned about "success" and "building buildings" and "humongous [material] things." He argued that this does not reflect Jesus' gospel.

> [The gospel of Jesus] is a gospel of ultimate success through obvious failure. That's why the cross is at the center of the gospel. The cross is not a gospel of success. Jesus did not succeed. He failed. But God took that failure and transformed that failure into success.
>
> I feel today with so much focus on building buildings and all the other humongous things that we do that we fail to see that the cross is at the heart at what the black church ought to be about. It was not very difficult for the black church to see that during the time at which it was born. Because being a slave church—that was not success. It was obvious failure there.
>
> I would like to see the church not be so concerned about its success. But much more concerned about a kind of success through failure. I would want to put my emphasis there. I'm concerned that the church does not get too concerned about its own survival because Jesus said that people who seek to save their life shall lose it. But if you lose your life, for the sake of the least of these then you will find your life.[90]

Cone's condemnation of the prosperity gospel further seeped into the political world when he declined an invitation to attend the 2006 graduation ceremony at the Interdenominational Theological Center (ITC) in Atlanta. Cone declined the invitation when it was announced that Bishop Eddie Long, of New Birth Missionary Baptist Church (a black megachurch in Atlanta), would be the commencement speaker. Long is a graduate of ITC. In protest to the decision to invite Long, Cone declined the invitation—particularly because of Long's preaching of the prosperity gospel.[91] Comparing Long to Martin Luther King Jr., Cone said, "King devoted his life to the least of these. . . . King could have been just like Bishop Long with all the millions he has, but he chose to die poor. He would not use his own message or his own movement to promote himself."[92]

Examples of prosperity theology in black megachurches

An examination of black megachurches clearly shows that the prosperity gospel is the dominant orientation in a number of black megachurches. The three tenets of the word of faith theology that Milmon Harrison lays out— (1) know who you are in Christ, (2) positive confession, and (3) divine health and material wealth—are expressed in the church documents of several black megachurches. Of the mission statements that I examined, 20 percent made reference to at least one of these tenets.

Know who you are in Christ. The first of Harrison's word of faith tenets is that Christians should "[k]now who they are in Christ." This means that the Bible serves as a contract between God and the believer. "These benefits of being in Christ are legally guaranteed and protected by *spiritual* law. Believers are entitled to expect a better life as a result and reward for being in relationship with God through Christ."[93] This tenet is promoted in a number of black megachurches.

In an interview, Rev. Frederick K. Price (from Crenshaw Christian Center) explains that born-again Christians have to uphold their side of the contract (which is faith) in order for God to deliver on his part—prosperity.

> If you've got one dollar faith and you ask for a ten-thousand dollar item, it ain't going to work. It won't work. Jesus said, "According to your [faith]," not according to God's will for you, in His own good time, if it's according to His will, if He can work it into his busy schedule. He said, "According to your faith, be it unto you."[94]

In his book *Breaking the Spirit of Poverty: Six Steps to Take You from Poverty to Prosperity*, Ed Montgomery (the pastor of Abundant Life in Houston) provides another example of this perspective. Montgomery explains how believers can move from a state of poverty to having all their material needs met by God, or as he puts it, how they can achieve "freedom from poordom." Montgomery, writing "from a black man's perspective," explains that God wants African Americans as a group to be as economically prosperous as white Americans as a group. He writes,

> God does not choose for some people to be rich while others remain in bondage. When I came to the realization that there were no cultural, ethnic, or racial barriers in God's economy, this good news set me free. God responds to

faith, anyone's faith. Therefore, I learned that He would respond to my faith and this liberated me.[95]

The "good news" is that African Americans have control over their circumstances. The reason that they are disproportionately among the poor is because they "accept the circumstances of home evictions, unemployment, debt," and so on. But poverty is not merely "the lack of money." "Poverty is a spirit." It is an affliction.[96] Therefore, by obeying the commands that God sets forth for the righteous and having faith that they are *supposed* to be prosperous and not poor, they can break this spirit. They too can live the prosperous life.[97]

Positive confession. Harrison's second tenet of word of faith theology is positive confession. Positive confession is the act of "naming it and claiming it." This means to vocally proclaim that what you desire from God will be provided to you by God. This tenet of the prosperity gospel stems from new thought metaphysics and mind science. Not only positive speaking but also positive thinking are important. Word of faith church members' "thoughts and self-talk are to be guarded, governed, and kept positive and 'scriptural.' Believers are encouraged to be diligent in maintaining a positive mental attitude and inner dialogue. Mental discipline, mental 'hygiene,' or self-censorship, should be an ongoing practice as demonstration of one's faith."[98]

The "name it and claim it" doctrine is very common in black megachurches. In word churches time is set aside in the worship service for congregants to verbally name and claim their blessings. A number of them have "financial faith confessions" for this purpose.

New Life Christian Center Church (in Houston) practices word of faith theology. They have a "financial faith confession" that illustrates both the importance of financial prosperity and the importance of positive confession.

Father I thank you that you have a financial plan for the believer's prosperity called Tithes and Offering. I set my heart to participate in your plan to bless my life. I have given the tithes of my increase and I believe I receive the windows of heaven's blessing for my life and my family. I thank you Father for creative wisdom and insight into financial affairs. I have given for the support of the man and women of God who teach me the Word of God; therefore I believe I receive a first class lifestyle. I give to spread the gospel in the earth; therefore I believe I receive the maximum return on my seed. I confess this ministry is debt free and I give for the support of the debt freedom of this ministry, therefore I thank you Father for supernatural wisdom, supernatural increase and supernatural debt cancellation in my life. I have vowed and given my vow therefore I decree a thing and it is established unto me and the light of God's favor shines upon my path. I thank you Father, I believe I receive your best in my transportation, in my life and in my career for your Word declares whatsoever good any man doeth the same shall he receive of the Lord. I thank you Father for abundance in my life and abundance for this ministry. I hold fast to my confession of faith in Jesus' name. Amen.[99]

This confession clearly exemplifies the prosperity gospel theology as it makes reference to God's promise of abundance to people and the material reward for supporting the church financially. The fulfillment of the promise is directly connected to the willingness of people to donate money to the church and to the minister and his wife.

Health and wealth prosperity. Harrison's final word of faith theological tenet is that born-again Christians are entitled to material wealth and divine health. Word of faith teaches that reports of Jesus' poverty are erroneous. In fact Jesus was materially wealthy. Just as God blessed Jesus with material wealth, God wants his followers today to be materially prosperous. When born-again Christians donate money to the church they should expect a material increase in return. This is referred to as "sowing a seed." According to word of faith theology, donating money through tithes and offerings should be considered both an investment in the giver's material prosperity and a sign of the giver's faith that God will return the material investment exponentially.[100]

Although the prosperity gospel refers to prosperity in all areas of life, including health, finance, and relationships, finance holds a privileged position, and these churches place a lot of emphasis on explaining how their members may go about receiving financial blessings, and many of these churches have "seed" ministries to this end. The principal behind seed giving is that as you give money to church, you are planting a "seed" that will grow in proportion to the amount that you planted. Giving to the church then becomes a personal financial investment. Several of the churches have ministries that help members budget their finances, including how they can tithe and plant seed money and still satisfy their household bills.

A good example of the seed-sowing beliefs in action occurred during my visit to Abundant Life Cathedral in Houston. During the church service the copastor (and wife of Pastor Ed Montgomery) Saudra Montgomery aggressively encouraged the congregation to give "seed money" to the church. She explained that giving a certain amount of money would cause the giver to receive that money back one hundred times over. She started the offering by asking, "Who is ready to be a millionaire? Who is ready to give $10,000?" As the crowd warmed up and began to stir, she called out, "Who is ready to receive

$100,000? Who is ready to give 1,000?" She continued to call out the denominations of bills until she got to those who wanted an increase on whatever they had to give. The focus of giving money to the church was on the expectation of an increasing return on the donation. Abundant Life also had a "Millionaires in Progress" ministry that emphasized the importance of tithing and of "planting seed money" in the church with the end goal of becoming wealthy.

It is clear that the tenets of the prosperity gospel are promoted in a number of black megachurches. In fact, a number of the most well-known leaders in the word of faith movement are black megachurch pastors including Keith Butler in Detroit (Word of Faith International Christian Center) and Creflo Dollar in Atlanta (World Changers Christian Center), as well as several others. It is important to note that the prosperity gospel is like other theological orientations in black megachurches in that it is a *thisworldly*—not *otherworldly*—theology. It teaches that it is God's will that people live the prosperous life here on earth.

Are all black megachurches word churches?

The black megachurch phenomenon and the word of faith movement are often spoken of and written about as if they are interchangeable. This is the case with journalistic treatments as well as many scholarly works that examine either of these two topics. The evidence presented in this chapter, however (which explores the multiple and varied theological orientations present in black megachurches), shows that clearly not all black megachurches are word of faith churches. The question becomes, why this mischaracterization?

The mischaracterization occurs for three reasons. First, a number of black megachurches (especially the most high-profile ones that have television ministries) are in fact word of faith churches. Second, many of them do actually explicitly express one or more tenets of the prosperity gospel—even if they abandon the others. The third reason that scholars and journalists generally group all black megachurches into the word of faith category is because while the majority of black megachurches are not actually "word of faith churches," explicitly promoting all three of the tenets of word of faith theology, they exude prosperity with their large buildings and celebrity pastors and therefore *implicitly* send the message that material prosperity is pleasing to God.

The grandiose megachurch structures and campuses upon which many of them are built alone emanate prosperity. The average megachurch worship service is highly professionalized. The services utilize professional musicians (sometimes celebrity recording artists) and technology specialists for lighting, filming, and broadcasting. The everyday operation of megachurches includes a number of full-time employees such as accountants, receptionists, and other office workers. These churches are big productions. This reminds one of James Cone's disparagement of many black churches for being too occupied with "success" and "building buildings."

The pastors of megachurches also emanate prosperity with their personal celebrity status. Many of them also drive expensive cars, have large, expensive homes, and wear flamboyant and expensive clothing and jewelry. The personal prosperity of many megachurch pastors implies that having wealth and flaunting it—living the high life—are acceptable and in fact pleasing to God.

Televangelist, businessman, and megachurch pastor Bishop T. D. Jakes is a good example of all of the three reasons why megachurches are often all labeled prosperity or word of faith churches. Jakes' prosperity-flaunting lifestyle implicitly promotes the gospel of prosperity even though he has spoken out against aspects of it.

T. D. Jakes is probably the best known of black megachurch ministers. Jakes' church, the Potter's House in Dallas, has a reported twenty-eight thousand members, yet this is only part of Jakes' influence.[101] Jakes has a national television ministry and through it is in the homes of millions of Americans. He has also sponsored conferences that have drawn nationwide participants. He has a conference for women, Woman Thou Art Loosed, a conference for men, the Man-Power Conference, and MegaFest, which brings together men and women. Jakes has multiple for-profit business projects and has written a number of books that have reached the best-sellers list; one of them, *Woman, Thou Art Loosed*, was turned into a movie.

In a book on Jakes sociologist Shayne Lee details Jakes' life and ministry and Jakes' significance in American culture and politics. He writes that Jakes is from humble beginnings in West Virginia and that he has the classic Horatio Alger–type life story of "pulling himself up by the bootstraps" and making it big through ingenuity and hard work.[102]

Lee shows that Jakes does not apologize for his celebrity status or his material success. In fact, Jakes defends his opulent lifestyle. Lee quotes Jakes' response when he was criticized for his prosperous lifestyle in the *Charlestown Gazette*: "If you're successful, it's not unusual to have a nice home. There are many prominent ministers who are successful. I don't think that is necessarily suspicious."[103]

Lee also shows that Jakes embraces certain aspects of word of faith theology—particularly the "sowing of seeds," with the expectation of individualized material prosperity in return. Lee quotes Jakes as saying, "God knows where you need your miracle harvest, and now is the time to sow your Miracle Faith Seed."[104]

While clearly Jakes embraces certain aspects of the prosperity gospel, Jonathan Walton argues that Jakes is not a word of faith preacher and points out instances where Jakes has rejected and disassociated himself from the prosperity gospel. Walton quotes Jakes as saying, "Christianity's foundation is not built upon elite mansions, stocks and bonds, or sports cars and cruise-control living. . . . To make finances the symbol of faith is ridiculous."[105]

Like a number of other black megachurches, the Potter's House may not be a "word church," but it is clearly influenced by word of faith theology. Even in black megachurches that have a liberationist theology some of the terminology of the word of faith theology is used, like "seed giving" and "supernatural increase." While the vast majority of black megachurch pastors do not consistently preach prosperity to their congregations, and this theme is usually not apparent in the theological literature of their churches, many black megachurch pastors are personally heavily criticized for their extravagant lifestyles. Aspects of the prosperity gospel are often strategically used to explain the good fortune of the pastors themselves and their extravagant lifestyles even when they do not regularly preach the "prosperity gospel."

Cheryl Gilkes' observations enhance our understanding of the broad influence of the "prosperity gospel" beyond churches that fall explicitly in the word of faith category. She observes aspects of the prosperity gospel primarily in middle-class black churches with relatively young congregations and makes the argument that these people are on more than just a quest for good fortune. Instead she claims that the prosperity gospel is a "culturally relevant religious explanation of one's good fortune." It is a way to reconcile the guilt feelings that young black urban professionals feel about their material success when so many African Americans, particularly those in their own families, are doing poorly.[106]

Prosperity gospel and public engagement

As I just explained, the size and opulence of the church edifice and celebrity status of the ministers (characteristics that virtually all megachurches have in common) implicate black megachurches with the prosperity gospel even when the church documents, pastors' sermons, and other evidence do not reflect prosperity teachings.

In fact, there are levels of "prosperity gospel" as a part of the theology of these churches (like black theology, neo-Pentecostalism, and prophetic theology). For example, while most churches expressed a belief that individuals have some spiritual power over their lives, they did not promote the idea that the causes for misfortune are individual and that poverty is a curse for those without enough faith.

Social scientists have observed that the "prosperity gospel" likely has a negative impact on certain aspects of public engagement. Word of faith churches tend to be apolitical and do not want to significantly alter the basic structures of American society. These groups see the economic system of capitalism, for example, as basically good, and those who suffer under it and who are poor are this way because they are afflicted with mental and spiritual poverty. This is the same with sexism and racism. This theology is individual oriented and promotes the idea that individuals, not societal structures, must change for their situation to change. Thus these churches tend to abstain from public engagement activities (like community development, electoral politics, or protest politics) that focus on affecting social structures.[107]

An examination of five churches in which the "prosperity gospel" is obviously the central part of their theology paints a corroborating picture. These black megachurches expressed the prosperity gospel in their mission statements, they preached it in their sermons, and they are associated with high-profile prosperity gospel or word of faith movements. These "prosperity gospel" black megachurches were more focused on individual economic empowerment than responding to the "knock at midnight." They were not likely to engage in extensive public engagement efforts. For example, at the time of this writing only one of the five had a CDO. Interestingly, the focus of this CDO, which would be considered public engagement, was a job bank, which is focused on the individual. For the most part these five churches generally did not do any community outreach or public engagement beyond food delivery on holidays. Their focus was not on developing communities but rather on bringing people into the church and changing their lives through conversion and positive thinking.

Examples of the prosperity gospel are evident in black megachurch mission statements, sermons, and books written by megachurch pastors. This theology is the most well known to be associated with the black megachurch movement, and so it is no surprise that it turned up as a dominant theology. The grandiose buildings and spectacles, along with celebrity status of the pastors and sometimes of members, implicate churches with prosperity preaching. As one would expect, the prosperity gospel depresses public engagement.

There are five dominant theological orientations in black megachurches. This is evident in mission statements, responses to survey questions, participant observations, and church documents. These theological orientations serve as motives for public engagement. Black theology and prophetic theology inspire public engagement. Prosperity theology and nondenominationalism depress public engagement. What follows is a discussion of what I call the politico-theological typology of black megachurches. This will help to make sense of how the theology affects public engagement.

A Politico-Theological Typology of Black Megachurches

Black megachurches are particularistic niche churches. On one hand, they fulfill the needs and desires of the transplanted black suburbanites. They are professional, accessible, and thisworldly. However, withstanding these common characteristics, this chapter has revealed the ways that black megachurches are also very diverse and particularistic. I began this chapter with the question of why some megachurches are involved in extensive amounts of public engagement activities and others are not. I wanted to explain how the theological orientations of these churches serve as motives for public engagement. I have shown that there are five different dominant black megachurch theological orientations and that these different theological orientations encourage different levels and types of public engagement.

In their study of black churches Lincoln and Mamiya explained their theory of black church theological orientations. It was their argument that there are six pairs of dialectical polar opposites that black churches fall along. Their dialectical model of the black church offers a dynamic view of black churches that emphasizes their complexities and how they participate in public life.[108]

In this tradition, this research has revealed a set of four continua along which black megachurch theological orientations fall: black theology versus color-blind theology, social gospel versus prosperity gospel, nondenominationalism versus denominationalism, and communal versus privatistic. Identifying black megachurches on this set of continua leads to a better understanding of the plurality of black megachurch theological orientations and how these orientations relate to their public engagement. It is not my claim that the churches fall on either one end or the other of one or another of these continua. Instead, each black megachurch falls somewhere in between each of these continua. Characterizing black megachurches by their politico-theological orientations helps us make sense of how the theology of a black megachurch relates to its politics. Next I explore the boundaries of these four continua.

Black Theology versus Color-Blind Theology

"Black theology" and "color-blind theology" represent the two ends of the first black megachurch politico-theology continuum. On one end lies black theology, and on the other end lie churches that identify themselves as "multicultural," "race neutral," and "color blind" and that resist the label "black church."

Many black megachurches have clearly been influenced by black theology, and several of them are in fact leaders in the practice of black theology in the black church. Black theology is evident in the worship styles, symbols, décor, traditions, and rituals of many of these churches.

On the other hand, there are black megachurches that do not practice black theology and even resist the label "black church." This became apparent as I interviewed black megachurch ministers while researching this project. Before interviewing black megachurch representatives I let the respondent know that I was doing a study of "black" megachurches. Several of the respondents retorted that they were in fact not "black" churches. Instead, they were churches "for all people," and they went on to name the different races of people represented in their churches. One black megachurch assistant pastor stated that although their church was overwhelmingly made up of African American members (two or three nonblacks attended the church) the senior pastor tried not to emphasize the racial differences and instead focused on "moving beyond race." One secretary refused to pass a call along to an assistant minister because she rejected the label "black church." One church even highlighted racial diversity on their website where they presented the racial composition of their church (90 percent were black).

Color-blind theology discourages public engagement. Color-blind theology not only deemphasizes "race" but also the legacy of "racism" on black communities. It therefore employs an individualistic/nonstructural approach to understanding social problems—an approach which deemphasizes public engagement. On the other hand, black theology encourages public engagement. Recall the key tenets of black theology: interpreting Christianity from a "black perspective," belief in a "black" Christ, and working for the liberation of the oppressed. According to black liberation theology, the black church should actively work to end economic, social, and political oppression and seize control of black communities. Black theology encourages a structural and collective analysis of society and social problems. These tenets clearly influence a church to be more publically engaged. The data show that churches that have higher levels of black theology are more likely to engage in building and renovating

affordable housing and commercial development, vehicles used to revitalize suffering black communities.

Prosperity Gospel versus Social Gospel

The second continuum is the prosperity gospel versus the social gospel. As
described above, the prosperity gospel is promoted in many megachurches.
Some of the important tenets of the prosperity gospel are that God wants his
followers to be prosperous, the faithful will be prosperous, and believers can be
prosperous economically and otherwise by transforming behaviors and beliefs.

On the other end of this continuum is the social gospel. The social gospel
tradition takes it as a given that there is social inequality and injustice in society.
The social gospel tradition promotes the idea that the church should be involved
in addressing these inequities and injustice. Much like black theology, the social
gospel promotes the idea that the example of Jesus teaches his followers to be
champions for those who are at the bottom of the socioeconomic hierarchies, as
he was.

The social gospel and the prosperity gospel have some interesting com-
monalities. Both examine material realities as important to Christian beliefs.
Harrison points out that material concerns are important traditionally in the
black church. He asserts that black churches have always had the double duty
of material and spiritual concerns. The key difference between the combining of material and spiritual concerns for the social gospel and the prosperity
gospel is the root of suffering. For the social gospel the root causes for suffering are systemic and are not evidence of the individual's lack of faith or good
works. This is why the social gospel leads to greater public engagement. Pro-
moters of the social gospel believe that it is the responsibility of the church to
address systemic inequality, and public engagement is a way to do this.

On the other hand, according to the prosperity gospel, the root of suffering
is the individual, and consequently the end of suffering lies with the individual.
Personal transformation is what leads to a materially prosperous life. Christ
Universal Temple's (Chicago) mission statement reads,

> We Believe that, rather than devoting our primary efforts to providing for the
> needy of the world, the time has come to make available to all people every-
> where a teaching that will enable them to provide for themselves by learning
> to release the divine potential within them.

This statement places an emphasis on individuals as responsible for their
financial situation and away from structures of society. It also emphasizes that

individuals have the power within themselves to change their financial situation by changing their thought processes.

Consequently the prosperity gospel suppresses most public engagement. Only activity that focuses on improving the individual, like financial counseling or a job bank, is not suppressed by the prosperity gospel. But even this is minimal, as the focus of the prosperity gospel is on transforming the individual's beliefs so that he or she can be prosperous. For "name it and claim it" theology, the key is to transform individual beliefs and thinking, and God will do the rest. Public engagement does not play an important role in fulfilling the prosperity gospel.

Denominationalism versus Nondenominationalism

The third continuum is nondenominationalism versus denominationalism. Of course denominationalism means to affiliate with a denomination and nondenominationalism means to be independent of denominational affiliation. The empirical evidence showed that regardless of denomination (Baptist, Methodist, Pentecostal, etc.) black megachurches that had a denominational affiliation were more likely to participate in public engagement activities than nondenominational churches.

There are several possible explanations for why this is the case. For the first explanation let us turn to the actual denominations to which denominationally affiliated black megachurches belong. The vast majority of them belong to either historically black denominations or liberal mainline white denominations. Historically black denominations (even if they are conservative or evangelical) were invariably developed in the context of or in response to either slavery or racial apartheid. They were generally founded out of protest to the treatment of black people in white churches or as an act of black independence or nationalism. Historically they have served as the primary social institutions for black Americans and have traditions of public engagement.

The vast majority of denominationally affiliated black megachurches that are in majority white denominations are in mainline denominations like the United Church of Christ and the United Methodist Church, which have legacies of political progressiveness—possibly making them more likely to engage in public activities. Even if the individual churches were recently established, their connection to these white liberal denominations and historically black denominations gives them access to public engagement traditions. So for black megachurches, belonging to a denomination encourages public engagement.

On the other hand, nondenominational churches do not have access to the denominational traditions and obligations. Furthermore, they are more likely to identify with the more conservative white evangelical traditions that tend to focus on personal transformation rather than structural transformation. A number of nondenominational black megachurches identify with the word of faith movement—which also depresses their public engagement.

Denominationalism makes black megachurches more likely to engage in public life. Nondenominationalism influences black megachurches to be less likely to participate in public engagement activities. This difference can be said to parallel the evangelical/mainline divide in the white church. Non-denominational black megachurches tend to be not as publically engaged as denominationally affiliated churches, and when they are it is on behalf of issues concerning individual personal morality.

Communal versus Privatistic

The fourth theological orientation continuum is the communal versus privatis-tic continuum. This final continuum is taken from Lincoln and Mamiya's 1990 study where they use "communal and privatistic" to describe one of their dia-lectical polarities. According to Lincoln and Mamiya, a communal theological orientation focuses on "all aspects of lives of their members, including political, educational and social concerns" and the larger community.[109]

On the other hand, a privatistic theological orientation tends "toward a pri-vatism, a more personal and individualistic sense of religiousness," and focuses on "individual well-being" and "withdrawal from the concerns of the larger community." Whereas most megachurches seem to regard a practical everyday message as important and thus are thisworldly churches, their area of focus lies on this communal/privatistic continuum.[110]

While the above examines the four black megachurch continua separately, it is important to keep in mind that each church falls along each of the four continua and therefore exhibits a combination of these characteristics. The closer churches fall toward the prosperity gospel, nondenominational, color-blind, and privatistic ends of the continua, the less likely they are to participate in activities that could be considered answering the knock at midnight. Like-wise, the closer they fall toward the social gospel, denominational, black theol-ogy, and communal ends of the continua, the more likely they are to answer the knock. In actuality black megachurches fall on a complex matrix of these conti-nua that helps us to understand how their political orientations are influenced by their theological orientations.

Conclusion

This chapter had two basic concerns: to describe dominant black megachurch theological orientations and to determine if and how a particular theological theme affects the church's public engagement activities. Five theological orientations stand out in black megachurches: a prophetic theological orientation, black theology, neo-Pentecostalism, nondenominationalism, and the prosperity gospel.

The theological orientation of black megachurches does have some impact on whether churches participate in some public engagement activities. For example, as one would expect, black megachurches with a prophetic theological orientation are more likely to have ministries specifically addressed to political and social needs; they are more likely to do commercial development and more likely to have built, maintained, or renovated affordable housing. Likewise, churches that are more racially conscious are more likely to do commercial development and housing development. Nondenominational churches are less likely than churches that are part of a denomination to establish a CDO. Prosperity churches focus their public involvement on increasing the prosperity of members of the church on an individualized basis and are likely to focus on personal transformation rather than community transformation.

Politico-theological continua of black megachurches further explicate the relationship between theological orientation and public engagement. Black megachurches fall along four politico-theological continua: black theology versus color-blind theology, social gospel versus prosperity gospel, denominationalism versus nondenominationalism, and communal versus privatistic. Churches that have black theology, social gospel, denominational, and communal orientations are most likely to participate in public engagement activities. Churches that lean toward color-blind theology, prosperity gospel, nondenominationalism, and privatism are least likely to participate in public engagement activities. Understanding the theological orientations of black megachurches helps us to understand why some churches engage and others do not.

CHAPTER 4

"PROGRESS NOT PROTEST"
Black Megachurches and Community Development

The mission of The Abyssinian Baptist Church is to win more souls for Christ through evangelism, pastoral care, Christian education, social service delivery, and community development.

—Abyssinian Baptist Church, Harlem, New York

The repertoire of black church public engagement activities comprises three broad categories: protest politics, electoral politics, and community development. The tradition of black churches' participation in protest politics was best exemplified during the Civil Rights Movement as activist black churches served as meeting places, trained leaders, and mobilized black communities to protest against racial apartheid.[1] As African Americans gained greater access to the electoral sphere, activist black churches became increasingly engaged in electoral politics. Activist black churches in post–civil rights America hold candidate forums and distribute voter guides, and in more than a few cases their ministers have run for public office.[2] The examination of the public engagement activities of black megachurches reveals that many also practice a third approach—the community development strategy.

Abyssinian Baptist Church represents a clear case of a church that since the late 1980s has sought to answer the "knock at midnight" through community

development. Abyssinian has a long tradition of social activism. In fact it was
founded as a result of a protest. In 1808 African American and Ethiopian sea
merchants walked out of First Baptist Church of New York in protest of segregated seating in the worship service. They subsequently formed their own church
and named it "Abyssinian" after "Abyssinia," the ancient name for Ethiopia.[3]

Calvin Butts III, Abyssinian's senior pastor, has continued this tradition,
and throughout the 1980s and 1990s Butts, from his platform as first the executive minister and then senior pastor, practiced a somewhat confrontational
politics. He has been an outspoken critic of former Mayor Rudolph Giuliani,
even publically calling him a racist. He organized and led a number of protests
and boycotts against racism in employment and law enforcement, malt liquor
advertising billboards in Harlem, negative rap music lyrics, and a variety of
other issues. Over time, however, Butts has led his church toward more of an
emphasis on the community development approach and cooperating with government rather than confronting it. In 1989, when Butts became senior pastor
of Abyssinian, the church established the Abyssinian Development Corporation (ADC). It has since become a leading participant in community revitalization efforts in Harlem.[4]

Calvin Simms, a *New York Times Magazine* reporter, asked Butts about the
increased emphasis on community development in a 2006 interview. Simms
pointed out the change in Butts' approach to public life and asked why he no
longer seemed to practice a "King era protest" style of politics. Butts' response
was that the activist black church had matured beyond strictly focusing on the
protest politics of the civil rights era and even the electoral strategies that followed. "Many of us feel that we have outgrown that." He explained that while
sometimes protest is still necessary "to make sure that people focus on issues
that are negatively impacting the community," in order to truly address the
issues of the twenty-first century many activist black churches have embraced
the community development strategy. According to Butts, these churches focus
on "progress not protest."[5]

The community development approach differs from both electoral politics and protest politics in that while participation in electoral politics refers to
supporting or participating in elections and protest politics refers to political
dissent and application of pressure to the system from outside the electoral
sphere, the community development approach consists of the direct production of goods and services and the building of assets. Abyssinian participates in
a number of community development activities including real estate development, a home ownership program, and a small business development program.

Abyssinian has developed multiple units of housing, has engaged in commercial development projects and a head start program, and partners with the New York Board of Education to help run a public school. The most telling evidence of the church's partiality to community development is their establishment of a community development corporation (CDC), the ADC. It is through the ADC that Abyssinian collaborates with government, local and national foundations, and private sector partners to deliver social services and produce many of their community development projects.

Abyssinian is not alone in pursuing this approach to public engagement. In fact (in 2000) the majority of the black megachurches in this study had developed separate nonprofits for community development—what I call broadly "community development organizations" (CDOs).[6] These CDOs vary in their focus, their clientele, the size of their budgets, and the diversity of their programs. Some of them are prototypical CDCs like ADC and the West Angeles CDC (in Los Angeles), which focus on housing and other physical development. Others focus on education and mentoring programs, social service delivery, and employment services. But invariably these CDOs are formed to counteract the lingering challenges facing black communities that, despite the progress of the Civil Rights Movement and post–political incorporation, still exist. Urban fiscal stress, crisis in public education, unemployment, concentrated poverty, and the lack of affordable health care and housing are just some of the issues that a subset of black megachurches try to address through their CDOs.

Like Abyssinian, black megachurches are increasingly and strategically utilizing the community development approach to public engagement and increasingly developing CDOs as the vehicles for their public engagement activity. Black megachurch CDOs do not focus primarily on housing like the prototypical CDC. They are generally more diverse in their programs. However, these organizations help black megachurches build the capacity to carry out their missions. They make it easier for these churches to collaborate with government, foundations, and other organizations of civil society to provide social services and engage in community development projects. Besides facilitating this collaboration, establishing a CDO also serves as a symbol of these churches' commitment to community involvement. CDOs help to brand black megachurches as "activist" and consequently help the churches attract members who are interested in joining an "activist" church. While collaborating with government allows churches to engage in more extensive projects than they would usually be able to do on their own, sometimes the consequences can be counterproductive to the "prophetic role" of the activist church.

The previous chapter discussed the motivational aspects of black megachurch public engagement. Theological orientation serves as the "motive" for black megachurch engagement in public life. This chapter explores the community development activities of black megachurches and the organizations they form as contributing to the "means" aspect of black megachurch public engagement. When black megachurches have CDOs, they are more likely to participate in a number of activities including commercial development, housing, voter registration, advocacy, and employment services. These organizations contribute resources required to participate in certain types of activities.

In order to give a sufficient background for the discussion of black megachurch CDOs, what follows is a brief overview of the community development movement and CDCs in the United States and a brief summary of the role of black churches within that movement. After the overview I explore the diversity of CDO types that black megachurches have developed. Finally, I examine the symbolic and instrumental reasons that so many black megachurches have chosen this approach as well as some political implications for their choices.

The Context of Community Development and CDCs

Community development is an elastic term that can be used to describe a range of activities aimed at enhancing the quality of life for residents in low- and moderate-income neighborhoods. Ferguson and Dickens delineate that the improvement of five assets should be included in definitions of community development: physical capital, intellectual and human capital, social capital, financial capital, and political capital.[7]

This broad definition is useful and more accurate than most other definitions, which describe only housing and economic development projects. For this chapter, however, community development is used in the broad way to refer to physical development, economic development, and direct provision of human services and in contrast to protest politics and electoral politics.

By any definition black churches have a strong community development tradition. However, the modern community development movement refers to efforts aimed at revitalizing distressed urban communities, and while there is a wide range of actors directly involved in this work, the leading actors have been CDCs.

Three Waves of CDCs

The first CDCs emerged during the 1960s. The Bedford-Stuyvesant Restoration Corporation in Brooklyn, New York, and the Hough Area Development

Corporation in Cleveland, Ohio (both in black neighborhoods), were two of these very early federally funded CDCs. There were dozens of these "first-wave" CDCs. They were similar in that they grew out of neighborhood organizing efforts often in response to "redlining, urban renewal and urban riots."[8] These CDCS had broad agendas for community revitalization. They were nurtured by the activism of the 1960s, but also by federal funding that was inspired in 1966 when Senator Robert Kennedy walked through the Bedford-Stuyvesant area of Brooklyn, New York, dramatically noting the deterioration that had occurred there and the need for community revitalization. This initiated the Special Impact Program of the Office of Economic Opportunity and the Model Cities Program, which gave federal funding to these first-wave CDCs.[9]

A second wave of CDCs saw tremendous growth and change in the CDC movement. This second wave was less connected to the community organizing efforts of the 1960s, and these CDCs also saw a narrowing of activities. These second-wave CDCs not only participated in less organizing and advocacy but also provided fewer social services and engaged in less economic development than their first-wave counterparts. However, second-wave CDCs were well funded like the first generation, and many engaged in housing development.

Despite the severe cut in federal funding to CDCs in the 1980s during the Reagan and Bush administrations, the number of CDCs continued to grow.[10] CDCs established since the 1980s are considered the third generation of CDCs. They are distinguished by their increased professionalization (and their leaders are more likely to be professionals than activists). These "third-wave" CDCs focus on commercial development and most significantly on housing. In fact they are credited with being the primary developers of affordable housing across the United States. The National Congress for Community Economic Development estimated that by 2003 CDCs had built or renovated over one million units of housing.[11]

Third-Generation CDCs Focus on Housing

Currently, the vast majority of CDCs focus most of their efforts on housing and to a lesser extent commercial development. In a national survey of CDCs Vidal found that 90 percent of them engage in some aspect of housing development whether it is the renovation of old housing or the development of new housing.[12] Even if these CDCs engage in other types of community development activity, in the majority of these organizations housing is the primary activity, serving as an "entry point" into development activity.[13]

This focus on housing has been attributed to the gap between what the market and public sector provide and what communities need. Vidal and Gittell describe CDCs as "gap fillers." They help to fulfill the demand for low-income housing that government should be providing but does not provide.[14] Consequently they became more important after the general decreases in federal funding to cities, starting in the 1980s.[15] CDCs were willing to do "creative financing" that is needed to provide low-income housing.[16] They sought out and were successful at attracting funding from the private sector, and even as federal funding to CDCs was cut, CDCs continued to develop low-income housing. Once CDCs began to do housing, their expertise in housing continued to grow and became a source of more funding.[17]

CDCs have been judged as effective producers of affordable housing and community development in areas struck by disinvestment. Bratt contends that aside from creating a number of low-income housing units and putting together the creative financing to support such projects, CDCs have also developed a "community-sensitive" model of low-income housing. Many CDCs participate in both commercial and housing development while promoting "community" interests and community empowerment.[18]

Others have pointed out that CDCs are more productive than more confrontational, protest-oriented community-based organizations. For example, Robinson claims that CDCs can "nudge" the typically insensitive "pro-growth machine" toward more "community-sensitive" alternatives—particularly solutions that combine the interests of business, governing officials, and local communities. He argues that CDCs can best contribute to urban redevelopment by "getting off the barricade and into the boardroom." He further argues that it is important for community-based organizations to move government and business "towards proactive community-sensitive pursuits."[19]

Housing and Only Housing?

CDCs are not without their critics. Some observers of the CDC phenomenon have argued that housing is the activity CDCs most frequently engage in because it is less financially risky than extensive commercial development and more politically expedient than community advocacy or organizing.[20] Essentially, CDCs have been successful in attracting funding for low-income housing development because housing development has been less controversial. Others acknowledge that CDCs have an overall positive impact on low-income communities but point out that it is difficult to raise funds for the advocacy activities that benefit poor people. They call for a movement toward more complementary relations between the advocacy and economic development traditions of CDCs.[21]

Others make the argument that the community development movement has been co-opted through CDCs. These critics argue that CDCs have become detrimental to the communities they are supposed to serve by countering community interests. They claim that instead of promoting the agendas of community residents, CDCs carry out the agendas of business and political leaders. Because CDCs are not governed by residents, they develop a landlord/tenant relationship with community members. Other critics point out that even when CDCs intend to represent community interests, the average CDC is not able to make a real dent in the problems of declining communities because they do not have the resources to deal successfully with the problems of urban redevelopment.[22]

Black-Church-Affiliated CDCs

Black churches have been a part of the CDC movement from the earliest days. According to Stoutland, early, first-wave CDCs had three basic sources: (1) black social movements, (2) the Alinsky tradition, and (3) "religious roots" such as "the Opportunities Industrialization Center formed by the Rev. Leon Sullivan of the Zion Baptist Church in Philadelphia."[23] Many of the first-wave CDCs were affiliated with black churches. Both the Civil Rights Movement and the Alinsky-affiliated organizations emphasized the use of the black church as an organizational resource.[24] In addition, some of the most active Alinsky-model community organizations were started in black churches or by black ministers. For example, the Woodlawn Organization mentioned in the previous chapter (TWO) began as a community organization led by the late Rev. Arthur Brazier, the former pastor of Apostolic Church of God (a black megachurch in Chicago).

Black-church-affiliated CDCs (like other CDCs) have increased in number since 1989, and the majority of black-church-affiliated CDCs can be characterized as third-wave CDCs.[25] Frederick explains this expansion as an attempt to address the needs of black communities in inner-city America—which had been marginalized by neoconservative retrenchment policies and black middle-class flight.[26] Owens points out that public policy developments like the 1996 welfare reform legislation, which included the "charitable choice" provision, and the George W. Bush administration's faith-based initiatives also added to the environment that encouraged the growth of black-church-affiliated CDCs.[27]

Of course not all black churches create CDCs. The motivational factors that determine whether a particular church will form a CDC are like those for public engagement in general discussed in the previous chapter. Black churches form CDCs because community engagement is a part of their theology, a part of ministering to the "total man" and "making the word flesh."[28]

Ministers play a key role in the decision of black churches to form CDCs and have a great deal of influence on the CDCs' missions and agendas.[29] Owens argues that ministers who start CDCs are motivated by political, professional, and programmatic goals. They use CDCs to address the need for more afford-able housing (programmatic goals); but they also use CDCs to help increase their own status, reputations, and relevance, which have waned since the Civil Rights Movement (political and professional goals). CDCs also help black churches preserve the financial and legal integrity of their church while still accepting government and private grant money for community development.[30]

Studies of black-church-based CDCs reveal that they have had a signifi-cant impact on community revitalization in low-income communities. These CDCs are harnessing resources beyond those of the particular church. They have facilitated the expansion of church community development activities from an almost exclusive focus on social service provision to more economic development activities such as increasing the affordable housing stock and con-structing community loan funds.[31]

In New York City, for example, Michael Owens found that black-church-affiliated CDCs collaborated with local government to create affordable housing in several low-income neighborhoods. In fact the black-church-affiliated CDCs were the primary institutions addressing the affordable hous-ing crisis in these neighborhoods. Through collaboration the CDCs became "conduits of 'substantive' resources from the larger external community" that led to the physical improvement of these neighborhoods.[32]

While Owens and others have shown that black-church-affiliated CDCs have made measureable improvements in low-income black neighborhoods, there is the potential for what Owens called "the negative face of collabora-tion, 'cooptation.'"[33] Paralleling the critique of CDCs in general, as organiza-tions come to depend on government funding, they risk co-optation. Instead of working on behalf of the people, they risk becoming what Martin Luther King Jr. called a "tool of government." The concern about co-optation prohibits some "activist" churches from seeking public funding for their activities.

Aside from the risk of co-optation, there is evidence that the political activities of black-church-affiliated CDCs are constrained by the fact that they seek government funding. Owens found that black-church-affiliated CDCs often refrain from engaging in activities that are overtly "political" in nature, such as voter registration, publishing the voting records of elected officials, and holding candidate and issue forums even though these are activities that are nonpartisan and therefore are allowable given their nonprofit status.[34] As with the critique of all CDCs, black-church-affiliated CDCs may focus on activities that are the least politically controversial.

The contributions and the challenges of the CDC model and black-church-affiliated CDCs in particular help to clarify the community development work of black megachurches. The majority of black megachurches have developed CDOs—separate nonprofit organizations whose missions are to fulfill some aspect of community development. Many of them are typical CDCs like those described above. Others do not focus on any aspect of physical or housing development (hard development) but may focus on social service provision, education, or counseling (soft development). I turn now to a description of black megachurch CDOs—first giving some general characteristics, then presenting three different types of black megachurch CDOs that the research uncovered.

Profile of Black Megachurch CDOs

While a majority of black megachurches have CDOs, there are some key characteristics that make certain black megachurches more likely to have CDOs than others. In chapter 3 I explained how the theological orientation of a church helps to influence whether a church will have a CDO. For example, churches that are affiliated with a denomination are more likely to have a CDO than churches that are nondenominational. Looking more closely at the CDOs shows that older churches (particularly churches that were founded before 1960) and churches whose ministers are more educated are more likely to have developed CDOs (see table 4.1).

Other factors that one might expect to be related to whether or not a black megachurch has a CDO do not seem to be related. For example, in her 1992 study of CDCs, Vidal found that that CDCs were not as likely to form in southern cities as in older industrial cities in the Northeast and Midwest.[35] However, among black megachurches located in the South, 71 percent have a CDO. One might also expect CDOs to be much more prevalent in inner-city areas than in suburban areas. However, there is a very little difference between the proportion of suburban black megachurches that have CDOs and those located in inner cities that have CDOs. This may be due to the fact that most

TABLE 4.1

BLACK MEGACHURCHES WITH COMMUNITY DEVELOPMENT ORGANIZATIONS

		% with Community Development Organizations
Age of church	Founded before 1960	71.0
	Founded after 1960	45.2
Pastor's education	Advanced degree	73.0
	No advanced degree	40.0
Church attendance	Fewer than 3,000 per wk	60.0
	More than 3,000 per wk	51.4
Regional location	Located in the South	71.4
	Not in the South	51.4
Metropolitan context	Inner-city area	63.9
	Suburban area	56.5

Data compiled by author.

of the "suburban" areas in which black megachurches are located are "inner-ring" suburbs. Many of these inner-ring suburban areas are undergoing many of the same socioeconomic problems that urban areas are undergoing—such as deteriorating schools, lack of employment opportunities, and poverty. In fact, Dennis Judd and Todd Swanstrom argue that the disparity in resources, average family income, and quality of life between inner-ring and outer-ring suburban areas is moving toward a disparity similar to the inner city/suburb divide.[36]

The fact that the black megachurches with affiliated CDOs tend to be older churches corresponds to Chaves' findings that older churches are more likely to be activist churches.[37] The fact that the churches that have more highly educated ministers are more likely to have CDOs points to the role that seminary education plays in socializing a minister to be inclined to engage in community development. Furthermore, development and successful maintenance of a CDO take skills that are more readily honed in academic programs. The leader-centered model that black churches subscribe to makes it likely that the personal characteristics of the minister (education background and theological orientation) will influence the churches' activities.

The data point to the conclusion that churches with CDOs tend to compose a subset of "activist" churches. As we would expect, churches with CDOs are more likely to participate in public engagement activities. This is the case even when these activities are done not through the CDO but through the churches themselves.

The Activities of Black Megachurch CDOs

My interviews with several black-megachurch-based community development organization (BMCDO) executive directors and my review of the mission statements, histories, goals, and objectives of several BMCDOs revealed that they generally adopt a broad perspective of "community development" beyond an emphasis on housing and other "physical development." Table 4.2 lists the various activities in which BMCDOs take part. Most engage in at least one economic, commercial, or housing activity. Most engage in at least one human development or soft development activity. Housing and children's programs (tutoring, day care, etc.) are the most frequently cited activities.

While many BMCDOs do engage in low- and moderate-income housing development (in fact, along with "child care and tutoring programs," this is the most often cited activity), housing cannot be said to dominate BMCDO activity. Most black-megachurch-affiliated CDOs take part in multiple activities. Furthermore, several focus exclusively on social service provision and do not engage in any housing or other physical or hard development activities. BMCDOs can be placed in three categories.

Typology of Black-Megachurch-Affiliated CDOs

BMCDOs vary considerably. Yet all fit easily into three categories: prototypical CDCs, thematic CDOs, and service delivery CDOs. The prototypical CDCs primarily focus on physical development or "hard development" (either housing and/or commercial). The thematic BMCDOs either target a particular population or target a particular community issue and engage in community development activities that address this problem or community issue. Finally, service-oriented BMCDOs primarily focus on "people" and not "place." These CDO programs generally focus on support programs for children and families, job training, or social service provision.[38]

Prototypical CDCs

Several of the BMCDOs are traditional CDCs. They target a neighborhood geographical area and engage in a combination of community economic development activities including housing, commercial development, business development, and social service provision, with an emphasis on housing. Housing is their "entry" activity and the activity in which they have made the greatest

TABLE 4.2

FREQUENCY OF PUBLIC ENGAGEMENT ACTIVITIES PARTICIPATED
IN BY BLACK-MEGACHURCH-AFFILIATED COMMUNITY DEVELOPMENT
ORGANIZATIONS (CDOs)

Activity	% of Black-Megachurch-Affiliated CDOs Involved in Activities
Adult education	24.2
AIDS hospice	3.0
Business incubator	11.4
Business resource center	6.1
Business tenants	12.1
Business total	24.2
Child care/tutoring/child programs	48.5
Clothes closet	24.2
Commercial development	16.7
Community development corporation companies	15.2
Counseling or support groups	30.3
Daily staple giveaway	15.2
Emergency financial assistance	15.2
Entrepreneur training	18.8
Food distribution	33.3
Health clinic	15.2
Homeless programs	21.2
Housing	48.5
Housing counseling	24.2
Housing rehabilitation	12.5
Immediate needs transportation	12.1
Job referral	27.3
Job training	30.3
Legal services/criminal justice	18.2
Low-income housing	31.3
Moderate-income housing	15.6
Political advocacy and organizing	18.2
Senior center or day care	12.1

Activity	% of Black-Megachurch-Affiliated CDOs Involved in Activities
Senior housing	25
Transitional housing	18.2
Uniform vouchers	3
Welfare to work program	12.5

Percentages do not sum to 100 because CDOs engage in several activities.
SOURCE: Data compiled by author.

impact. Many of their other activities either support the housing development efforts or stem from the housing development efforts.

ADC, discussed at the beginning of this chapter, is worth examining in greater depth. As I already stated, ADC is affiliated with Abyssinian Baptist Church in Harlem, which has a tradition of extensive engagement in the community. In addition to Rev. Calvin Butts, discussed at the beginning of this chapter, Rev. Adam Clayton Powell Sr., and Rev. Adam Clayton Powell Jr. provide excellent examples of this activist tradition. Powell Sr. was the senior pastor of Abyssinian from 1908 until his son Adam Clayton Powell Jr. became the senior pastor in 1937. During Clayton Powell Sr.'s tenure as senior pastor, Abyssinian built the first community recreation center. During the Great Depression, while he was still assistant pastor, Powell Jr. established an extensive and well-known food bank and relief program that aided thousands of people. When he became senior pastor Adam Clayton Powell Jr. continued to carry on the tradition of social ministry and became a U.S. congressman in 1946 where he championed socially progressive legislation such as minimum wage and antipoverty programs and preached that the black church should be active in the black freedom movement.

The community development activity that Abyssinian engages in through the ADC builds upon this socially and politically activist, "prophetic" tradition. ADC is one of the most productive CDCs in urban America.[39]

ADC was officially incorporated in 1989, though they started some activity in 1986. Like other third-wave CDCs, ADC started with housing and housing rehabilitation as their primary activity. Their mission statement reads as follows:

> The mission of the Abyssinian Development Corporation is to improve the quality of life in Harlem by: Increasing the availability of quality housing to people of diverse incomes. Enhancing the delivery of social services,

particularly to the homeless, elderly, families and children. Fostering economic revitalization. Enhancing educational and developmental opportunities for youth. Building community capacity. The thrust of ADC's overall program is geographically focused in Central Harlem, from 126th to 139th streets, between Fifth and St. Nicholas avenues. A fundamental tenet of ADC's philosophy is a rejection of the "deficit model" view of Harlem. We see a place with many assets, both human and physical, that are the foundation for the community's revitalization.[40]

ADC has rehabilitated over one thousand units of affordable housing. They purchased and renovated apartments for seniors, a set of row houses that were turned into cooperatives, a complex for formerly homeless families, brownstones for moderate-income families, low-income rentals (a significant percentage reserved for formerly homeless people), and a set of condominiums for moderate-income families.[41]

ADC leaders have mastered the art of combining various funding sources to finance their projects and have received grants from the Department of Housing and Urban Development, the city of New York, the state of New York, Local Initiatives Support Corporation, and private developers. ADC began its activities with a $50,000 grant and now operates with a multi-million-dollar budget. Abyssinian, through the ADC, influenced the implementation of affordable housing initiatives in the 1990s by becoming an important and influential partner with the city of New York's Department of Housing Preservation and Development.[42]

Though housing has been their primary activity, ADC's activities have expanded beyond housing. Karen Phillips, the former executive director, explained that "true revitalization means more than just providing shelter. His [Rev. Calvin Butts'] vision was to create a real community—homes for people of all incomes, good schools, thriving businesses and top notch cultural institutions."[43] There are a number of programs that support this comprehensive focus. ADC has partnered with the New York City Board of Education and opened the Thurgood Marshall Academy for Learning and Social Change (a day school for students in grades 7–12) and more recently added a lower school. ADC also has ventured into commercial development. It has partnered to build a Pathmark grocery store and the Harlem Center, which houses several commercial businesses. ADC also sponsors several community tenant associations and block associations.[44]

The West Angeles CDC in the Crenshaw neighborhood of Los Angeles is another prototypical CDC. West Angeles CDC was founded in 1994 as part of the outreach ministry of West Angeles Church of God in Christ (COGIC). West Angeles counts itself among a group of faith-based institutions that "seek to promote social change through Christian community development." Through collaboration with an impressive list of local government offices, like the Los Angeles Housing Department, the Los Angeles Unified School District, the Los Angeles Community Development Commission, the federal government, commercial businesses, civic associations (including other churches), philanthropists, and West Angeles COGIC, West Angeles CDC has built or renovated more than 150 units of residential housing. It also sponsors home-ownership courses and entrepreneur training. West Angeles CDC has conflict resolution programs for youth, periodic free legal counseling, and a domestic violence prevention/education program.[45] There are a number of these proto-typical CDCs that black megachurches have developed.

Thematic Black-Megachurch-Affiliated CDOs

Several BMCDOs target a particular population or social problem and provide multiple services to address this population or problem. The "thematic" CDO really exemplifies the comprehensive aspect of community development by attacking a particular issue or social problem from different perspectives.

One example of a thematic BMCDO is affiliated with St. John's United Methodist Church (in Houston): the Bread of Life Homeless Project. As is indicated by the name, the Bread of Life Homeless Project targets the homeless population at the edge of downtown Houston.

In 1992 the United Methodist Church sent Rev. Kirbyjon Caldwell, the senior minister at Windsor Village United Methodist Church, a black megachurch in southwest Houston, on a temporary assignment to St. John's United Methodist Church, on the edges of downtown Houston, to help revive it. St. John's had been a predominantly white church that as the neighborhood changed dwindled down to only a handful of members, who occupied a sanctuary that could accommodate eight hundred. Within a year, Revs. Rudy and Juanita Rasmus (husband and wife copastors) took over leadership of the church, and it rapidly grew from a congregation of nine to over nine thousand members. St. John's is located right next to the "Pierce Elevated" in Houston, a section of Interstate 45, named so because it goes over Pierce Street. Underneath the Pierce Elevated is a concrete lot where from the 1980s people who were homeless gathered and camped.[46] Early in its revival St. John's decided to serve the homeless population that surrounded the church, and in December 1992 Revs. Juanita and Rudy Rasmus formed the Bread of Life Homeless Project as a separate nonprofit.

While Bread of Life began as a homeless food distribution program it rapidly expanded to provide an array of services to improve the stability of people who are homeless. Bread of Life uses biblical scripture as its mandate to engage in its activities, particularly Matthew 25:35, 38, and 40: "For I was hungry and you gave me food; I was naked and you clothed me. . . . [I]n as much as you did it to one of the least of these my brothers, you did it to me." It is important to note that about one-third of the members are currently or formerly homeless.[47]

St. John's also operates a facility "Daybreak," where they provide shower and laundry services, a health clinic, adult literacy and GED programs, substance abuse counseling, clothing, and other necessary items. In 2006 they opened Resurrection House, a thirty-bed transitional living facility. Under construction is single-room-occupancy apartment housing—Knowles-Rowland Temenos Apartments (named for singers Beyoncé Knowles and Kelly Rowland, who partnered with St. John's through their foundation and personal donations to complete the project). The Bread of Life Homeless Project also partners with the city of Houston to distribute food through their food bank. They also have an HIV/AIDS testing, prevention, and education program.

The Bread of Life Homeless Project engages in these activities with the cooperation of and financing from several government agencies including the city of Houston Department of Health and Human Services and the Harris County Community Development Agency. Other funding comes from the Houston Endowment Inc., the Brown Foundation, and St. John's United Methodist Church itself. They are staffed by a mixture of paid staff and volunteers, some of whom have also been beneficiaries of the programs.

Project WAITT (We're All in This Together), which is the major project of Brentwood Community Foundation, is another community development project that targets a particular population. This CDO is an affiliate of Brentwood Baptist Church (also in Houston). Project WAITT targets people living with HIV/AIDS. They provide services such as a food pantry, rental assistance, mortgage assistance, utilities assistance, temporary and permanent housing, and nutrition and health counseling. Project WAITT combines "hard" physical development—building temporary and permanent affordable housing—with extensive "soft" development activities such as financial assistance and social service provision.

"Service-Oriented" BMCDOs

The service-oriented BMCDOs focus exclusively on "people-based" services, either providing health services or a variety of social services, youth services, counseling, and so on. They focus on soft development as opposed to hard development activities. Instead of focusing on a "charity" approach, much of this service delivery is actually aimed at raising the economic viability of community residents.

Bethel Outreach Center (BOC) in Baltimore is one such organization. BOC is affiliated with the Bethel African Methodist Episcopal (AME) Church, which has a long history of social and political activism. Like Abyssinian, the Bethel AME congregation was first organized as a political act. A group of African Americans, who would eventually form Bethel AME Church, first worshipped with a white congregation but eventually left the predominantly white Methodist church because of intolerable discrimination and in 1797 formed the Bethel Free African Society, which eventually became Bethel AME Church. Lawrence Mamiya has described Bethel's history as a "journey toward and a struggle for freedom."[48] Although a member of the AME denomination, Bethel AME was founded before the establishment of a national AME church and actually sent the most delegates to the first national meeting of the AME church.[49] Some argue that Bethel AME Church was the first totally independent black church in Baltimore.[50] Also like Abyssinian, Bethel sponsored a food program that provided relief to black families during the Great Depression.[51] Members of Bethel AME, a prominent church in the history of African Americans in Baltimore, were the investors that funded one of the first large black-owned businesses in Baltimore—the Chesapeake Marine Railway and Drydock Company (in 1866).[52]

BOC was begun in 1979 by the missionaries of Bethel AME Church and was incorporated in 1987 as a separate 501(c)(3) entity. When its mission is compared to the mission of ADC, a prototypical CDC, it is clear that the mission of BOC is "people" as opposed to "place" targeted. All of the programs are geared toward improving an individual's quality of life and earning potential. They endeavor to do this through "direct aid, assistance and counseling, education and employment."[53]

The programs of BOC provide direct aid and include a clothes closet, a soup kitchen (which supplies hot meals on site and through a carryout service), and a food pantry (emergency food supplies) and the provision of supplies (blankets, food, and clothing to homeless people). BOC also has education and job training programs. They have a GED class, a sewing class, a computer literacy class, and a tutorial program for children and adults. BOC also engages in family support programs such as supportive services for HIV-positive women, parenting support, developmental child care for parents participating in any of

BOC's programs, bereavement counseling, and a uniform voucher program for students attending Baltimore City Public Schools.[54]

Other service-oriented CDOs include Cathedral Second Baptist CDC (Cathedral Second Baptist Church in New Jersey). This organization, founded in 1990, has a food program, counseling, support for college students, social service programs, and an ex-offender reentry program, all "soft development" activities.

These three types of CDOs, prototypical CDCs, thematic CDOs, and service-oriented CDOs, obviously help to focus their sponsoring black mega-churches' attention and much of their resources on particular kinds of activities. Therefore, the types of BMCDOs the churches create function as another aspect of black megachurch "particularism."

Churches with CDOs Are More Likely to Participate in Public Engagement

While there are black megachurches without CDOs that are considered "activist churches" because of their considerable participation in public engagement activities, as one would expect churches with CDOs are more likely to participate than churches without CDOs. We can reason that these churches would obviously be more likely to engage in "hard development" activities. These activities take large amounts of money that churches (without harnessing resources from various actors) do not often have. The CDO provides a way to harness these resources and channel them to community projects. When it comes to "hard development," 58 percent of churches with CDOs do affordable housing, while only 22 percent of those without CDOs had developed or managed affordable housing. Of churches with CDOs, 36 percent had done commercial development, and only 8 percent of those without CDOs had done some commercial development.

As table 4.3 notes, black megachurches with CDOs are also more likely to engage in most other public engagement activities than those that do not have CDOs. For example, 17 percent of black megachurches without CDOs had established credit unions compared to the 36 percent of black megachurches with CDOs. Of those without CDOs, 4 percent had business incubators compared to 21 percent of those with CDOs. When it comes to overtly "political" public engagement, 81 percent of those with CDOs had participated in voter registration, compared to 70 percent without CDOs. Of those with CDOs, 76 percent reported that they engaged in political advocacy or organizing, compared to 50 percent without CDOs. When looking at churches that

TABLE 4.3
BLACK MEGACHURCH-BASED PUBLIC ENGAGEMENT ACTIVITY
IN MEGACHURCHES WITH AND WITHOUT CDOs

Public Engagement Activity	% with CDOs	% without CDOs
Advocacy or political organizing	76	50
Affordable housing	49	22
Business incubators	21	4
Commercial development	36	8
Credit union	36	17
Employment	81	60
Food pantry	91	94
Political ministry	51	13
Voter registration	81	70

SOURCE: Data compiled by author.

have standing ministries dedicated to political and social activity, the difference is much more disparate. Of black megachurches with CDOs, 51 percent had social and political ministries, whereas only 12 percent of those without CDOs had these ministries. It is clear that for economic development, political advocacy and organizing, and hard development like housing and commercial development, having a CDO matters. Only when it comes to food provision is there no difference between those with CDOs and those without CDOs.

Although churches with CDOs clearly participate in public engagement activities at a greater rate than churches without CDOs, it is important to note that often these activities are not done within the CDO *but within the church itself.* Of the public engagement activities examined, housing and commercial development are done more frequently via the church-based CDO than the church itself. But both food delivery and social/political activities are more frequently participated in via the church. Table 4.4 looks at only churches with CDOs and shows the percentage of activities taking place within the CDOs and those taking place via the church.

Immediate Needs Activity

Of black megachurches that have affiliated CDOs, "immediate needs" public engagement activities are likely to be based out of the church itself as opposed to the CDO. For example, while 94 percent of black megachurches with CDOs

TABLE 4.4

SELECTED PUBLIC ENGAGEMENT ACTIVITIES OF BLACK MEGACHURCHES THAT
HAVE AFFILIATED COMMUNITY DEVELOPMENT ORGANIZATIONS (CDOs)

Activity	Church Engages in the Activity (Not CDO Based) (%)	Affiliated CDO Engages in Activity (CDO Based) (%)
Affordable housing	11	38
Commercial development	17	19
Food delivery	59	32
Political ministry	30	21

SOURCE: Data compiled by author.

distribute food, only 34 percent of BMCDOs have food distribution as one
of their programs. Most of these churches engaged in food delivery before the
incorporation of the CDO. This activity is a traditional one in black churches
and is normally handled by missionary societies (almost always composed of
church women).

When food and clothing are distributed through the CDO it is done more
frequently than when it is distributed through the church. BMCDOs distribute food and clothing daily or weekly as opposed to only occasionally (e.g.,
around Thanksgiving or Christmas). BMCDO programs are generally more
expansive than church-based social service delivery and are often for a target
population. Their programs are usually financed by local governments in addition to church members. On the other hand, most of the programs that are
based out of the churches are financed solely by church members' donations of
food, clothing, and money.

Housing, Commercial Development, and Economic Development

Most of the largest and most significant housing and commercial development
projects are through CDOs. Producing one of these large-scale projects takes
expertise, access to resources, and political and economic clout. Generally the
church must recruit economic partners in the private sector and use their political clout so that local government will help them to facilitate their projects.

While the vast majority of black megachurches that engage in housing
and commercial development have CDOs, *not all of this activity takes place*

using the CDO as the vehicle. Commercial development and housing are also practiced outside of CDOs. Most black megachurches that have CDOs and participate in housing do so through their CDO (70 percent), but 30 percent of black megachurches that have CDOs and also engage in housing participate in their housing development through the church (and not the CDO). For example, Union Temple in Washington, D.C., rehabilitated several units of housing in their surrounding neighborhood of Anacostia before they even established a CDO. Although housing development was a long-term objective of the Union Temple Community Development Corporation, they began with housing counseling—coordinating a project aimed at placing low- and moderate-income people into affordable homes across the D.C. area, with a particular focus on Anacostia.[55]

Political Engagement

Although black megachurches with CDOs are considerably more likely to participate in more overtly political engagement activities than are other black megachurches, this activity is usually done in the church itself rather than through the affiliated CDO. BMCDOs generally do not engage in political development. Only 21 percent of BMCDOs include political or social advocacy as one of their program activities.

That said, several BMCDOs do take part in more overtly political and advocacy activities. For example, one Washington, D.C., BMCDO periodically holds candidate forums for local elections and issue forums to provide local citizens with information about relevant political issues. This BMCDO regularly invites candidates for local election and allows them a forum within which they can express their views to the public. This also provides the public access to the candidates. There are also BMCDOs that target specific issues. For example, one Los Angeles BMCDO organizes people around the issue of the environment, another organizes around the issue of juvenile justice, and still others sponsor voter registration drives. Others advocate for homeless people and for AIDS victims.

Instead of creating their own separate CDOs, there are a few black megachurches that are active members of community organizations affiliated with the Industrial Areas Foundation (IAF) . These organizations are among those particularly involved in political organizing and advocacy work. The IAF is a group of nationally networked community organizations founded by the late Saul Alinsky in 1940. IAF organizations are based on a community organizing model that focuses on the issues that local residents deem important—issues that affect people's everyday lives and where they can see a measurable improvement. They operate from the motto "Never do for a community what it can do for itself" and insist on citizen participation akin to the participatory democracy models (like Ella Baker proposed in her life's work in civil rights and community organizing). One of the earliest IAF organizations, TWO, which was mentioned earlier in this chapter, had Bishop Arthur Brazier as its first executive director. At the time Brazier was also the newly appointed pastor of the Apostolic Church of God (a black megachurch in Chicago).[56]

St. Paul Community Baptist Church, a black megachurch in New York, is a member of one of the IAF affiliates in Brooklyn—East Brooklyn Congregations (EBC). The pastor of St. Paul, Rev. Johnny Ray Youngblood, was a leader of EBC, and a number of St. Paul's church members worked actively in the organization. The EBC participated in "voter registration, candidate nights, and mass rallies attended by candidates and elected officials."[57] Through one of his sermons where he did an exegesis of the prophet Nehemiah, Rev. Youngblood was the "unwitting originator" of the idea for the EBC's best known achievement—the Nehemiah Homes Project.[58] The Nehemiah Homes Project (which includes twenty-three hundred units of housing in east Brooklyn) became a model for affordable housing development that was later copied in cities like Baltimore and Los Angeles. Through political organizing the EBC garnered support for the building of the Nehemiah homes, and one rally attracted over five thousand people. This helped to convince Ed Koch, then the mayor, that the Nehemiah Homes Project was worth the city's investment.[59] Even before the development of their housing project, the EBC was involved in political organizing and advocacy work like advocating for community policing and for better business practices among merchants in the community. For example, they got grocery stores to stock better food in the community of east Brooklyn underserved by public and commercial institutions.[60]

Unlike EBC, most BMCDOs *do not* engage in overtly political activity (electoral or advocacy). Still, it is important to emphasize that black megachurches with CDOs are more likely to engage in political engagement activities than those without CDOs. Of all churches with social and political ministries, over 80 percent also have affiliated CDOs.

The establishment of CDOs represents a trend toward making community development a more formalized and permanent part of black church life. This trend amounts to the "institutionalization" of community development. This is significant as the "institutionalization" raises two important questions. First, why would megachurches choose to "institutionalize" community development, particularly through a CDO? Second, what are the political implications of engaging in public life using a CDO as the primary vehicle? The answer to the first question rests with the instrumental and symbolic uses of the CDOs. The answer to the second question lies with the bureaucratization of public engagement and the political challenges that come with establishing and maintaining funding for CDOs.

Instrumental and Symbolic Uses of the BMCDO

The fact that even when black megachurches establish CDOs they do not do all of their community development through the CDOs raises the question of why they create them. Interviews with several black-megachurch-affiliated CDO executive directors revealed both instrumental and symbolic reasons for the establishment of CDOs. The instrumental purposes are to keep foundation and government grant funds separate from the church funds and to attract resources from funders who are reluctant (like some foundations) or prohibited (like government in some cases) to award capital directly to religious organizations. The symbolic purpose is to serve as a symbol of the "activist" church. The churches use the CDO to harness necessary funds to engage in community development projects, but they also serve to attract potential members who want to attend an activist church.

Traditionally the black church has been the one black institution that is financed, led, and controlled by African Americans.[61] CDOs provide a way to separate the indigenously raised church funds from the foundation and government "community development funds," which they reason helps them to maintain this independence. Preserving their independence is an attempt to protect the "prophetic voice" that this independence has helped to foster in many black churches.

Furthermore, a number of government grants are not available to religious organizations because of the doctrine of the separation between church and state. Thus, churches have an incentive to form CDOs—as this will allow them access to greater funding opportunities for their development projects. In addition to government funding, there are philanthropic organizations that prefer to award grants to faith-based organizations that demonstrate a respect for separation between church and state. In addition to attracting funding from government and philanthropic sources, black-megachurch-based CDO executive directors find that, legally, it makes it easier to accept grants when they keep the funding separate.

In recent years, particularly under the George W. Bush presidential administration, the doctrine of separation of church and state has been weakened. This is evident in the expansion of charitable choice and the Bush administration's emphasis on faith-based initiatives. Charitable choice was originally a provision of the 1996 welfare reform Personal Responsibility and Work Opportunity Act, which was signed into law by Bill Clinton. The charitable choice provision allowed state and local governments to use the block grant funds that were provided under the new welfare law to contract out social service provision to faith-based organizations without forming a separate nonprofit organization. George W. Bush expanded this provision and as soon as he took office established the White House Office of Faith-Based and Community Initiatives to investigate and support the expansion of faith-based organizations' applications for government grants to provide social services. The Office of Faith-Based and Community Initiatives continued with the Obama administration and was renamed the White House Office of Faith-Based and Neighborhood Partnerships.

Faith-based initiatives have been met with mixed reactions among black megachurches (which I discuss in detail in the conclusion to this book). When interviewed, one California BMCDO executive director thought that faith-based initiatives could have a positive impact overall if they encouraged more churches to become involved in community development. Another New Jersey BMCDO executive director expressed reservations about inexperienced churches receiving government funds without forming separate nonprofit organizations.

As noted above, black megachurches with CDOs are more likely to engage in all types of public engagement activity—even though they often carry out these activities through the church itself and not its affiliated CDOs. They use the CDOs to garner resources to engage in community development, which is their instrumental function, but the CDOs also serve a symbolic function. In fact, the formation of a CDO (while not necessarily a precursor to engagement) signals the church's commitment to community revitalization. A CDO serves as a symbol of an activist church. This is important for the theological "particularism" of black megachurches described in the previous chapter. As noted earlier, even the type of CDO that the black megachurch creates is important to its "particularism." Symbols of activism like having a CDO attract potential community development partners as well as individual congregants who are interested in attending an activist church. These CDOs send a message to the community. One Washington, D.C., executive director put it this way: "Forming a CDC is a statement that lets this city know what we are about although we've been doing community development for some time."[62]

Black megachurches form CDOs for both symbolic and instrumental reasons. They are able to garner funds through the CDOs, but the CDOs also serve as symbols of the activist church.

Political Challenges of the Black-Megachurch-Affiliated CDO

BMCDOs face many of the same political challenges that CDOs in general face. As noted above, the CDC literature is full of discussions of these challenges. Much of the work of CDCs requires collaboration with government and other powerful actors like foundations and others in the private sector. The CDOs' collaboration with government in particular presents challenges to black activist churches when they want to criticize government or elected officials. Sanctions or the fear of sanctions may constrain the activities of black megachurches that use CDOs. Second, the use of the CDO means that black megachurch public engagement is becoming increasingly bureaucratized. This increased bureaucratization means that the work is more often done by professionals and that laypeople miss the opportunity to develop social capital and the enhanced sense of efficacy that come with participating in these types of activities.

Challenge to the Prophetic Voice

Recall the critique of third-wave CDCs' exclusive focus on housing. Some scholars argue that the emphasis that CDCs place on housing development and rehabilitation is driven by the desires of the funders as opposed to the needs of the community. Moreover, the focus on housing takes away from the organizing and advocacy functions of CDCs. Margaret Weir puts it this way: "[F]unders' priorities have strengthened CDCs while hastening the decline of community organizing as a major component of their activities."[63] According to some observers, this overemphasis on housing leaves a void in the political activism that is needed in low-income communities.

Establishing a CDO does not seem to deter black megachurches from participating in "political" activities. While the majority of the social and political ministries are not programmatic aspects of the CDOs, the churches that are most frequently engaged in political ministries also are most likely to have CDOs. The activist black megachurches often have CDOs, so instead of discouraging "political engagement," it seems that having a CDO and engaging politics go hand in hand.

Black megachurches, however, have a finite amount of organizational, political, and economic capital. Expending any one of these in one area may stop them from expending it in another. Thus, even if these churches intend to engage in political activities, if their capital is spent on physical development or housing or social service provision, they are likely less capable of "political engagement." In other words, resource constraints (political or economic) may cause churches to abandon one of the activities and leave a vacuum that the less politically active megachurches are not likely to fill.

The Case of Union Temple Baptist Church

Union Temple Baptist Church in Washington, D.C., provides a good example of the plight of churches trying to maintain a "prophetic voice" while trying to raise money from private investors and government in order to expand their economic development, housing, and social service activities.

Union Temple CDC was incorporated in 1999 with a D.C. municipal grant for a project aimed at increasing home ownership among low-income residents (through housing counseling), particularly residents already living in the area.[64] According to the executive director of the Union Temple CDC, the minister of Union Temple decided to start a CDC because he "realized the importance of being anchored in the community and changing the world through housing." Although the church was already involved in a "full range of activities that affect people's lives including housing, family support and address other social ills that serve as barriers to 'the good life,'" a CDC would attract more financing and serve as a symbolic measure. It "says that we are interested in doing community development."[65]

The pastor, Rev. Willie Wilson, and Union Temple had a strong relationship with D.C. City Hall under the Marion Barry administration (1978–1990, 1994–1998). Barry was a member at Union Temple, and Rev. Wilson served as his "spiritual advisor." Rev. Wilson and the Union Temple Baptist Church ushered Barry's way back into the mayor's office after he had served time in prison for a drug scandal. Rev. Wilson spearheaded Barry's 1994 political comeback campaign and brought his and the church's political resources in support of Barry's reelection.[66]

Much of the community development work that Union Temple was engaged in was in part facilitated by municipal grants. Prior to the municipal grant that supported the establishment of the CDC, the church received grants for a number of projects including a transitional housing facility and the renovation of several housing units. Having a good relationship with the mayor's office no doubt helped them to secure these grants. In spite of the relationship with the mayor's office and the receipt of these grants, Rev. Wilson and the Union Temple Baptist Church were able to maintain their "prophetic" voice, and Union Temple was one of the most outspoken churches in D.C.

What happens when a relationship with elected officials, once sweet, goes sour? When Barry's successor Anthony Williams ran for mayor, Rev. Wilson also endorsed and supported him (though to a lesser extent than he had Barry). However, when Anthony Williams made public his controversial plan to close D.C. General Hospital, they began to part ways. This conflict reached a climax when at a church-sponsored issue forum on the closing of D.C. General Hospital, to which Williams was invited to explain his plan, Wilson openly criticized Williams. Williams later claimed that he had been ambushed. The Williams administration retaliated by revoking Wilson's low-number license plate (a low number is given as a perk to friends and allies of the administration) and stated that Wilson, by his actions, proved he was "no friend of this administration."[67]

While taking away a special license plate is not a retaliation of any real substance, this symbolic act does indicate the potential for a real sanction against the church because of the use of its prophetic voice. Churches have to use political resources to garner financial support and cooperation from city governments in order to carry out their community development projects, especially those that are dependent on grants. The Union Temple example shows that, like economic resources, a church's political resources are limited. The political resources expended on trying to attract and maintain city government cooperation and grants have the potential to take away from those resources expended on expressing a "prophetic voice."

Michael Owens provides further insight into this issue in his examination of black church/municipal government partnerships in New York City. First, Owens observes that New York City officials intentionally tried to direct the activities of black activist churches in New York through municipal grants. They "hoped that allowing activist churches and related CDCs to participate in the execution of the Ten Year Plan might quell their direct challenges to the status quo in public policy and municipal practices."[68] Owens gives us two examples of sanctions exacted against black-church-affiliated CDCs when they criticized municipal government officials, like the Rev. Willie Wilson/ Anthony Williams incident described above. The first was against Canaan Baptist Church of Christ (a black megachurch in New York), whose affiliated CDC—Canaan Development Corporation—lost the opportunity to participate in a community development project a block from the church because

Canaan's pastor, Rev. Wyatt T. Walker, called then-mayor Giuliani a "fascist" on a local public affairs program. The second was Rev. Calvin Butts of Abyssinian. On the same television program Butts called Mayor Giuliani a racist. The Giuliani administration's response was to block a multi-million-dollar commercial development project (Harlem Center Mall) on which ADC had planned to collaborate with the city.[69]

These three examples show that an emphasis on the community development strategy is not without its drawbacks. These churches are the ones most likely to engage in politics, and therefore the silencing of their voices would be the most costly to struggling African American neighborhoods.

The Challenge of Bureaucratization

Lincoln and Mamiya juxtapose the bureaucratic and charismatic traditions of black churches.[70] Bureaucratic leadership is based on expertise. Charismatic leadership is based on the personal charisma of the leader. Black megachurch leadership is a part of the charismatic tradition. As described in chapter 2, black megachurch ministers were often also the founders of their churches, or at least were the leaders of the churches when they grew to reach "megachurch" attendance numbers. Their charismatic leadership is a partial explanation as to why these churches grew when others did not.

Consistent with the "charismatic tradition," ministers often were the impetus behind the establishment of the CDOs. However, the institutionalization of church-based community development has resulted in increased bureaucratization of church-based public engagement activities. On one hand, increased bureaucratization establishes a continuity of programs and an efficiency of programs that a reliance on charismatic leadership and informal networks does not. On the other hand bureaucratization can have a negative impact on social capital formation. Fred Harris argues that the increased bureaucratization and professionalization in black churches has the potential to decrease the amount of social capital that has traditionally been formed in these churches. This is because fewer people tend to have the opportunity to learn political skills, as professionals do the work that nonprofessional church members used to perform. With increased professionalization and bureaucratization, lay churchgoers do not have the opportunity to learn as many political and leadership skills.[71]

Much of the public engagement work that CDOs participate in does call for professional expertise—especially housing development and commercial development. The majority of the CDO executive directors are professional experts in community development work or social service delivery. For example (at the time of data collection for this project), the executive director of Shiloh Baptist Church CDC was a lawyer, with knowledge of the rules governing nonprofit organizations. The executive director of the Union Temple CDC had been a housing rights activist since the 1960s and had been active in the CDC movement since 1968. Before working at Union Temple he had built low- and moderate-income housing across the country for a few different CDCs. The executive director of ADC worked for the city of New York, building housing, before coming to work for ADC.

These executive directors were not only professionals in the community development field but also active members of the church and were lay members of the church or in ministerial leadership before they became directors of the CDOs. For example, Rev. A. Davis, at Shiloh, was also the executive minister of the church. Mr. Fred Grimes, the executive director at Union Temple CDC, was an active member of the church when he was approached by Rev. Wilson and asked to lead the CDO. Wilson approached him because he knew that he had expertise in the area. Ms. Karen Phillips, the former executive director of ADC, was an active member of Abyssinian and had been the director of the volunteers at the ADC before it was officially incorporated, when the pastor, Rev. C. Butts, asked her to take over as executive director.

In these instances the churches capitalized on the skills of their church members. Through the establishment of these CDOs, black megachurches are able to harness skills and resources within their churches to facilitate community improvement but may lose some opportunities for developing the skills of laypeople who were not already professionals in the field. Ultimately, these CDOs may undermine some of the important benefits of public engagement for laypeople (e.g., building social capital and increasing political efficacy).

Conclusion

Black megachurches are increasingly participating in the community development approach to public engagement. This is evident in the number of projects they engage in and the number of CDOs that they have recently developed. Many of these organizations are not typical CDCs. They do not focus exclusively or primarily on housing. Instead BMCDOs vary. Some of them are typical CDCs, focusing on place-based development, and their entry activity was housing. Others are thematic in their focus. They target particular populations or particular issues and provide a range of services like food, employment services, and housing. And finally, a significant number of BMCDOs are focused primarily on "soft" rather than "hard" development. These CDOs may engage in job training or adult education, but generally their focus is people based rather than place based.

BMCDOs have both instrumental and symbolic functions. Instrumentally, CDOs make it easier for the churches to garner funds to engage in development projects from different sources. They also serve as a symbol that the church is an activist church to potential partners and to the broader community. This is important for "niche" churches that draw members from entire metropolitan areas (not particular neighborhoods). Their activist orientations are an important component of their "particularism," and for folks who are interested in attending an activist church the CDOs help to convince people to pass up multiple churches each Sunday to worship with them.

CDOs formalize and professionalize public engagement activities and provide a greater continuity of programs. But by relying on professionals who are church members, black megachurches that do most of the public engagement through CDOs may miss the opportunity to hone the political skills of non-professional community workers.

Black megachurches that have CDOs must also use caution when they want to express a prophetic voice and criticize government, elected officials or the status quo in general. As the three examples (Union Temple, Abyssinian, and Canaan Baptist) illustrate, these churches are subject to sanctions if they criticize people in power. The political capital expended to attract government funds may take away from the political capital that might have been expended using their prophetic voice—organizing and advocating on behalf of important community issues. When churches collaborate with government they may have to make important trade-offs concerning the use of their political capital.

CHAPTER 5

DUAL GENDERED SPHERES AND PUBLIC ENGAGEMENT IN BLACK MEGACHURCHES
Women Carving Out Space to Make a Difference

Women occupy a most peculiar position in the black church. Although they consistently make up the majority of members of black churches, for the most part they lack access to formal positions in ministerial and lay leadership. In the broader black church (and in black megachurches), women hit the "stained-glass ceiling."[1] While historically black churches were generally founded in response to racism, discrimination, and segregation in the larger culture, black churches have not been able to see their way to gender equality. Lincoln and Mamiya colorfully illustrate this phenomenon by observing that men occupy the pulpits while women are relegated to the pews.[2]

Despite this deeply entrenched sexism in their places of worship, women in the black church have acquired organizing and leadership skills through their parallel and auxiliary organizations. Ironically these organizations were formed as a result of their exclusion from full and equal participation in black church life. Through them black women have traditionally done advocacy work, organized for social change, and provided social services to their communities. In fact, according to Evelyn Brooks Higginbotham, it was the public engagement activity of black women that was largely "responsible for broadening the public arm of the black church and making it the most powerful institution of racial self-help in the African American community."[3]

These gender dynamics in the black churches can be described as dual gendered spheres.[4] Dual gendered spheres refer to separate arenas of leadership, labor, and authority in black churches where men are allowed to operate in one sphere and women are relegated to another. This chapter explores two aspects of the dual gendered spheres in black megachurches. First is the restriction of women from areas of ministerial and lay leadership in churches. Second is the space that women have created for leadership development, community involvement, and community transformation in spite of this restriction and their treatment as the "second sex."

Women lack equal access to formalized positions of ministerial leadership in black megachurches, like in the black church in general, yet they play a leading role in the public engagement efforts of black megachurches. I concentrate specifically on the megachurch-based community development organizations (BMCDOs) described in the previous chapter and show that there is a "womanist" influence on megachurch-based public engagement activity in which these BMCDOs participate. BMCDOs are likely to espouse and practice a more integrative approach to public engagement than CDOs in general (which are predominantly led by men). Therefore, it makes a difference in the public engagement agenda and programmatic thrusts of these organizations that so many women are leading their efforts.

By writing a separate chapter focused on gender it is not my intention to "ghettoize" the discussion but instead to emphasize the important role that women are playing in the public engagement efforts of black megachurches. Below I begin with a brief review of the tradition of patriarchy and an overview of the dual gendered spheres in black churches. That is followed by an examination of the "stained-glass ceiling" in black megachurches. Finally I explore BMCDOs and evaluate their activities from a gendered perspective.

A Tradition of Patriarchy

Many historically black denominations explicitly restricted women from ordination at their inception. The founders of these denominations reasoned that God had not intended for women to be equal to men in this regard through the use of biblical scripture. Perhaps one of the most often cited scriptures used to justify women's subordination in churches is the statement attributed to the Apostle Paul in 1 Corinthians 14:34: "Let your women keep silent in the churches: for it is not permitted unto them to speak." Many black church leaders used this Scripture to argue that women should not be permitted to speak from the pulpit, reserved for the *men* of God. Clarence Taylor observes that in the late nineteenth and early twentieth centuries in black churches in Brooklyn "[t]he Pauline view and the social custom that women were not suited to lead was practiced with little deviation."[5] Gilkes describes the attempt to silence women and bar them from certain areas of power and authority in black churches and the consequential "confrontation between women and the larger system" as "the politics of silence."[6]

Historically women have challenged their subordinate roles in black churches.[7] Interestingly, even the Pauline scriptures have been used to challenge gender discrimination. An early example is abolitionist and free black woman Maria Stewart, who pointed out the danger of applying scriptures without consideration of the context in what amounts to an early version of "womanist theology." In her "Farewell Address to Her Friends in the City of Boston" (delivered September 21, 1833) she speaks on the importance of women's voices in speaking out against slavery:

> What if I am a woman; is not the God of ancient times the God of the modern days? Did he not raise up Deborah to be a mother and a judge in Israel? Did not Queen Esther save the lives of the Jews? And Mary Magdalene first declare the resurrection of Christ from the dead? Come, said the woman of Samaria, and see a man that hath told me all the things that ever I did; is not this the Christ? St. Paul declared that it was a shame for a woman to speak in public, yet our great High Priest and Advocate did not condemn the woman for a more notorious offense than this; neither will he condemn this worthless worm. . . . Did St. Paul but know of our wrongs and deprivations, I presume he would make no objection to our pleading in public for our rights.[8]

According to Mary Sawyer, Stewart "took up public speaking on behalf of women and the enslaved, addressing, as well, the severe restrictions imposed on 'free' blacks. Without fail her exhortations were couched in the language of religious morality."[9] Stewart was inspired by her religious beliefs to enter into the public sphere and engage in political activism. While many used biblical references to justify the restriction of women from the ministerial hierarchy, Stewart used the Bible to justify her and other women's roles as public activists.

More recently theologians and other students of the black church have pointed out the hypocrisy of patriarchy in black churches that have been at the forefront of challenging racism in mainstream Christianity. Womanist theologians argue that relying on the dictates of Paul without taking into account the historical context is hypocritical, especially for theologians claiming to practice "black liberation theology." This is because black liberation theology consistently rejects the use of Paul's statement "slaves obey your master" to justify slavery in the American South. Womanist theologians argue that if the Pauline scriptures should not be used by slave owners to justify slavery, they should not be used to oppress or vilify women.[10]

C. Michelle Venable-Ridley points out that relying on the dictates of Paul can be problematic for the black community in general but especially for black women. Using a historical example, she argues that for the most part African Americans had an aural exposure to the Bible during slavery and "chose for themselves the texts that they included in their biblical canon."[11] Because of their use by those who wanted to maintain the slavocracy, the Pauline scriptures were often excluded from the enslaved African's biblical canon. Venable-Ridley points to Howard Thurman to emphasize this point. When explaining why his grandmother (who had been enslaved) would not allow him to read Paul to her, Thurman's grandmother said,

> "During the days of slavery," she said, "the master's minister would occasionally hold services for the slaves. Old man McGhee was so mean that he would not let a Negro minister preach to his slaves. Always the white minister used as his text: 'Slaves, be obedient to them that are your master . . . as unto Christ.' Then he would go on to show how it was God's will that we were slaves and how, if we were good and happy slaves, God would bless us. I promised my Maker that if I ever learned to read and if freedom ever came, I would not read that part of the Bible."[12]

Womanist theologians also argue that the overreliance of male-centered examples in the preaching traditions of the black church is problematic because this practice generally vilifies women and girls. Instead, black preachers and theologians should make a concerted effort to utilize a race and gender perspective to construct "a normative understanding of the relevance of the Scriptures to black women's struggles and triumphs."[13] Just as the story of the Jewish oppression in and eventual "exodus" from Egypt is often used as analogous to African Americans' experience of slavery in the United States, an attempt should be made to relate black women's particular experience of oppression to the Bible.[14]

Womanist theologians look to women of African descent in the Bible, like Hagar, an enslaved woman of Egyptian heritage who had been forced to have the child of Abraham and Sarah (who owned her) so that they would have an heir. According to Old Testament scholar Delores Williams, Hagar struck a first for freedom when she ran away from her household because of Sarah's ill treatment. While in the wilderness she named God "El-Roi," God who hears. While she was instructed to go back to Abraham's house so that she could have her baby in safety, she was later expelled from the household with her young son. While in the wilderness with no family connections and protection, Hagar was blessed and taken care of by God, who provided for her. Hagar was "exploited and disinherited by the oppressor, but blessed and empowered by God."[15] Ethicist Cheryl Sanders points out that many African American women can identify with and receive encouragement from Hagar's plight, as she was a single mother trying to raise her child amidst exploitation and in other adverse circumstances.[16]

Although patriarchy and sexism in black churches have been contested, patriarchy (albeit to varying degrees) is alive and well in the black church and megachurch. For example, when interviewed one black megachurch pastor opined that because all of Jesus' twelve disciples were men, Jesus obviously did not mean for women to be authority figures in the church. When questioned about whether women should be allowed to be the senior pastor of a church, he responded, "Show me in the Bible where God said women should preach. There is nowhere in the Bible that says this and if it is not in the Bible, then women should not preach." In another black megachurch I observed in Prince George's County, Maryland, hierarchy based on gender was explicitly taught to the congregation—specifically to the children of the congregation. Each Sunday this church has a children's lesson incorporated into the main service. One Father's Day the children were called to the front of the church, and from them four volunteers were selected. The children who volunteered were to participate in a skit that would teach the rest of the children and the congregation at large about God's strategy for communicating his will. The four volunteers turned to face the congregation as they each held a sign reading "God," "Father," "Mother," or "Child." The children went on to perform the skit, and the objective was to communicate that God speaks to the fathers who are the heads of households, who in turn speak to mothers, who in turn communicate God's will to children. To portray this in the skit, the God character said "Jump!" to the father character, who started jumping and in turn told the "mother" to jump. The "mother" started jumping and turned to the children and said, "Jump"—and the children of course began to jump. This particular skit was interesting not only because of the subject matter but also because of the manner that was used to get this message across. Acting out a skit will presumably instill these ideas about a sacredly sanctioned gendered hierarchy much more deeply than a sermon could—especially in children.[17]

Dual Gendered Spheres in Black Churches

Dual gendered spheres are partially the result of the tradition of patriarchy in black churches discussed above. Two spheres of leadership, labor and authority, have formed based on gender that are both separate and unequal, and scholars are increasingly exploring these separate spheres in black churches. They have observed that women have been restricted, by organizational bylaws or custom, from certain areas of lay and ministerial leadership. However, in spite of this women have been able to create a space from which they can develop leadership skills and have some power to influence black churches and to have an important impact on their communities.

In one exploration of the dual gendered spheres, Jualynne Dodson finds that while women were excluded from the formal ministerial hierarchy of the African Methodist Episcopal (AME) church, this does not mean "women were powerless in the exercise of denominational power."[18] In fact in her study of the founding of the AME church, Dodson finds that although the records on the founding rarely mentioned women's activities, men and women adopted a form of surrogate leadership in the AME church. The male leaders in the AME church served as surrogates for collaborative leadership between men and women. This "surrogate leadership" model was adopted in response to the "nature and constraints the larger U.S. society place on nineteenth-century African American organizational development." Thus, black churches used "surrogate leadership" in order to interact with the larger patriarchal American white society with limited conflict. She states,

> A patriarchal society would not deliver its resources through female leadership structures. African American communities have always possessed fewer resources and needed access to those of the larger society. The communities were also aware of the patriarchal nature of the U.S. and therefore employed a male surrogate, perhaps less qualified and representative of their will to publicly implement the decisions and desires of the collective.[19]

An example of this "surrogate leadership" in the AME church is the Daughter's Church, which had to approve the bishops' appointment of ministers. Although this was not a formal check on the bishops' power, Dodson claims that it was just as powerful. In essence Dodson makes the argument that there was a sort of strategic complicity, of black women, in their own marginalization.[20]

In her very extensive work on black women in black churches, Cheryl Gilkes describes the dual gendered spheres as a "dual-sex system" and argues that although separate spheres for men's and women's leadership and authority exist in a "clearly patriarchal" context, they do not identically replicate the patriarchal system found in the larger American society and are more akin to west African gender relationships.[21] For Gilkes, in the dual-sex system women's roles often carry status that is near equal to the status that men's roles carry.[22] According to Gilkes, an example of this parallel and almost equal role that black women play in some black churches is the "church mother." These church mothers are "occasionally pastors, sometimes evangelists, but most often leaders of organized church women." The church mother's role varies, but she is always an older woman who is presented as an "example of spiritual maturity and morality to the rest of the congregation."[23]

While in most churches the "church mother" is an informal position, in the Church of God in Christ (COGIC) church it is an institutionalized formal role, and Gilkes argues that the institutionalization of this role led to the strengthening of the women's department of the COGIC church, which she argues is the most powerful women's organization in any black denomination. Women were integral to the prospering of the COGIC church through their work in education and their organizational skills.[24]

Gilkes further argues that in the Sanctified church, women have both maintained a patriarchal tradition and fostered individual and social change. While women in the COGIC church are restricted from the highest positions of ministerial leadership (such as pastor, elder, and bishop) and assigned lower positions in a ministerial hierarchy (such as evangelist, church mother, and teacher), men and women do practice collaborative leadership in some areas. Furthermore, women exhibit some influence because these gender-assigned groups were almost parallel organizational structures. The reason for this is that the COGIC church (which is a Pentecostal church) carries the egalitarian nature of the Pentecostal interpretation of the gospel and of who can be called to ministry.[25] In this tradition, *who* is called is not of question, but rather in what form he or she may express this calling.[26]

In her seminal work on the founding of the National Baptist Convention, Evelyn Brooks Higginbotham gives yet another example of how gender hierarchies and dual spheres affect the public engagement of black churches. In her discussion of the black Baptist church in the early part of the twentieth century, Higginbotham shows that black women were introduced to the public sphere through working with their churches. Higginbotham looked beyond ministerial leadership and "exceptional women" to lay activity and leadership of black Baptist women and found that through the women's clubs and church auxiliary organizations women "initiated race-conscious programs of self-help," which contributed to molding the significance of the black church as provider of social services and community action. For example, social welfare programs and educational institutions used the church to resist racial oppression in the larger society and gender oppression. In some ways their activity accommodated the status quo, but in other ways it resisted it—blurring the lines between accommodation and resistance. In essence black churches exhibited what she calls a "dialogic" relationship between patriarchal oppression of women and the facilitation of black women's activism—with accommodation and resistance happening all at once.[27]

While there are a number of examples of women exhibiting activism, participating in decision making, engaging in community politics, providing social services, and learning political leadership skills from within this separate "women's" sphere in black churches, Fred Harris emphasizes the fact that these separate women-only organizations always have less power than their male counterparts and that in fact there is a severe negative impact of these separate spheres for black women's leadership in secular politics. Not only do these separate spheres perpetuate the "stained-glass ceiling" in black churches, but also the sanctioning of these separate spheres makes it more difficult for the black community to accept women in secular political leadership positions. As an example of this, Harris discusses the plight of black women leaders in the modern Civil Rights Movement such as Ella Baker and Septima Clark. These activists were constantly challenged in their decision making and leadership because of the movement's domination by the Southern Christian Leadership Conference (SCLC), which had an organizational structure modeled on the black Baptist church. Both Baker and Clark said that the norms of the black Baptist church undermined their leadership in the SCLC. Because women were not accepted into leadership positions, these women would not be accepted even if they were responsible for designing the various programs or had more information on the subject than the male leaders. By sanctioning a gender hierarchy using the authority of the church and biblical scripture, women are not taken seriously in secular life. Therefore, overall, the gendered hierarchy in black churches not only is detrimental to black women in black church life but also has an overall negative impact on the black political landscape.[28]

While patriarchy is clearly a part of the black church tradition, it has not been passively accepted by black church women but has been contested from its inception. Furthermore, the dual spheres or dual-sex systems gave black church women the organizational skills and a platform from which to contest their oppression and led them to establish organizations for societal change. In spite of patriarchy, black women have created an alternative view of womanhood that affirms community activism and participation in the labor force.[29]

The dual-sex system is clearly evident in black megachurches. In black megachurches women are for the most part restricted from the highest levels of ministerial leadership, either by doctrine or by tradition. Women in black megachurches hit the stained-glass ceiling. Women in black megachurches also disproportionately do the work of community outreach and community development. And to a large extent they disproportionately shape how black megachurches engage in public life.

The Stained-Glass Ceiling: Women's Ministerial Leadership in Black Megachurches

The "stained-glass ceiling" refers to the invisible (and formal) barriers that exclude women from certain areas of leadership in a church hierarchy. In black churches, formal barriers to ministerial leadership vary. Black Baptist congregations generally do not have any formal rules barring women from entering the ministry, but their informal rules and practices certainly restrict women's ministerial roles. Black Methodist denominations (AME, Christian Methodist Episcopal [CME], and African Methodist Episcopal Zion [AMEZ]) all ordain female ministers and are generally more liberal than Baptist and Pentecostal churches when it comes to women in ministerial leadership. All churches in the predominantly white, mainline denominations also ordain women—and actually the United Methodist Church was the first major denomination to elect a black woman (Leontyne Kelly) as a bishop.[30] While some Pentecostal churches have been the most vehemently against female leadership, others have been the most responsive to female leadership. Drake and Cayton observed that the Pentecostal churches in Chicago in the early twentieth century had many women pastors.[31] Traditionally, women often were the founders of Pentecostal churches, although many times, after they founded the churches, male leaders were sent to take over formal pastoral leadership of the church.[32] On the other hand most Pentecostal churches severely restrict women from serving in ministerial positions. COGIC and Bible Way Temple (both of these denominations have megachurches) formally restrict women from ministerial leadership.[33]

Black megachurches vary in the level to which the ministerial "stained-glass ceiling" will allow women to rise. Although most black denominations now ordain women and almost 80 percent of black megachurch ministers said that they approved of women being pastors of churches, this high rate of approval

is not consistent with the actual number of women at the highest levels of ministerial leadership in black megachurches as pastors. Black megachurches, like
black churches in general, overwhelmingly have male senior pastors.

Pastors' Views of Women's Ministerial Leadership
in Black Megachurches

Black megachurch ministers differ as to whether they believe that women
should be the senior pastors of churches, reaching the highest levels of church-
based ministerial leadership, or if they should be ordained as ministers to
serve on any level. This historical debate has been the source of the splitting
of denominations and ministerial alliances. For example, in 1919 a conservative faction broke away from the Pentecostal Assemblies of the World (PAW)
because PAW ordained women.[34] More recently (in 1997) one such debate
was carried out publically when three pastors were expelled from a Washington, D.C., ministers' conference, the Missionary Baptist Ministers' Conference
(which had about four hundred clergymen), because of their participation in
the ordination ceremony of a woman, Rev. Anita O'Brien-Russell. Rev. Max-
well Washington, the president of the Missionary Baptist Ministers' Conference at the time argued that when referring to bishops, the Bible uses only the
male pronoun he.[35] Therefore, ordaining women was to him clearly against the
will of God.

These expulsions as punishment for ordaining women were not new. Pastor H. Beecher Hicks of Metropolitan Baptist Church (a D.C. black megachurch) had been expelled from the Missionary Baptist Ministers' Conference
in 1984 for ordaining a woman. Several of the ministers who had been expelled
joined with other more progressive ministers to form the "Washington Metropolitan Ministerium," whose president was Dr. Wallace Charles Smith, pastor
of Shiloh Baptist Church, another black megachurch in Washington. Smith
said that the new organization was not so much a reaction to the conflict over
women in leadership as a proactive measure to aggressively act on behalf of
social justice issues. However, he did note that "[the Washington Metropolitan Ministerium] is the first African American clergy group which openly wel-
comes women in leadership positions. Women are very much a part of our
executive committee, and they chair some of our key committees."[36]

Although it is impossible to conclude that black megachurches are liberal
on women in leadership based on these cases of two megachurch pastors taking
a stand for women in leadership, based on answers to survey questions and the
number of women in ministerial positions in black megachurches it appears

that black megachurches are more liberal on women's roles as leaders than are black churches in general (see figure 5.1).

In *Something Within* Fred Harris compares Lincoln and Mamiya's survey of black ministers to the National Black Politics Study of African Americans' public opinion. He found a large disparity between the opinions of the African American public and black ministers regarding women in ministerial leadership. While only 52 percent of black ministers were in favor of women pastors of churches, 78 percent of respondents in the National Black Politics Study felt as if there should be more women clergy. This difference was especially profound in the COGIC church. Only 22 percent of COGIC ministers supported women as pastors of churches, whereas 84 percent of the COGIC laity supported more women clerics.[37]

Both Lincoln and Mamiya's study and Harris' study found that denomination is a key variable in determining whether black churches approved of female clergy or approved of women pastors of churches. In Lincoln and Mamiya's study 91 percent of Methodist ministers and 89 percent of the Methodist laity approved of women clerics and women pastors. However, only 29 percent of Baptist ministers and 22 percent of COGIC ministers approved of women pastors of churches. According to Fred Harris' study, 77 percent of Baptist and

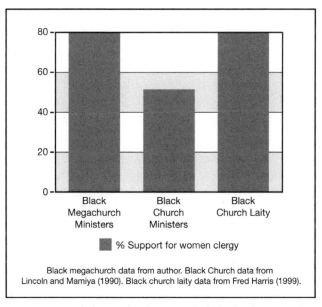

Figure 5.1—*Black Megachurch Ministers,' Black Church Ministers,'
and Black Laity Support for Women Clergy*

84 percent of COGIC laity agreed that churches should allow more women to become members of clergy.

Overall, megachurch pastors were more in favor of women in the ministry than black church pastors in general. In all, 79 percent of the black megachurch survey respondents agreed that women should be able to be pastors of a church. This is a higher percentage than those for both the black church laity and the black ministers.

There is a significant time lapse between the Lincoln and Mamiya data and the black megachurch survey, as the Lincoln and Mamiya data were collected during the 1980s. Still the difference in the megachurch ministers' responses, while reflecting the passage of time, probably reflects real differences in black ministers' and black megachurch ministers' attitudes toward women as pastors of churches.

Even with the generally high black megachurch approval rating for women pastors, it is still apparent that denomination is a key variable in whether a minister approves of women pastors.[38] Of those black megachurches surveyed (which included black churches in United Methodist, Pentecostal, AME, Baptist, and nondenominational churches) all of the megachurch ministers who disapproved of women pastors (28 percent) were from either nondenominational or Baptist churches.

Of those Baptist and nondenominational ministers who did not approve of women pastors of churches, the intensity and basis for their objections varied. For example, some pointed to the Bible for justification. Others were more reluctant to give even any justification. One assistant minister said that the official policy of the church did not bar women and that the senior pastor had some working relationships with women pastors; however, the pastor was not "about to let any women preachers in *this* church." Others seemed uncomfortable and refused to answer the question. This indicated to me that they probably were not in favor of women pastors but did not want to say this was the formal church policy, especially when a woman was asking the question. In fact, all three (two Baptist and one nondenominational) of those who refused to answer the question do not have any women ministers in their churches. The fact that two of the three were Baptists is significant as it further points to a glass ceiling. Officially most black Baptist churches do not have ordinances against ordaining women, but according to Lincoln and Mamiya, "the general climate has not been supportive of women preaching and pastoring churches."[39]

At least one megachurch minister who responded that he disapproved of women pastors indicated that he interpreted "pastor" to mean the senior minister of a church.[40] When I asked him if he thought women should be pastors of a church, he responded that they can preach but should not be "pastors" of a church. In the COGIC church such a distinction is extremely important and probably accounts for some of the difference in the clerical and laity responses. Women in the COGIC church are not to be senior ministers of a church or hold the titles of elder, bishop, or pastor, but it is acknowledged that they can preach or teach the word of God. In fact they often established churches and served as an interim "pastor" of these churches under the title "evangelist" until a male "pastor" could be sent to assume the pastorate. In the COGIC church one can agree that more women should be members of black church clergy while at the same time disapproving of women pastors of churches. This distinction is also key to understanding the stained-glass ceiling. Discrimination against women's ministerial leadership becomes more evident the higher women get in the ministerial hierarchy.[41]

Women in Ministerial Positions

Whether churches are in favor of women in the ministry or not, the fact is that there are few women senior pastors of megachurches.[42] As Konieczny and Chaves note, women pastors are generally concentrated in smaller congregations with fewer organizational and economic resources. Predominantly black churches are more likely than predominantly white churches to have a female pastor, and these churches are more likely to be independent nondenominational churches than they are to be affiliated with a denomination. Women's pastoral leadership is more likely to exist at the "entrepreneurial margins than at the bureaucratic center of the religious world."[43]

During the time these data were collected, the two black megachurch women senior pastors were Pastor Johnnie Coleman, pastor of Christ Universal Temple, an independent word of faith church, and Pastor and Apostle Betty Peebles, pastor of Jericho City of Praise, an independent Pentecostal church, both of whom have since died. Rev. Coleman (discussed in chapter 3) was the founder of Christ Universal Temple, and Betty Peebles' husband was the founding pastor of what was then Jericho Baptist Church and is now Jericho City of Praise. After Pastor Peebles' husband and son died, she took over pastorate of the church. They moved from Washington, D.C., to Prince George's County, Maryland, removed "Baptist" from their church sign, and built a very large City of Praise that is located adjacent to the Washington football team's stadium. While aside from a few exceptions women are not the senior pastors of black megachurches, they do occupy various ministerial leadership positions.

Women serve as copastors (usually the "pastor's" wife). They also serve as associate ministers and executive ministers and in other assistant-level positions.

The position of first lady of the church, or the pastor's wife, has traditionally offered some power and leadership responsibility. For example, the wives of the bishops of the AME church, CME church, and AMEZ church direct the women's programs in their districts. This is also true of the COGIC church. In fact, Gilkes argues that in the COGIC church it became a practice for COGIC pastors to look for leadership and organizational skills in a wife to administer the affairs of the church.[44] This is also carried out in local congregations. In many instances the first lady or pastor's wife directs the women's departments in local congregations.

In a variation of the traditional role of first lady in black churches, in several of the megachurches studied the pastor's wife serves in a ministerial capacity, often as "copastor" of the church. I found that 29 percent of the pastors' wives were also ministers—the majority of them copastors. Interestingly, copastor varies in its meaning in terms of the authority and responsibility that these copastor women have.

A few of these copastor relationships mean that the husband and wife share the pastorate on almost equal terms. For example, both Catherine and Billy Baskin in New Way Fellowship Church are called "Bishop." And in fact when explaining their history they said that although they began as a Baptist church they were never "common Baptist." "This allowed us to develop a ministry that went beyond ordinary Baptist practices. If it was of God, of Christ, of the Holy Spirit, we were willing to follow after it . . . includ[ing] the inclusion of women in ministry and leadership."[45] Another example is Revs. Juanita and Rudy Rasmus at St. John's United Methodist Church (Houston). Part of the mission of St. John's is to "remove the barriers of classism, *sexism*, and racism from the worship experience."[46] Addressing sexism as a barrier is a rare theme in the missions of black megachurches and indicates their commitment to gender equality.

In the vast majority of the megachurches that are copastored, however, the woman/wife/copastor is clearly a distant second in command to the man/husband/pastor. Often these copastor wives are ministers to the women only. In these churches the husband's title is "senior pastor" and the wife's title is "copastor." This indicates a hierarchy inconsistent with parity that the "co" in copastor implies. In most of these churches, the husband and wife were also cofounders of the church.

TABLE 5.1
WOMEN IN FORMAL MINISTERIAL POSITIONS IN BLACK MEGACHURCHES

Formal Ministerial Position	% of Black Megachurches with at Least One Woman in These Positions
Senior pastor	.03
Copastor	21.0
Associate pastor (second in command, including copastor)	40.0
Assistant ministers	73.0
Wife a minister in ministry	29.0

N = 45. Data compiled by author.

Even though the "co" in copastor is somewhat of a misnomer, an impressive percentage of black megachurches had women as second in command—whether their title is copastor or associate pastor (or some other title). Including the churches that are copastored by the pastors' wives, 40 percent (almost half) of black megachurches had women who were second in command to the senior pastor at the time of this writing (see table 5.1). Furthermore, the vast majority of megachurches (73 percent) had at least one woman minister serving in some capacity. The more common ministries that women lead were community outreach, youth and children, counseling, education, and of course women's ministries.

Although this proportion of black megachurches with women ministers seems relatively high, the ratio of women to men in the ministry in black megachurches is relatively low. One must keep in mind a unique aspect of megachurches. They generally have relatively large ministerial staffs ranging from three to more than twenty. And although a few of the churches had almost an equal number of men and women on their ministerial staffs, many of them only had one woman. Men composed the majority of those on the ministerial staffs of black megachurches.

Just like the approval for female pastors, in megachurches denominational affiliation is a key factor that indicates whether a church has women as part of the ministerial staff. Table 5.2 shows that all of those churches that do not have at least one woman on the clerical staff are nondenominational, Baptist, or Sanctified.

TABLE 5.2
APPROVAL OF WOMEN PASTORS BY DENOMINATION

Megachurch Denomination	% of Pastors Approve
Nondenominational	73
Baptist	70
Black megachurches in white denominations (United Methodist, Disciples of Christ, United Church of Christ)	100
African Methodist Episcopal	100
Sanctified church (Bible Way Church, Pentecostal Assemblies of the World, Church of God in Christ)	25

N = 31. Source: ITC/Faith Factor Project 2000 (Megachurch).

Although nondenominational, Sanctified, and Baptist megachurches are the only ones that express any disapproval of women pastors, these churches are very diverse. In fact some of the most progressive churches concerning gender are nondenominational, Sanctified, or Baptist. Of nondenominational black megachurches, 43 percent had women copastors. Recall that it was a Sanctified denomination, PAW, that in 1919 splintered because some of their leaders chose to ordain women. Baptist churches are also diverse in their views on women. Of the Baptist churches, 32 percent have women who are second in command to the senior pastor—whether they are copastor or the first assistant to the senior minister.

The Gendered Nature of Black Megachurch Public Engagement

A Tradition of Public Engagement

The dual-sex systems of black churches refer not only to the positions of leadership that are designated for women and men, as just described, where women are subject to the "stained-glass ceiling," but also to the sphere that women have carved out for themselves to affect communities in spite of the restrictions placed on them. The black church public engagement activities that are the concern of this book (electoral politics, social service provision, community development, organizing and advocacy) are interestingly connected to the women's sphere as much of the public engagement activity in black churches lies within the women's sphere—especially regarding social service provision. Many aspects of community outreach like missionary work, feeding the poor and hungry, and educational programs fall into the realm of "women's work."

Through their church missionary societies and auxiliary activities women have provided welfare services and instilled a practice of self-help programs that were manifested in the black women's club movement.

In the antebellum period, black women were active in antislavery societies that were established through their churches. After the Civil War they were especially active in the early African American mutual aid societies, many of which were based in black churches. They were active "despite the 19th century conventional standards that emphasized their domesticity," which said that a woman's proper place was in the home—away from public life. Their church and auxiliary work provided community services to people in need, often orphans, community service projects, social programs, and capital for loans to black entrepreneurs.[47]

In the twentieth-century black church, women carried on with their emphasis on community work. Gilkes observes that in the COGIC church women participated in community work "in order to foster group survival, growth, and advancement."[48] This work was extremely multifaceted and was manifested in education and employment advocacy and training. It was also manifested in working with organizations such as the NAACP, the Urban League, Student Nonviolent Coordinating Committee, the YWCA, and the National Association of Colored Women's Clubs. The work was a form of social action through which women affected their communities and tried to achieve social change. Gilkes writes that "if it wasn't for the women, racially oppressed communities would not have the institutions, organizations, strategies, and ethics that enable the group not only to survive or to maintain itself as an integral whole, but also to develop an alien, hostile, oppressive situation and to challenge it."[49]

Traditionally women have played a critical role in black church–based public engagement. As we would expect, megachurch-based public engagement activities reflect this critical role. As described in the previous chapter, CDOs have been the vehicle of choice for many black megachurches seeking to address the social, political, and economic challenges of contemporary black America. Women are leading these organizations, and when they do it makes a difference.

A Gendered Look at Megachurch-Based CDOs

Black megachurches utilize the CDO to participate in public engagement activities that include social service provision, community economic development, and political activities (electoral politics and political advocacy). It is no surprise that women are playing a very important role in the public engagement activity of black megachurches and their increasing use of the CDO. A gendered look at these organizations, one that encompasses the context of the dual spheres of leadership, labor, and authority is therefore important to really understand black megachurch public engagement.

Women are extensively involved in BMCDOs—in fact disproportionately so. Over half of the BMCDOs have women executive directors. This is especially significant in view of the fact that both minorities and women are underrepresented in executive director positions of most typical community development corporations (CDCs). Only 20 percent of CDCs have women executive directors.[50] The relatively large proportion of women-led BMCDOs is consistent with the idea that black women are at the forefront of black megachurch public engagement activities. It demands an exploration of the impact of gender on BMCDOs and an exploration of the differences between men-led and women-led BMCDOs.

Women-Led CDOs

In their study of women-led CDOs Marilyn Gittell et al. show that women-led CDOs have some characteristics that are different from those of the typical CDC. One of the most important differences is that women-led CDOs take on a much more holistic and comprehensive approach to community development. Unlike the typical CDC, which focuses primarily on housing, women-led CDOs offer multiple and varied programs.[51]

> Women-led CDOs in particular have taken on multiple roles in the community including housing and economic development, organizing, activism and advocacy, as well as human service delivery. The roles the organizations play and the programs which have been established reflect women's self-described "holistic" approach to community development.[52]

According to Gittell et al., women-led CDOs are also more likely to foster social capital than most typical CDCs. They further show that women-led CDOs have a more flexible and collaborative management style than their male-led counterparts and have staffs that primarily comprise women.[53]

According to Gittell et al., one of the important barriers that confront women as community development leaders is that the community development world tends to be sexist and male dominated. For example, where CDC budgets are larger, men are more likely to be executive directors, and members of the staff and organizations that are women led receive less funding than those that are men led. This is especially the case when these organizations undertake "hard" development activities such as housing and commercial development, which are more expensive than their "soft" counterparts.

The fact that women-led CDOs tend engage in so many different types of activities on average (instead of exclusively focusing on housing) may have a negative impact on the amount of funding these CDOs attract. In addition to the outright discrimination against women CDO leaders (which demonstrates funders' doubt of women's abilities to be successful community developers), women-led CDOs' multiprogrammatic focus may also discourage funders. Funders are sometimes reluctant to fund a multiprogrammatic organization. According to Gittell et al., one woman CDO leader was told that her multi-programmatic focus was "problematic." "[W]omen's focuses are multiple [and] most people wanted to hear focus."[54]

Black Megachurch CDOs and Women-Led CDOs

As described in the previous chapter there is a striking difference between typical CDCs and BMCDOs. CDCs typically participate in housing (which serves as the entry-level activity), commercial real estate or business enterprise development, and one social service or advocacy work area. They have made their most outstanding contributions in the area of affordable housing.

TABLE 5.3

TYPICAL COMMUNITY DEVELOPMENT CORPORATIONS (CDCs), WOMEN-LED COMMUNITY DEVELOPMENT ORGANIZATIONS (CDOs), AND BLACK MEGA-CHURCH CDOs COMMUNITY DEVELOPMENT ACTIVITY

Community Development Activity	% CDCs[a]	% Women-Led CDOs[b]	% Black Megachurch CDOs
Housing development	87	68	48
Commercial real estate development	67	20	17
Job training/placement	52	45	45
Business enterprise development	58	—[c]	26
Organizing and advocacy	35	over 50[d]	19
Social services	41	—[c]	51

[a]National Congress for Community Economic Development, Coming of Age: Trends and Achievements of Community-Based Development Organizations (Washington, D.C.: NCCED, 1998).
[b]Gittell, Bustamante, and Steffy, Women Creating Social Capital.
[c]Not available.
[d]There are different activities that fall under the realm of "organizing and advocacy." For all of them the value is over 50%.

On the other hand, BMCDOs do not focus primarily on housing. Table 5.3 shows that instead of the typical CDC, BMCDOs much more closely resemble women-led CDOs. They are generally more comprehensive in their approach and have a broad array of public engagement activities in which they participate. Like women-led CDOs, BMCDOs are also holistic and take an integrative approach to community development—one that incorporates human development and "hard" development and often has a multiprogrammatic focus. As was discussed in the previous chapter, many of the BMCDOs mention holistic development as a part of their missions.

The Role of Gender in Megachurch CDOs

The fact that BMCDOs look more like women-led CDOs than typical CDCs is in part due to the number of women black megachurch CDC directors. As stated earlier, a slight majority of BMCDOs are women led. Also, the majority of the paid staff members of BMCDOs are likely to be women—as are the majority of the volunteers. As explained earlier, traditionally black women have been responsible for much of the public engagement in the black church.

CDOs represent a new development in this traditional landscape. Church-affiliated CDOs are formal and more bureaucratized than other vehicles for public engagement. More importantly, CDOs have to interact with the white-male-dominated community development world in order to attract and retain funding. Therefore, establishing a megachurch-based CDO in some ways transfers the public engagement activity from the female-dominated sphere to the white-male-dominated "community development world." In this way the transition to CDOs "masculinizes" black megachurch public engagement.

In an example of the increased bureaucratization and formalization of community work, I noticed that it was the case for many BMCDOs that women had developed the organization and set the agenda and were already doing the public engagement work through a volunteer church-based organization like a missionary society before the CDO was separately incorporated and received funding (like was the case for Bethel AME Outreach Center in Baltimore).

Gittell et al. found that in many cases women initiated and led the public engagement efforts when there was no funding or salaries and the labor was voluntary, but when funding was secured and positions became salaried a man was hired.[55] Sometimes the discrimination that women face in the white-male-dominated community development world may lead to a strategic use of gender discrimination that some women in the Gittell et al. study reported that they practiced—a type of "surrogate leadership" (similar to what Dodson describes). In this surrogate leadership, men may be the ones to interact with the potential funders on behalf of a CDO that is codirected with women; or women executive directors may send a male member of the staff to meet with certain people, whom they felt would not be responsive to women leaders.[56]

One black megachurch in Houston may have utilized a similar strategy. This church has three CDCs. Two of them were started and then were directed by the pastor's wife. Several years later the third corporation was established, as an umbrella organization for the other two. At the time of this writing it was male led. Though the third is the umbrella organization, it is misleading not to recognize that these other two organizations that actually have the community development programs were started by a woman and were started years before the umbrella organization; however, male leadership appeared to be at the highest level.

There are many examples of black megachurches in which women organized community work efforts through their missionary societies or other "outreach" organizations, set public engagement agendas, and were already doing the work through a volunteer church-based organization like a missionary society before it was separately incorporated and received funding.

Comparing Men-Led and Women-Led Megachurch-Based CDOs

To shed further light on the impact of gender on the programmatic thrusts of BMCDOs it is important to examine the differences between men-led and women-led BMCDOs. Upon examination of the programs of these CDOs it became clear that there are some distinct differences between women- and men-led groups. First of all, women-led BMCDOs had a broader, more holistic programmatic thrust than did the men-led BMCDOs. Whereas the women-led BMCDOs averaged seven different activities per church, the men-led BMCDOs averaged three. This supports Gittell et al.'s finding that women-led CDOs are more holistic, broader, and usually multiprogrammatic in their approach.

Not only is there a difference in the number of programs that men- and women-led CDOs take on, but also there is a difference in the activities that they are more likely to participate in. There were several activities that women-led CDOs were more likely to engage in—especially social service activities. In fact, there were several activities—health clinics, homeless shelters, services for homeless people, and daily staple giveaways—in which men-led BMCDOs in this study did not participate at all. The results of bivariate correlation analyses showed that whether the executive director was male or female was related to

TABLE 5.4
BLACK MEGACHURCH COMMUNITY DEVELOPMENT ORGANIZATIONS (CDOs),
BLACK MEGACHURCH WOMEN-LED CDOs, AND BLACK MEGACHURCH
MEN-LED CDOs: PERCENTAGE OF PARTICIPATION AND VARIOUS PUBLIC
ENGAGEMENT CDO ACTIVITIES

CDO Activity	Black Megachurch CDOs (%)	Black Megachurch Women-Led CDOs (%)	Black Mega-church Men-Led CDOs (%)
Social service provision*	52	70	29
Food distribution	36	47	21
Health clinic/services**	16	29	0
Homeless shelter	10	18	0
Service to homeless	23	41	0
Daily staple giveaway**	16	29	0
Counseling or support groups**	32	53	7
Emergency financial assistance*	16	29	0
Employment services			
Job referral	29	41	14
Job training	32	41	21
Entrepreneurial training	20	21	19
Adult education programs	26	35	14
Welfare to work	13	13	14
Housing	45	47	43
Housing counseling	29	29	21
Senior housing	23	25	21
Low-income housing	27	31	21
Business activity	26	29	21
Community development corporation companies	16	18	14
Business resource center	7	0	14
Business tenants	13	24	0
Commercial development	17	29	7
Community organizing/ advocacy	19	18	21

CDO Activity	Black Megachurch CDOs (%)	Black Megachurch Women-Led CDOs (%)	Black Mega-church Men-Led CDOs (%)
Legal services/criminal justice	19	12	29
Children and seniors			
Programs for children/ tutoring, child care	52	59	43
Senior center	13	18	7

*Correlation between activity and executive director's gender is statistically significant at .05.
**Correlation between activity and executive director's gender is statistically significant at .01.
Data compiled by author.

whether the BMCDOs did social service of any kind and whether they provided health services. The BMCDO's executive director's gender was related to whether the BMCDO participated in social service provision in general and, within social service, to participation in health clinics and services, services to the homeless, daily staple giveaways, emergency financial assistance, and counseling services and support groups (see table 5.4).

The Sexual Division of Labor

A look at the sexual division of labor is instructive in explaining the differences in the activities of men-led and women-led BMCDOs. The sexual division of labor is the separation of labor roles by sex. This division of labor is evidenced in the dual gendered spheres in the black church ministerial leadership, discussed earlier, and is also evidenced in the public engagement activities conducted via CDOs. The fact that women-led CDOs are more likely to participate in social service provision is due to their tradition in providing social services—especially through churches and the sexual division of labor, which dictates that women are responsible for "caring" and "nurturing" work.

For example, women-led megachurch-based CDOs were more likely to engage in health care provision and providing social services, which are extensions of social reproductive work that women are responsible for in a sexual division of labor. Emergency financial assistance and daily staples are also a part of nurturing a household that extends to the public sphere.

Although women-led BMCDOs are more likely to do certain activities and there is a comparable number of men- and women-led BMCDOs, men-led BMCDOs are not really more likely to do any certain types of activities.

Especially interesting is that men-led BMCDOs are not more likely to do the "hard development" activities such as housing development and rehabilitation or commercial development, in spite of the fact that women are disadvantaged when they attempt to infiltrate the construction business and the hard development networks (although black men have trouble infiltrating these networks as well). So although women-led BMCDOs engage in more of the social service and soft development activities, they participate in "hard development" to the same extent as men-led BMCDOs. This is more evidence of the fact that these women-led BMCDOs are broader and more holistic in their approach. The evidence also implies that women are doing more black megachurch community development, and they are in many ways leading in these efforts—as is consistent with the dual spheres tradition. This also reflects some of the intricacies of the sexual division of labor, in which although women are responsible for the social reproductive functions, they are increasingly responsible for the economic production functions (and black women have a tradition of labor in this area as well).

Black women have traditionally done the outreach and are carrying on this tradition in BMCDOs, and gender roles greatly influence black- BMCDOs. Women disproportionately lead BMCDOs (in comparison to typical CDCs). BMCDOs provide a model for holistic community development, which takes into account various aspects of one's life.

Conclusion

There is a strong tradition of patriarchy and discrimination in black churches and black megachurches. This tradition is supported by biblical interpretations and church traditions and culture. Although there has been constant conflict over gender roles in the church, this discrimination has resulted in gendered spheres in which black women and men are assigned to certain roles based on sex. These gendered spheres have also led to a "stained-glass ceiling" that limits women's access to certain levels of power and influence in the church, especially formal ministerial leadership.

These gendered spheres, however, have not stopped women from developing leadership skills, displaying influence in their churches, and affecting their communities through public engagement—in fact leading in these efforts. This is evident in the realm of BMCDOs. Women disproportionately lead BMCDOs when compared to typical CDCs. Their overparticipation in the new trend of community development is not surprising given their traditional roles in the black church. Furthermore, women-led BMCDOs are more likely than the men-led BMCDOs to pursue a multiprogrammatic approach and to work in the areas of health care, social services, and counseling—areas designated for women in a sexual division of labor.

The facts that these BMCDOs are black church based and that much of the black church public engagement activities are "women's work" as dictated by the "dual political spheres" mean that these activities are dominated by women. On the other hand, the community development world—at the level of executive director (especially the more funding the organization has)—is heavily male dominated due to the sexual division of labor. This dictates that BMC-DOs' leadership should be dominated by men. So while the black church basis of the BMCDO "feminizes" the BMCDO leadership, the male-dominated community development arena "masculinizes" it.

In any case, BMCDOs are influenced by the "dual spheres of labor" that designate women as responsible for community outreach work. Women make up the majority of the volunteers and paid staff members of church-affiliated organizations. Furthermore, all BMCDOs s resemble women-led CDOs more than typical CDCs—which indicates that they are also influential in decision-making processes. Finally women-led BMCDOs engage in more activities than do men-led BMCDOs. This suggests that women greatly influence black megachurch public engagement.

CHAPTER 6

CONCLUSION
Black Megachurches and Black Politics
in the Twenty-First Century

The black megachurch is arguably the most exciting black social organization to arise in the latter half of the twentieth century. Like the storefront church phenomenon that developed during the Great Migration, the black mega-church phenomenon has grown due to what Andrew Wiese calls the "next great migration"—the 1980s and 1990s suburbanization of much of black America.[1] Just as migrants established storefront churches to help them accli-mate to the new urban environment "up north" at the turn of the twentieth century, so have megachurches developed to respond to the needs of the black suburban migrants almost a century later.

Black megachurches are accessible to these suburban migrants. The churches are open, welcoming, and convenient to them. Black megachurches are thisworldly and respond to the temporal as well as spiritual needs of their congregations. They provide the professional worship experience that members of this demographic expect and the enthusiastic worship style that they desire.

Black suburban migration is not only a product of geographic shifts in black populations but also reflects the post–civil rights expanded black middle class. Thus, black megachurches also reflect a "class migration." Even the casual observer will agree that the grandiose physical structures of black megachurches are alone a testimony to the aggregation of material resources and wealth that has been possible only in post–civil rights America. As an older black woman put it when she found out I was studying them, "Can you believe that black people can come together and build something this beautiful? This wasn't possible in my day!" And she is right. Maybe a handful of these churches could have existed (and very large churches did exist) forty years ago, but not the numbers that they exist now. African Americans did not have the relative freedom in civil society, nor did they have the aggregated resources to build or sustain them.

While these churches clearly reflect the gains of the Civil Rights Movement, what about their public engagement? Do they address the challenges that persist for black people in post–civil rights America? Are these churches engaging public life in a way that would allow them to address the most urgent needs of black communities? Forty years after the civil rights struggle, does the black megachurch rise to the challenge that Dr. King set for the black church back in 1963—to "answer the knock at midnight"?

The Nuances of Answering the Knock

To answer these questions it was first important to address one of the greatest misconceptions about black megachurches—their assumed uniformity, the notion that they are all identical in "thought, word, and deed." This is particularly interesting in the face of the most recent "black church" literature, which has increasingly embraced a heterogeneous black *church*. Black *mega*churches, on the other hand, are assumed by both lay observers and academics alike to lack this heterogeneity.

The foregoing chapters have shown that there is a wide variety of black megachurch experiences, theological orientations, and strategies for participation in public life. Instead of being a homogeneous group, black megachurches are what Omar McRoberts calls "particularistic spaces." These churches are differentiated by the bundles of services and opportunities they offer, their dominant theological orientations, their ministries, their public engagement, their reputations, and even their architectural designs. This particularism operates almost like a brand. In one metropolitan area there might coexist the Afrocentric church, the social justice/civil rights church, the psychological/self-help church, the political church, the hip-hop church, the socially conservative evangelical church, and the word of faith church—each one of them with megamemberships. Potential members are attracted to the particularistic characteristics of one megachurch over another. They are attracted by the opportunity to be a part of the churches to participate in the activities, to benefit from the services the megachurches offer, and/or just to be associated with the church and in a sense live vicariously through the church's reputations. The particularistic and multidimensional black megachurch fits nicely with other recent studies that observe the black church through a pluralistic lens as opposed to a unitary or dichotomous one. Just like there is not one "black church" that is either the liberator or the opiate of the masses, there is not one black megachurch that either responds to or ignores the knock at midnight.

When it comes to "answering the knock," on one extreme there are black megachurches that focus primarily on personal and individual transformation, and while they are thisworldly these churches do not respond to "the knock" per se because they strictly address the insular needs of their congregations. On the other extreme there are black megachurches that try to address issues in a communal fashion, providing services and goods to those in need and dealing with issues of social justice in the way that Martin Luther King Jr. called for.

The theological orientations of these churches serve as motives for their public engagement. Theological orientations prescribe both ways of understanding society and the roles that churches should play in society. The social gospel, black liberation theology, communal theological orientations, and denominational ties all influence churches to participate in activities that could be described as "answering the knock." On the other hand the prosperity gospel, a color-blind theology, a privatistic theology, and nondenominationalism are theological orientations that make it less likely that churches will participate in these activities.

The activist churches—those that are aggressively engaged in public life—try to address issues like poverty, racism, and racial disparities in education, health, and life chances on a structural level as well as a personal one. They try to address the needs of black communities through a broad array of ministries. These include affordable housing projects, commercial development, and promoting civic engagement and increasingly the community development approach. A majority of them have established community development organizations (CDOs) which they use to bureaucratize and institutionalize their public engagement. These CDOs allow churches to harness resources from government and others to participate in more extensive public engagement activities than churches would be able to do on their own. Black-megachurch-affiliated CDOs also serve as symbols of the church's interests in community development and of the fact that they are activist churches.

Most interesting about the community development approach and black-megachurch-affiliated CDOs is the way they reflect the traditional patriarchal structures, gendered spheres of leadership, labor, and authority in black churches. Black-megachurch-affiliated CDOs most often take a "holistic" approach to community development, which tends to resemble the approach of women-led CDOs. They are also more likely to be led by women than CDOs in general. This reflects the fact that the public arm of black megachurches tends to be a part of the "women's sphere."

Those who expect the activist black megachurches to fill the gaps left by the Civil Rights Movement should be aware that these churches struggle with prioritizing their activities given limited capacity and limited political capital. For example, when churches form CDOs and accept government funding, the leaders and representatives of these churches are limited in how they criticize government policies, even when they feel such policies are detrimental to their communities. The leaders of activist churches make strategic decisions that sometimes result in sacrificing some forms of public engagement for other forms, often constricting their prophetic voices.

So when it comes to whether the black megachurch is answering the knock at midnight—and responding to human need—we see that the answer is nuanced. While they are generally thisworldly churches catering to the black working- and middle-class suburban migrants, the differences among these churches are profound and include their varying orientations toward public engagement. Furthermore, examining black megachurches also reveals important debates in contemporary black politics about methods and philosophies that should be employed to "answer the knock." The next section explores some of these debates as they have taken place in select black megachurches.

Fruits and Fissures

The examination of black megachurches reveals that they not only are a result of the gains of 1950s and 1960s social movements but also reflect some of the divergent views of a black political agenda and political strategies that should be used to address the challenges or "midnights" that remain. They reflect the "fruits" of the Civil Rights Movement but also the fissures of contemporary black politics.

Debates about the public role of black megachurches parallel debates concerning a more general black public agenda. For example, should black megachurches focus on getting black elected officials in office or community economic development? Should they engage in protest politics? Are a reassessment and rededication of "family values" and a socially conservative morality really needed for the revitalization of black communities? Should black

megachurches promote a traditional "social justice" agenda? Should they promote a deracialized politics? A black nationalist politics? Should they cooperate with government or serve as the "gadfly" and press their agenda from the
. outside? Or should there be some combination of these goals and strategies?

The funeral of Coretta Scott King and the black megachurch where it was
held (New Birth Missionary Baptist Church in suburban Atlanta) together tell
a story about both the fruits of the Civil Rights Movement and some of these
divergent strands in black politics. New Birth is located in DeKalb County,
which is a majority-black suburb of Atlanta. It is important to note that the
Atlanta metropolitan area has one of the largest black suburban populations in
the country, which grew by more than seven hundred thousand in the 1980s
and 1990s.[2] It is also a city where black power, at least in the form of black control of city hall, has been the status quo since 1973, when Maynard Jackson was
elected to his first term as mayor. It is representative of the "New South," and
Atlanta's large black suburban population reflects African American post–civil
rights social mobility.

New Birth Missionary Baptist Church has been in DeKalb County since
1983 and with twenty-five thousand members is one of the largest churches
in the country. It has experienced the rapid growth consistent with the typical megachurch. In 1987, when Bishop Eddie Long first came to New Birth,
there were three hundred members. Four years later, in 1991, membership had
grown to eight thousand. New Birth has over forty ministries and church auxiliary organizations including a day school that enrolls children from PK3 to
eleventh grade. In 2000 New Birth built a $50 million, ten-thousand-seat sanc-
tuary. New Birth is accessible, professional, and thisworldly and is organized to
meet the needs of the 1980s–1990s expanded black middle class in Atlanta. As
such, its very existence is the consequence of the Civil Rights Movement that
made Dr. King and Mrs. King cultural icons.

Yet there was controversy surrounding the selection of Eddie Long's New
Birth for Coretta Scott King's funeral that in turn exposed some of the fissures
in black politics. The source of much of the anxiety was political stances that
Long had taken that were supported by Rev. Bernice King (Coretta Scott King
and Martin Luther King Jr.'s youngest daughter), an elder at New Birth who
considers herself Long's "spiritual daughter."[3]

Recall from chapter 3 that theologian James Cone had criticized Long
and refused to attend a function where Long was to be the keynote speaker
because of Long's "prosperity teachings." But perhaps the most illustrative
example of a controversial political stance was the December 2004 Reigniting the Legacy March led by Eddie Long and Bernice King. The controversy

surrounding this march came about because of the message it articulated. The march denounced same-sex marriage and supported a constitutional amendment that would define marriage as a union between a man and a woman. For some, this socially conservative agenda was contrary to the traditional Civil Rights Movement agenda. Long, though, did not see this as contradictory to the traditional Civil Rights Movement but totally consistent with this tradition. From Long's perspective, the "midnights" that remained were not due to structural inequalities and persistent racial discrimination but instead due to corrupt moral values and black people's failure to take advantage of opportunities that had been given to them. On the eve of the march, Long stated that this was the direction that most thought black political activism should take. He said that "a strong segment of society 'wants to go back to basic, fundamental moral beliefs'" that were the basis of his Reigniting the Legacy March.[4]

The Reigniting the Legacy March was rife with civil rights–era symbolism that supports Long's view of an evolving Civil Rights Movement. The "legacy" of course was to refer to the Martin Luther King Jr. civil rights legacy. The marchers traveled from the King Center (where Bernice King lit a torch from her father's grave site) to Turner Field. Yet to 1960s civil rights figures like U.S. Representative John Lewis and NAACP chairman Julian Bond, its message perverted the civil rights legacy. They argued that the Reigniting the Legacy March was actually contrary to their perspective of civil rights, which promoted equality and the opening up of the society. Bond was quoted as having said, "With so many problems afflicting black Americans, you wonder, what harm is done by people in love?"[5]

The opposition to New Birth's politics was enough to keep Bond away from Coretta Scott King's funeral. He argued that Coretta Scott King had embraced the idea of gay rights as civil rights. He said, "I knew her [Coretta Scott King's] attitude toward gay and lesbian rights. . . . I just couldn't imagine that she'd want to be in that church with a minister who was a raving homophobe."[6] Coretta Scott King's funeral was a moment that illustrated both the fruits and the fissures of black politics in the post–civil rights era.

Black Megachurches and Black Politics in the Twenty-First Century

Of course, black communities since the Civil Rights Movement are not just basking in the successes of their upward mobility. Even when looking at suburban DeKalb County from the last example, there is evidence of racial disparities and inequality that parallel pre–civil rights disparities. Most African American suburbanites in DeKalb County live in the inner-ring suburban neighborhoods where there has been disinvestment in the housing stock and the commercial districts. They pay higher taxes, receive fewer services, and have a lower rate of homeownership and higher poverty rates.[7] The majority of African Americans attend almost all-black schools that perform lower than their white counterparts in DeKalb County.[8] And in the city of Atlanta—sometimes touted as the "black Mecca"—in 2004 the child poverty rate was the highest in the country. As Journalist Bruce Dixon wrote for the *Black Commentator*, "For almost half of Atlanta's children, 'black Mecca' never happened at all."[9]

The paradox of black progress is not limited to Atlanta but can be found throughout the country. Despite the gains in economic and political power (even the election of a black president of the United States) there are widening intraracial gaps among the African American middle class, the working poor, and the so-called "underclass." Furthermore, the racial disparities between whites and blacks persist.[10]

The Civil Rights Movement brought an end to Jim Crow segregation and produced a significant increase in black participation in electoral politics. The passage of the Voting Rights Act of 1965 resulted in millions of new black voters, which in turn resulted in a remarkable increase in black elected officials. The primary mode of black political participation shifted from movement politics to electoral politics. But toward the close of the twentieth century, students of black politics recognized that electoral politics was not bringing the progress that was hoped for during the 1960s and 1970s. According to political scientist Robert C. Smith, "[D]uring [the] twenty five year period of the new black politics, the life-chances and condition of the bottom third of black Americans grew worse by almost any measure of well being." As some became better off and benefited greatly from the end of Jim Crow segregation, others did not seem to benefit but instead became more "segregated, impoverished and increasingly . . . marginalized, denigrated and criminalized."[11] As African Americans moved from "protest to politics" and from "exclusion to inclusion," the important political challenges became how to make black politics meaningful for not just the black middle class but also black working-class and poor people and second how to close the persistent racial disparities.[12]

Those who study black politics have suggested strategies for a post–civil rights black politics that would address these dilemmas. For example, Ralph Gomes and Linda Faye Williams suggested forming political coalitions with white and other working-class groups. Because working-class whites especially tend to be reluctant coalition partners with blacks, they argued that there would first have to be a political economy education campaign for working-class whites, showing them how they would benefit from such a coalition. Browning, Marshall, and Tabb suggested coalition politics with liberal generally middle-class whites as the way to increase black political incorporation and increase the services blacks receive from local governments.[13]

Ronald Walters and Robert C. Smith both suggest that electoral politics alone is not sufficient to deal with these dilemmas. According to Smith, all black politics in the post–civil rights era has been focused on system integration. This system integration, incorporation, or inclusion has really been co-optation of the leadership classes. As a result African Americans have been unable to get substantive policy changes from the system—only symbolic changes. Black electoral politics has been "irrelevant" for the masses of blacks, and black leaders have to be more accountable to their black working-class, poor, and more marginalized constituents. Walters suggested that instead of concentrating solely on electoral politics, this strategy should be combined with outside agitation and pressure on the system—a political "gadfly" that has been lacking in postincorporation black politics.[14]

Most recently Cedric Johnson has argued that "black ethnic politics has run its course as an effective means to confront inequality."[15] Johnson agrees with Smith that the post–civil rights emphasis on systemic politics has not served blacks well. The primary focus on black identity politics has been detrimental to the struggle for systemic change. Johnson claims that progressive and democratic goals of black politics have also been sacrificed for "racial unity." Appeals to race-first identity politics or "racial unity" have minimized the important diversity among African Americans, ignored the sharpening class divisions, and pushed the agenda of the most privileged while leaving the needs of the most marginalized unanswered. Therefore, instead of race-first political strategies he advocates for an emphasis on "popular democratic struggles" that confront neoliberal capitalism.[16]

Scholars are not the only ones who have recognized that the strategy of electoral politics has not produced on a level consistent with the aspirations. Activists, clergy, celebrities, and everyday people try to diagnose and provide a prescription for the paradox of black progress. Black megachurches at the beginning of the twenty-first century have contributed to the debate, and an examination of their participation in the first three elections of the twenty-first century provides excellent fodder for the further discussion of divergent perspectives and strategies of addressing post–civil rights dilemmas. For example, in 2000 several black megachurches looked toward cooperating with government and engaging in community development through George W. Bush's faith-based initiatives as a strategy to fill some of the gaps left by focusing primarily on electoral politics. In 2004 several black megachurches engaged in the "culture wars." Their political engagement was motivated by the perspective that slippage in black people's moral values was the reason that black communities were suffering, and they advocated for socially conservative social policy like restrictions on same-sex marriage and abortion rights. The 2008 election of President Barack Obama was the most dramatic election for displaying the roles of black megachurches in public life. Black megachurches participated in electoral politics by mobilizing voters, providing resources, and spreading political messages. Trinity United Church of Christ (a black mega-church in Chicago) and its former pastor, Rev. Jeremiah Wright, played key roles in the election of Barack Obama to the presidency of the United States by contributing resources and enhancing his political persona. These debates are not isolated to the examples I provide or to the specific presidential election year but provide good illustrations of ongoing debates in black politics.

2000: Cooperating with Government

When George W. Bush ran for his first presidential term in 2000 as a "compas-sionate conservative," one of his most publicized platform agenda items was "faith-based initiatives." Once in office, Bush established the Office of Faith-Based and Community Initiatives to investigate and promote ways to make it easier for churches to apply for and receive government funding to provide social services. Bush pitched faith-based initiatives to black ministers and made headlines when shortly after his election in 2000 he met with thirty minis-ters (several of them African American and Democrats) at the First Baptist Church in Austin to discuss and gain support for his party and the faith-based initiative plan. The apprehensions about faith-based initiatives ran the ideo-logical gamut and went from concerns about blurring the line of separation between church and state and involving government in proselytizing, to con-cerns about the "wrong" groups having access to faith-based grants, to concerns about the possibility of funding for secular and government social service pro-vision being reduced and allocated to faith-based organizations.[17] But where the black church was concerned the main trepidation came from the suspicion that the Bush administration and the GOP were trying to pit black preach-ers against black political leaders, trying to co-opt black preachers, and try-ing to purchase their support and the support of their church members.[18] The leadership from the historical black denominations (e.g., Progressive National

Baptist Convention, National Baptist Convention, Church of God in Christ [COGIC], African Methodist Episcopal [AME], African Methodist Episcopal Zion), representatives from the Congress of National Black Churches, and national leaders like Jesse Jackson and Al Sharpton were not invited to the meeting. In fact neither was the press. This sharpened the suspicion that Bush's overture to some black pastors was an attempt to divide and conquer the black electorate.[19] Reflecting this interpretation the *Washington Post* headline the day before the meeting read, "Bush to Host Black Ministers: Faith-Based Initiatives May Circumvent Civil Rights Leaders."[20]

Four black megachurch ministers attended that original faith-based initiatives meeting with George W. Bush—Rev. Kirbyjon Caldwell of Windsor Village United Methodist Church in Houston, Rev. Carlton Pearson of Higher Dimensions Church in Oklahoma,[21] Rev. Floyd Flake of Allen AME in Queens, and Bishop Charles Blake of West Angeles COGIC in Los Angeles. Pearson was a celebrated Pentecostal pastor who had attended Oral Roberts University and had been mentored by Oral Roberts himself. Caldwell, Blake, and Flake were all extensively involved in community development projects already. Their churches had all already established CDOs, indicating their willingness to participate in the activities envisioned by faith-based initiatives. Allen AME Neighborhood Preservation Development Corporation was founded in 1976, Windsor Village's Pyramid Community Development Corporation in 1992, and the West Angeles Community Development Corporation in 1994.

Rev. Caldwell's participation in the election of George W. Bush and his public support of Bush were particularly interesting. Windsor Village United Methodist Church is overwhelmingly composed of working- and middle-class African Americans who consider themselves to be Democrats. In fact, in Texas in 2000 blacks gave George W. Bush only 5 percent of their votes—which was even lower that the national record low percentage of votes (9 percent) that black voters gave the Republican presidential candidate in 2000.[22] Despite this, Caldwell enthusiastically supported George W. Bush in the 2000 presidential election. He introduced Bush at the 2000 Republican National Convention and gave the benediction at his 2001 and 2005 inaugurations. Despite the disapproval of most of his congregation and of Houston's black community, Caldwell maintained support for Bush even after the controversial election results in Florida and subsequent Supreme Court decision. In a postelection sermon at Windsor Village in December 2000, Caldwell addressed his critics, admitting that his support of Bush had "created a stir within some pockets of the Houston community." In this sermon he called Bush "the new Republican" and praised his tax plan, his performance as governor of Texas, and his position on "race." He also criticized Al Gore for his "position on race" and tax plan and stated that African Americans should beware because "Al Gore is no Bill Clinton," acknowledging the black community's identification with Bill Clinton.[23]

Under the leadership of Caldwell, Windsor Village has clearly taken advantage of state, federal, and local funding and private resources to engage in extensive community economic development in the Hiram Clarke area of Houston. While George W. Bush was governor of Texas, Windsor Village cooperated with government to build hundreds of affordable single-family homes in the Hiram Clarke neighborhood—a subdivision called Corinthian Pointe. They also developed the Power Center, a business park that houses one of the few banks in the area, a private school (the Imani School), a Women, Infants, and Children Nutrition Program office, a banquet and reception hall, a health clinic, and other small businesses. Windsor Village has continued with their community development efforts. They added additional homes to Corinthian Pointe, partnered with the city for a public elementary school, partnered with the YMCA to build a local YMCA branch that houses the only community swimming pool in the area, and built an additional business center (the Kingdombuilders Center).

The community development approach is one way that megachurches have weighed in on the debate about how to respond to the persistent problems that elude black electoral politics. As I discussed in chapter 4, through community development black megachurches have contributed to actual material improvement in many underserved black neighborhoods. They feed people, house them, and provide health care and youth services in the inner city and in inner-ring suburbs. In some cases they have contributed to commercial development, addressing the blight that has captured many of the metropolitan areas where black people live. The community development strategy has clearly led to tangible benefits.

Eva Thorne and Pastor Eugene Rivers placed black churches that engage in extensive community development, like Windsor Village, at the center of a post–civil rights "new black politics." They argued that this "new black politics" utilizes a community development approach and addresses the issue of how black politics can help the "least well-off." Thorne and Rivers advocated black churches working with Republicans if it would allow them to secure resources for community revitalization, even if the leadership and memberships of the churches did not agree with the Republican Party on most of the party's positions.[24]

Cooperation can help churches gather the resources they need to carry out their community development projects, but there are clearly challenges to cooperating with government. One is the threat of outright co-optation. Anxiety about this very real threat was echoed again and again throughout my interviews with black megachurch leaders; even those whose churches were already engaged in community development projects with government were concerned about this. If you cooperate with government, do you become the "tool of government" as Martin Luther King Jr. warned against? Can you criticize government policies or the actions of elected officials when you are also accepting government funding?

Recall from chapter 4 the examples of politically progressive activist ministers being sanctioned for speaking out against local government. When Rev. Willie Wilson (Union Temple Baptist Church in Washington, D.C.) spoke out against closing D.C. General Hospital he was slapped on the hand by then-mayor Anthony Williams and lost his special license plate. When Rev. Calvin Butts called former New York mayor Rudy Giuliani a racist the Abyssinian Development Corporation lost the city's cooperation on a $49 million project (the Harlem Center Mall) they had planned to develop.[25] One of the drawbacks to cooperating with government is that the threat of sanctions may discourage black megachurches from using their prophetic voices.

Furthermore, Owens warns that cooperation can lead to the demobilizing of black communities. Black communities may come to feel that because churches are engaging in community revitalization, there is no role for the state in community revitalization and may not pressure government for the resources to support their communities. Furthermore, they may settle for incremental changes that come from cooperative politics and opt out of conflict politics that might lead to structural transformation.[26]

While cooperating with government to engage in community development became a publicized issue with George W. Bush's faith-based initiatives, many black churches were already participating in community development projects that entailed cooperating with government before Bush's presidency.[27] In fact black churches and mainline Protestant churches are more likely to apply for government funds to engage in community programs than more conservative white evangelical groups that compose the Republican electoral coalition.[28] Furthermore, the more socially conservative black church is less likely to participate in public engagement activities than the prophetic theologically oriented, socially liberal church. Therefore when black megachurches decide to do community development they may be conflicted. The conflict is between working within the system and cooperating with government versus maintaining an independence from government and challenging inequality and oppression in society. Drew Smith calls this a tension between "maximizing opportunities and minimizing constraint."[29]

Many of the black megachurches that are doing community development are the same churches most likely to engage in electoral politics and also the same churches that are most likely to speak out against government and engage in protest politics. These churches make strategic choices to try to balance the opportunities to cooperate with government with the need to resist oppressive government policies and advocate for their communities. When they choose community development, they may have to sacrifice their prophetic voices, and when they use their prophetic voices they might lose the resources necessary for large-scale community development.

2004: Black Moral Pathology Thesis

After the 2004 reelection of George W. Bush against John Kerry, the exit polls showed that a plurality (22 percent) of voters thought that "moral values" were the most important policy issues facing the nation. These moral values were largely interpreted as references to same-sex marriage and abortion. Exit polls showed that moral values were more important to voters than the economy (20 percent), terrorism (19 percent), the war in Iraq (15 percent), and health care (8 percent).[30] Same-sex marriage was an especially hot-button issue. Eleven states passed ballot initiatives to restrict same-sex marriage by amending their state constitutions.[31]

Journalists reported that the United States was engaged in "culture wars"— where there is a profound political cleavage between those who are committed to "traditional values" and those who have more modern views of society. While many political scientists have concluded that the significance of the 2004 exit poll results was exaggerated and that the notion of culture wars is an oversimplification of American politics, studies have also shown that the "moral agenda" has been an effective mobilizing tool.[32] Since the 1980s the Republican Party has latched onto the ideas of "traditional family values" and has tried to define the Democratic Party as the party "that has forgotten God, family, and decency."[33] Even if it has been slightly exaggerated, there was a significant public discourse about moral values in 2004, and while most African American Protestants gave their overwhelming support to John Kerry and the Democrats (as they had in 2004), there were a number of high-profile moments of support for the moral agenda by a number of black megachurches and black megachurch pastors. They argued a "black moral pathology" thesis as an explanation for post–civil rights disparities. They claimed that the old civil rights battles were necessary but that they had been fought and won. Improving black people's morality would lead to better life chances for black people in the post–civil rights era.

One of the best examples of the black moral pathology thesis at work is New Birth's Reigniting the Legacy March described earlier in this chapter. Long (New Birth's pastor) acknowledges that there are still racial disparities in U.S. society, but he does not view *racism* as an important feature of contemporary American life or as a primary cause for the disparities. Instead, as Jonathan Walton points out, Long sees black people as being held back by their *preoccupation* with racism and America's racial past instead of the actual effects of racism in the present. Black people simply need to "forgive and forget" and realize that they are "already in the Promised Land."[34] Furthermore, lapsing moral values and diminishing moral fortitude are the real reasons for contemporary black suffering. Black communities suffer because they do not work hard enough, do not take advantage of their opportunities, and have strayed from "traditional family values." Consequently, Long and others who promote the moral pathology thesis believe that "getting over race" and correcting the lapsing moral values in black communities are the keys to addressing racial disparities.

In February 2005 (a couple of months after the New Birth march) a group of black ministers calling themselves the High Impact Leadership Coalition met in Los Angeles. This group of about one hundred ministers was led by politically conservative evangelical Bishop Harry Jackson (from Prince George's County, Maryland). While Jackson was not a leader of a megachurch, he did have the support of a handful of black megachurch leaders, including Fred Price, whose Crenshaw Christian Center hosted the event. After the meeting the ministers unveiled "the Black Contract with America on Moral Values."[35] This document (obviously channeling the GOP's 1994 Contract with America) highlighted six important "values" (really public policy goals) that the nation should focus on that would benefit black America. These included prohibiting same-sex marriages and abortions, encouraging school vouchers and charter schools, increasing homeownership, increasing intervention in African politics (particularly in the Sudan), prison reform, and extending health care. Jackson claimed that this set of values combined a concern with "justice" and a concern for moral values that are of particular importance to the black community.[36]

Topping the list was the "moral issue" of same-sex marriage. According to Jackson same-sex marriage would lead to a further decline in heterosexual marriage in black communities to the detriment of these communities. In an interview with *Washington Post* reporters he explained, "What tends to happen is that people tend to devalue the institution of marriage as a whole. People start rearing kids without two parents, and the black community already has this incredibly alarming and, if I may say, this shameful number of babies being born without fathers."[37] For Jackson the "moral values"—same-sex marriage and abortion—are the reasons that African Americans would find a better home with the Republican Party and why he personally voted for George W. Bush in 2004. According to Jackson, black communities would be better served by the Republican Party, which placed these values at the forefront of their agenda. He said, "It seemed like the Democratic agenda had been hijacked by a militant homosexual agenda without even caring about what was going on with African Americans."[38] Like the Legacy March, the Black Contract with America on Moral Values is guided by the perspective that focusing on moral values, very narrowly defined as banning same-sex marriage and secondarily abortion, as the primary strategy should be used to combat racial disparities.

Obviously, social conservatism is not new to black political ideology and is particularly entrenched in black churches. Kelly Brown Douglas, in her book *Sexuality and the Black Church*, argues that white racism led to an attack on black humanity through an assault on black sexuality. The result is that most black churches ignore sex and sexuality. This makes them ineffective in dealing with issues like sexual abuse, teenage pregnancy, and HIV and AIDS. Instead black churches have tended to reinforce patriarchy, sexism, and homophobia and have failed to truly be an agent for the full liberation of black people in America.[39]

Cathy Cohen explains how the marginalization of gay men and lesbians in black churches particularly impeded black churches from being effective against HIV/AIDS. AIDS was early portrayed as a "gay man's disease," and because homosexuality is seen as an abhorrence, pathology, and a sin in black churches, they (and other mainstream black organizations) did not acknowledge the devastation of this disease to gay black men and others in black communities. Furthermore, AIDS was not seen as a "black issue." Cohen claims that black issues have to be "embraced publically by community institutions and leaders are thought to be linked to, or conform to, middle-class/dominant constructions of moral, normative, patriarchal citizenship."[40] Thus, the issues of the most marginalized in black communities have a difficult time becoming "black issues" worthy of concern by black mainstream institutions and elites. Cohen claims that because AIDS was seen as a "gay" disease and not a "black" disease, black churches generally stood by while AIDS ravaged black communities.[41]

Ignoring issues pertaining to sex and sexuality and defining them as "not black issues" are consistent with most of the black megachurch participation in the 2004 moral values discourse. Even though most black megachurch members and leaders were not out protesting against the rights of same-sex couples to marry and may not have even been in favor of the ballot initiatives, in large part this was *not* because they *supported* the rights of same-sex partners to marry. Instead, they did not perceive the "moral campaign" as a "black issue." In addition, many of them viewed the moral campaign as distracting and a Republican ploy to divide and conquer the Democratic electoral coalition. Civil rights activist and minister Rev. Joseph Lowery summarized this perspective nicely in a sermon he gave at Howard University's Rankin Chapel. He said, "Gay marriage, that's not our issue! Our issues are jobs, income, housing, education, climate control. I'm not worried about who somebody is sleeping with."[42] The right of homosexual people to marry or not was not a "black issue" any more than AIDS was a "black issue" for most black churches during the period that Cohen writes about.[43]

Political mobilizing around the moral values agenda though is a step beyond the inaction on issues that are associated with marginalized groups or ignoring or even pathologizing homosexuality. What are new and developing and more frequent are black megachurch political mobilization and public policy advocacy based on conservative social politics and a moral pathology thesis. The marches, public statements, and support of conservative ballot initiatives from the pulpit have only increased since 2004 when moral values dominated the public discourse.

Apostle A. R. Williams and the church where he is pastor, World Overcomers Christian Church (a black megachurch in Memphis), provide good illustrations of the moral pathology thesis at work as an explanation for the problems of black Memphis and black America. Williams does not ignore sex or sexuality. Instead, on a regular basis he graphically and explicitly preaches about sexuality and what he perceives as morally proper and improper sexual relations. For example in one of his sermons, "How to Keep Your Husband So the Ho Don't Get Him," he sparked a bit of controversy when he brought a bed onto the stage at World Overcomers and he and his wife performed a marital skit explaining the importance of and giving directions for how a wife should attend to her husband in the bedroom.[44]

Williams saves his most explicit and graphic sermons, however, for preaching against the "evils" of homosexuality. In two of his sermons, "Can a Gay Person Be a Christian?" and "The Case against Same Sex Marriage" (both accessible online via the church's website) he does not soften his contempt for gay and lesbian people with a "love the sinner, hate the sin" philosophy. Instead he uses what might best be described as shock and scare methods in these sermons—referencing feces, urine, male and female sex organs, rape, and pedophilia all under the auspice that he is "telling it like it is" about homosexuality. In these sermons he describes what a "Christian nation" should look like juxtaposed to "a gay nation"—its antithesis. For Williams heterosexuality is natural and right according to God. (He said that if you are not sure about this you should "check your plumbing" and then you should realize that "it takes a socket and a plug to equal electricity.") On the other hand, homosexuality is not only deviant behavior and a sin but also a "gateway sin," and once the church and the state are more accepting of homosexuality all other social ills will follow. In a sermon called "The Case against Same Sex Marriage" he warned the congregation that if they do not watch out "this will be a gay nation," and he wants the black community in particular to be aware of this threat. "Black people did not move in the Civil Rights Movement until they killed Emmett Till, then they got scared. You wait until they abuse and rape your daughters and sons, then it will be at your front door." He claimed that "next generation will be the gay generation" because public school curriculums will have to include the "gay lifestyle." Williams even used the moral pathology thesis to blame victims of HIV and AIDS for their disease. He says that "sometimes AIDS is God's last ditch effort to save gay men." "There will be more gay people in heaven than we think because they repent on their dying bed." Apostle A. R. William's use of the moral pathology thesis extends beyond HIV and AIDS. He also blamed the victims of Hurricane Katrina in New Orleans, saying that New Orleans was "a sinful city." He said that the word "Katrina" means "to cleanse" and that Katrina was God's way of "cleansing the city."[45]

Not only does Williams express his contempt for and fear of "a gay nation" from the pulpit, but also he and World Overcomers have engaged in a considerable amount of moral values political mobilization particularly focused on challenging the expansion of rights to gays and lesbians. For example, in 2003 the church spent thousands of dollars to put a two-page ad in the Memphis *Commercial Appeal* to protest a Supreme Court ruling that invalidated all state sodomy laws. The headlines read "Court Says Sodomy (Homosexuality) is OK but What Does God Say?" In 2007 when a federal hate crime bill that would have extended protected categories to include sexual orientation was being debated, Williams was outspoken in his opposition to the measure. From the pulpit Williams encouraged his congregation to be activists on the

issue. In 2009 a Shelby County ordinance was proposed that would have pro-
tected the equal employment opportunities of people regardless of sexual orientation. Williams instructed his congregation, "We can't sit back and wait for
God to do everything. God looks for action on our part because he gave men
dominion here on earth." He also asked the congregation to pray that Barack
Obama would veto the federal hate crime bill (which had just passed in the
Senate). In the same sermon he expressed displeasure about the decision of
Memphis-based Federal Express to add sexual orientation to its antidiscrimi-
nation policies.

> "Knowing Federal Express's background ... Fred Smith ... making it a fam-
> ily organization and corporation and now to see that gay activists have eked
> into the power base and have now put it to where all kinds of orientations are
> open—is heartbreaking—and as big as they are they will influence all other
> corporations." He said, "The devil has put a stronghold over the company and
> it has got to be brought down."[46]

In 2006 World Overcomers became more visible in the city of Memphis and
beyond when they erected a seventy-two-foot replica of the Statue of Liberty
with some interesting modifications. Instead of a torch, World Overcomers'
Lady Liberty, which they call the Statue of Liberation, holds a cross in one
hand and a tablet with the Ten Commandments in the other. At the foot of the
statue are the words "America: Return to Christ," and the statue has a single
tear that signifies sadness with the direction that the United States is going. In
other religious nationalistic symbols they have a display in the church and on
their website highlighting "founding fathers" such as Thomas Jefferson, George
Washington, and other white men from the era who testify through their writings, speeches, and memoirs that the United States was meant to be a Christian
nation.[47] It is this religious nationalism that prescribes their active participation
in the moral values debate.

Some black megachurches and black megachurch pastors utilize the
moral pathology thesis to understand racial disparities and to develop ways
of addressing them. World Overcomers, the High Impact Coalition, and New
Birth are interesting though because they not only use the moral pathology
thesis to describe why these disparities exist but also are politically mobilized
around these moral values. While there are black churches that definitely are
linked to a social conservative tradition, in the past conservative orientations
were not politically mobilized. In fact a number of studies used "politically
active churches" as a trope for "politically progressive churches."[48] Engaging in
collective action around politically conservative causes is relatively new for the

Statue of Liberation. Image courtesy of Leon Caldwell

black church, and the assumption that a politically active black church is a progressive black church is no longer appropriate, if it ever was.

2008: "The Wright Effect"

Leading up to the historic 2008 U.S. presidential election, black megachurches continued to weigh in on the moral values debate, and they certainly continued to cooperate with government to do community development, but black megachurches' participation in electoral politics was the highlight of their activity. Black megachurches supported candidates, registered voters, drove voters to the polls, and encouraged voting from the pulpit. During the Democratic primaries both Hillary Clinton and Barack Obama spoke at black churches and black megachurches on the campaign stump. In South Carolina state senator Daryl Jackson, who is a pastor of a black megachurch (Bible Way Church of

Atlas Road), served as Clinton's state campaign director, and a member of Jackson's church, Anton Gunn, was the South Carolina political director of the Obama campaign.[49]

This election was like no other. The United States elected its first black president, Barack Obama, and during the general election black megachurch pastors publically prayed for Obama, endorsed his candidacy, and donated money to the campaign. Even Kirbyjon Caldwell from Windsor Village, who strongly supported Bush in 2000 and 2004, gave his support to Obama and donated to his campaign.[50]

Yet perhaps the most dramatic moments of the campaign and election stem from the relationship among Barack Obama, his former pastor Rev. Jeremiah Wright, and Obama's former church, Trinity United Church of Christ (UCC). In March 2008 news outlets ran loops of controversial excerpts from two of Jeremiah Wright's speeches and painted him as "anti-American." As a consequence, Wright was seen by many observers as Obama's Achilles' heel. I would like to suggest, however, that instead of an Achilles' heel, Jeremiah Wright and Trinity actually helped to propel Obama to his historic presidential campaign and ultimate victory in three key ways. First, they helped to shape the political persona of Barack Obama. Second, they also provided Obama with political resources and helped him to gain legitimacy in certain black circles, which made him "black enough." Last, Obama's political skills and his ultimate separation from the caricatured Trinity and the caricatured Jeremiah Wright allowed him to distance himself from the ideas of a certain type of black politics, which ultimately contributed to Obama's deracialization strategy. Instead of an Achilles' heel their relationship became a "sacrificial lamb," as one D.C. minister and activist put it.[51]

Legitimacy, Audacity, and Hope

In *Dreams from My Father*, Barack Obama explains what first brought him to Trinity UCC. He was working as a community organizer on the South Side of Chicago and was trying to organize black ministers and encourage them to join his organization. He recalled that one of the ministers, Rev. Philips, told him that he might be more successful at winning over black preachers if he were to join a church. Philips said, "What you're asking from pastors requires us to set aside some of our more priestly concerns in favor of prophecy. That requires a good deal of faith on our part. It makes us want to know just where you're getting yours from. Faith, that is." Philips, along with other ministers whom Obama spoke to, pointed him to Trinity UCC as a church he should visit and

Rev. Wright as someone he should talk to. Rev. Philips said, Wright's "message seemed to appeal to young people like [Obama]."[52]

Philips and the other pastors were correct. Not only did Obama visit Trinity, but he eventually joined and was baptized by Wright; Wright married Barack and Michelle Obama and baptized their children—Sasha and Malia. Joining a large, politically active black church on the South Side of Chicago no doubt helped to legitimize Obama in Chicago where he was basically an outsider—not in a sense of his racial or ethnic background but in the sense of the community politics. According to Obama, ministers were sometimes skeptical when he first called to talk to them about community organizing and they wondered "[w]hy this Muslim—or worse yet, this Irishman, O'Bama— wanted a few minutes of their time."[53] Joining Trinity and having Rev. Wright as a supporter likely helped him to be more successful as he started his political career and climb to the office of the presidency of the United States by first contributing to his local political legitimacy. Obama acknowledged the support of Trinity and Rev. Wright, and when he won the race for U.S. senator from Illinois in 2004 he immediately thanked his pastor, Rev. Jeremiah Wright, and acknowledged fellow "Trinitarians" in his election night speech.[54]

Trinity and Rev. Wright further helped to legitimize Obama on a national stage. During both the race for U.S. Senate and the presidential race, the media ran away with questions about Obama's authentic "blackness." Alan Keyes attempted to cast himself as the authentic black candidate and questioned Obama's blackness over and over during their 2004 race for Illinois sena- tor.[55] The media, however, particularly questioned whether Obama was "black enough" to gain the overwhelming support of African Americans that he would need in order to secure the Democratic nomination for president in 2008.[56] Whether this was largely a media fabrication or a real concern, Wright and Trinity added to Obama's black authenticity. As an example, one writer, Ta- Nehisi Coates, wrote that the debate over Obama's "authentic blackness" was nonsense but that for the record "Obama is married to a black woman. He goes to a black church. He's worked with poor people on the South Side of Chicago, and still lives there" and is black.[57] He pointed to the church along with other characteristics as evidence of "blackness" beyond just racial identity but rather a connection to a particular political agenda. Jeremiah Wright addressed the issue in a sermon he delivered at Howard University in January 2007 celebrat- ing the life and work of Martin Luther King Jr., Wright said, "Assassins' bullets may have taken Martin Luther King Jr. but God gave us a Barack Obama." Wright, a preacher respected nationally in "prophetic black church" and old guard civil rights circles, put Barack Obama squarely within the black experience for a national audience—not just Chicago or Illinois. He was saying to his listeners that Barack Obama was indeed "black enough."[58]

Even more interesting are the ideas that Wright, Trinity, and the prophetic black church contribute to Obama's political persona. In *The Audacity of Hope* Obama describes how the "black church" influenced him. The "historically black church" helped to shape his political persona by "deepen[ing] [his] resolve to lead a public life ... fortif[ying] [his] racial identity and confirm[ing] his belief in the capacity of ordinary people to do extraordinary things."[59]

Obama explains that it was the theological orientation and practices of the prophetic black church (of which Trinity is such a superb example) that drew him to Christianity. He wrote in his autobiography that through his experience with "the black church" he had "newfound understandings" about religious organizations in general and Christianity in particular.

> It was because of these newfound understandings—that religious commitment did not require me to suspend critical thinking, disengage from the battle for economy and social justice, or otherwise retreat from the world I knew and loved—that I was finally able to walk down the aisle of Trinity Church of Christ one day and be baptized. It came about as a choice and not an epiphany; the questions I had did not magically disappear. But kneeling beneath that cross on the South Side of Chicago, I felt God's spirit beckoning me. I submitted myself to His will, and dedicated myself to discovering His truth.[60]

He admired the black church's "power to spur social change" and wrote that it was an "active, palpable agent in the word." The social justice activities that the black church participated in were "the Word made manifest."[61]

Of course Obama's description of "the black church" is a description not of all black churches but of a subset of activist black churches or prophetic black churches. He was describing the type of church Trinity is—one whose dominant theological orientations are prophetic theology, the social gospel, and black liberation theology. Trinity's motto is "unashamedly Black and unapologetically Christian." Trinity also has a number of ministries promoting social justice and concern for the "least of these" and a number of ministries exploring the particular relevance of Christianity to people of African descent. Obama wrote that Trinity perpetuates an ethic of a "cultural community," by "assur[ing] its members that their fates remained inseparably bound, that an intelligible 'us' still remained."[62]

While the church as an institution had an important impact on Obama, Jeremiah Wright's contribution to Obama's political persona is in some ways even more compelling. Wright, who had served as the pastor of Trinity for over thirty-six years before he retired in 2008, had been the pastor of Trinity for seventeen years when Obama joined Trinity. He obviously had an unparalleled role in developing the church's theological orientation that drew Obama to Trinity. In his first meeting with Wright, Obama observed that it was Wright's "ability to hold together, if not reconcile, the conflicting strains of the black experience—upon which Trinity's success had ultimately been built."[63]

Perhaps the best example of Wright's contribution to Barack Obama's political persona is Wright's sermon "The Audacity to Hope." In the sermon, Wright tells the story of Hannah, from 1 Samuel 1:1-18. Hannah seemed like she had everything one's heart could desire, she had a husband who loved her very much and told her so. But Hannah was really living in hell and despair because of the jealousy of her husband's first wife, who hated and tormented her, and the fact that she had a barren womb. In spite of all this Hannah still fervently prayed and praised God. According to Wright, it took audacity to do this because in Hannah's temporal world there was no evidence that her prayers would be answered. Yet Hannah had a "vertical" relationship with God, and this is what gave her the audacity to hope that her prayers could be answered. Wright said that it was the Hannah-style "audacity to hope" that caused enslaved Africans to sing, "Overhead I hear music in the air. Overhead I hear music in the air. There must be a God somewhere" despite their enslavement.[64]

Barack Obama describes the experience of listening to Wright preach "The Audacity to Hope" in his autobiography. While listening to the sermon he experienced an epiphany of sorts, and it moved him to tears. First he connected Wright's sermon to his own life and to the lives of people he knew and had been working with as a community organizer in South Side of Chicago.

> I imagined the stories of ordinary black people merging with the stories of David and Goliath, Moses and Pharaoh, the Christians in the lion's den, Ezekiel's field of dry bones. Those stories—of survival, and freedom, and hope—became our story, my story; the blood that had spilled was our blood, the tears our tears; this black church, on this bright day, seemed once more a vessel carrying the story of a people into future generations and into a larger world.[65]

Then he began to see the universality of Wright's concept of hope and that it could transcend historical and racial bounds. He wrote,

Our trials and triumphs became at once unique and universal, black and more than black; in chronicling our journey, the stories and songs gave us a means to reclaim memories that we didn't need to feel shamed about, memories more accessible than those of ancient Egypt, memories that all people might study and cherish—and with which we could start to rebuild.[66]

Obama titled his 2004 keynote address at the Democratic National Convention and his second book *The Audacity of Hope*, after Wright's sermon. Obama juxtaposed the "politics of cynicism" with the "politics of hope," and "hope" became somewhat of a political mantra for him.[67] As he stated in his 2004 keynote address, he used the idea of hope and his sense that people wanted to have hope as a way to combat notions of cynicism, fatalism, and fear about what government can accomplish and about civil society more generally.

Obama's concept of hope is the hope that Wright talked about in his sermon; it is a "religious hope," one based in the prophetic black church tradition. "Hope in the face of difficulty. Hope in the face of uncertainty." In his 2004 address he said, "The audacity of hope! In the end, that is God's greatest gift to us, the bedrock of this nation. A belief in things not seen. A belief that there are better days ahead."[68]

Obama made it clear that the type of hope he was talking about is not just "blind optimism" or just ignoring social problems and wishing them away. For Obama hope is actually a precursor to political efficacy—the belief that one can make a difference in the political system or in civil society. Therefore Obama's hope requires action. Even though it is religiously based, it is far from otherworldly.

It's the hope of the slaves sitting around a fire singing freedom songs. The hope of immigrants setting out for distant shores. The hope of a young naval lieutenant bravely patrolling the Mekong Delta. The hope of a millworker's son who dares defy the odds. The hope of a skinny kid with a funny name who believes that America has a place for him, too.[69]

This theme of hope as a precursor to efficacy was central to Obama's campaign for president. He fluently used the concepts "hope" and "change" in his campaign and his campaign slogan "yes we can" implies that people can actually make differences through their public engagement even when it seems unlikely. Furthermore, each of Obama's victories was such a dramatic departure from what was expected that political efficacy was reinforced with each victory as the believers were rewarded for their "hope." In other words, the victories were support for why "hope" was a worthwhile sentiment—why one should hope. His electoral successes were evidence that change could come in America, and furthermore they built the sense of political efficacy so that every success he had—Iowa, the Democratic nomination—seemed unlikely yet inevitable. For Obama, "hope" is the reason to keep persisting and working because "change" can come even when it seems unlikely. "The Audacity to Hope" is probably the most important contribution that Wright and the prophetic black church tradition contributed to Barack Obama's electoral success.

Racialization and Deracialization

In addition to political legitimacy, political resources, and hope, Wright and Trinity played a nuanced role in Obama's strategy of "deracialization" in his campaign for the Democratic nomination. Deracialization theory basically contends that black candidates can win and have won elected office in contests that have majority white electorates when they deemphasize race in their campaigns. Studies have shown that deracializing can help to neutralize some of the reluctance that white voters have toward voting for a black candidate. Deracialization theory has been used to explain the successful African Americans in places with majority white electorates like Douglas Wilder in Virginia and Norman Rice in Seattle.[70]

A "deracialized" political campaign strategy requires that the black candidate deemphasize race in three ways. First, deracialized campaigns minimize their appeals to black communities. Second, the candidates "project a nonthreatening image" to white voters primarily by distancing themselves from black people identified as "racial partisans." Finally, they steer away from public policy issues that are race specific and that specifically target racism (e.g., bussing and affirmative action) or issues that have come to be identified with race like poverty, welfare, and the criminal justice system. Instead black candidates running deracialized campaigns emphasize issues that are considered able to transcend racial lines and are universal.[71]

Barack Obama's campaign for U.S. president clearly followed in this vein. Until forced to respond to the "Wright controversy" (explained below) the Obama campaign rarely mentioned race or racism. A cursory look at Obama's presidential campaign platform paints a corroborating picture. The "Organizing for America" campaign issues were the economy, Wall Street reform, new energy, health care, education, and comprehensive immigration reform.[72] While all of these issues clearly affect African Americans, none of them is a taboo issue according to a deracialization strategy. There was little to no discussion of issues like poverty, welfare, or the criminal justice system, which have been framed in the public discourse as "black issues."

While Obama enjoyed the support of the majority of black elected officials, he also kept those who were recognized as "black leaders" like Jesse Jackson and Al Sharpton at an arm's length. Even the controversy surrounding Jesse
Jackson's comments that were overheard by live microphones, indicating that
he wanted to dismember Obama because he was "talking down to black people"
(in his Father's Day address), illustrates the perspective that Obama's campaign
rhetoric was sometimes inconsistent with some traditional black political perspectives and that he was distant from some perceived "racial partisans."

As I explain below, when Barack Obama's relationship with Jeremiah
Wright was exposed and exploited by the media, it first counteracted Obama's
strategy of deracialization—painting Obama as not only a black *person* but
possibly a black radical. But when Obama distanced himself from the church
and denounced Rev. Wright, he was able to effectively re-deracialize his campaign. Breaking with Wright symbolically separated Obama from radical black
politics.

The Wright Controversy and Obama's Racialization

Clearly Obama and Wright's relationship went back further than the 2008
campaign and election; however, most Americans first heard of Wright during
the hotly contested Democratic primaries between Obama and Hillary Clinton. Excerpts from two of Wright's sermons were taken out of context and
looped over and over on national television, causing a storm of controversy.
Edward Herman and David Peterson note that the "Wright controversy" was
the most reported news item for the first 125 days of 2008 in the *New York
Times* and *Washington Post*. The frames for these news stories were "divisive,"
"crazy," "rant and rave," "destructive," "politics of the past," and "backward thinking." As excerpts of the sermons were looped on cable television and the Internet, Wright began to be judged as "un-American," "bigoted," "crazy," and "racist."
Trinity's church members were harassed, the church itself received a number of
bomb threats, and Rev. Wright was personally threatened.[73]

The media and some parts of the public were demanding that Obama
address how he could attend this church for twenty years. Hillary Clinton
said Wright's comments constituted "hate speech." In an interview with the
Pittsburgh Tribune-Review she said, "He would not have been my pastor....
You don't choose your family, but you choose what church you want to
attend."[74] While Trinity and Jeremiah Wright had helped to propel Obama's
political career in Illinois, the association with Wright was threatening to end
his career now that Obama was on a national stage. While at one time he may

have been considered "not black enough," he was fast approaching "too black" and too closely connected with the ideas of 1960s political leftism.

It is worthwhile to look at the sermons themselves to get a better understanding of the "Wright effect" on the campaign and election. One of the sermons, known by its most controversial statement, "America's chickens are coming home to roost," was actually titled "The Day of Jerusalem's Fall" and was preached on Sunday, September 16, 2001. In this sermon Wright preached about the tragic events on September 11 and addressed the question, "What should our response be, in the face of such unthinkable acts?" He compared September 11 to a biblical story in Psalm 137 in which Jerusalem was attacked, the walls of the city were breeched, and many were brutally and savagely killed. Their attackers and then captors (the Edomites) demanded the people of Jerusalem to sing the "Songs of Zion," and they responded, "How can we sing the songs of the Lord while in a foreign land?" Wright said that for the people of Jerusalem the day of Jerusalem's fall was a "[d]ay of pain, a day of anger, a day of rage, a day of terror, a day of outrage, a day of death, a day of destruction, a day of devastation . . . that changed their lives forever," just like September 11 was for Americans. For "people of faith" in Psalm 137 the response to their day of devastation was "revenge" and "payback." Wright referred to the eighth and ninth verses of Psalm 137, which read, "O Daughter of Babylon, doomed to destruction, happy is he who repays you for what you have done to us—he who seizes your infants and dashes them against the rocks." Wright notes that in the passage the people of Jerusalem moved from reverence to retribution and wanted retribution even from the innocent.[75]

Wright claimed that every public worship service he had heard until then echoed the feelings of the "people of God" in the Psalms—calling for retribution. But instead of revenge the moment after September 11 called for self-examination and social transformation. It was a time for the "people of faith" to focus on their personal relationship with God, loving their families, loving their communities, loving their church family, and loving one another, because one never knows if one will ever see one's loved ones again.[76]

The most controversial part of the sermon (and the thirty seconds that were played over and over in the media) was what Wright called "a faith footnote" to the primary text of his sermon. "I heard Ambassador Peck on an interview yesterday. Did anybody else see or hear him? . . . [H]e pointed out that what Malcolm X said when he was silenced by Elijah Mohammad was in fact true, he said America's chickens are coming home to roost." Wright continued,

We took this country by terror away from the Sioux, the Apache, Arikara, the Comanche, the Arapaho, the Navajo. Terrorism. We took Africans away from their country to build our way of ease and kept them enslaved and living in fear. Terrorism. We bombed Grenada and killed innocent civilians, babies, non-military personnel. We bombed the black civilian community of Panama with stealth bombers and killed unarmed teenagers and toddlers, pregnant mothers and hard working fathers. We bombed Qaddafi's home, and killed his child. Blessed are they who bash your children's head against the rock. . . . We bombed Hiroshima. We bombed Nagasaki, and we nuked far more than the thousands in New York and the Pentagon and we never batted an eye. Kids playing in the playground. Mothers picking up children after school. Civilians, not soldiers, people just trying to make it day by day.[77]

Wright shouted in "the black preaching style" crescendo of his sermon,

Violence begets violence. Hatred begets hatred. And terrorism begets terror-ism. A white ambassador said that y'all, not a black militant. Not a reverend who preaches about racism. An ambassador whose eyes are wide open and who is trying to get us to wake up and move away from this dangerous preci-pice upon which we are now poised.[78]

Taken in context this sermon is a warning against rushing to war to avenge the tragic events on September 11. Wright points to the "insanity of violence" as a cycle that is potentially never ending. Out of context "America's chickens are coming home to roost" served to paint an image of Wright as "un-American" because he was critical of the United States at a time of mourning.

The second sermon was preached two years later, on April 13, 2003, after the war in Iraq had begun. It was titled "Confusing God and Government" but has come to be known as the "God damn America sermon." In this ser-mon Wright claims that in the post-9/11 world Americans should not equate God's will with a particular government's agenda and should not continue in the war in Iraq. He argues that often "governments lie," "governments change," and "governments fail" and that God does not sanction oppressive actions that governments take (even the U.S. government). He gave examples of oppressive governments in the Bible and in world history and examples of when the U.S. government has been oppressive. The most controversial portion of the sermon and the portion that was looped on television was where he focused on the mistreatment of various groups by the U.S. government throughout history including women, Native Americans, Japanese Americans, African Americans, and poor people.

And the United States of America government, when it came to treating her citizens of Indian descent fairly, she failed. She put them on reservations.

When it came to treating her citizens of Japanese descent fairly, she failed. She put them in interment prison camps.

When it came to treating the citizens of African descent fairly, America failed. She put them in chains. The government put them on slave quarters. Put them on auction blocks. Put them in cotton fields. Put them in inferior schools. Put them in substandard housing. Put them in scientific experiments. Put them in the lower paying jobs. Put them outside the equal protection of the law. Kept them out of their racist bastions of higher education, and locked them into positions of hopelessness and helplessness.

The government gives them the drugs, builds bigger prisons, passes a three strike law and then wants us to sing God Bless America. Naw, naw, naw. Not God Bless America. God Damn America! That's in the Bible. For killing innocent people. God Damn America for treating us citizens as less than human. God Damn America as long as she tries to act like she is God and she is Supreme.[79]

To even the most desensitized listener, hearing Wright's words out of context looped over and over during the hotly contested Democratic primaries was a bit shocking. In actuality, when taken in context both of these sermons are squarely within the black prophetic tradition. They express a belief in the ideals of America, what it is supposed to represent—freedom, democracy, and justice for all. They also express the idea that throughout history actions of the U.S. government have betrayed these ideals. Complete with the critique of the U.S. government and the warnings of impending doom, they are not so different from the prophetic sermons preached by Martin Luther King Jr. during the Civil Rights Movement. For example, in a sermon delivered only two months before he was killed King said that nations are often caught up with what he called "the drum major instinct":

"I must be first." "I must be supreme." "Our nation must rule the world." (*Preach it*) And I am sad to say that the nation in which we live is the supreme culprit. And I'm going to continue to say it to America, because I love this country too much to see the drift that it has taken.

God didn't call America to do what she's doing in the world now. (*Preach it, preach it*) God didn't call America to engage in a senseless, unjust war as the war in Vietnam. And we are criminals in that war. We've committed more war crimes almost than any nation in the world, and I'm going to continue to say it. And we won't stop it because of our pride and our arrogance as a nation.

> But God has a way of even putting nations in their place. (*Amen*) The
> God that I worship has a way of saying, "Don't play with me." (*Yes*) He has a
> way of saying, as the God of the Old Testament used to say to the Hebrews,
> "Don't play with me, Israel. Don't play with me, Babylon. (*Yes*) Be still and
> know that I'm God. And if you don't stop your reckless course, I'll rise up and
> break the backbone of your power." (*Yes*) And that can happen to America.
> (*Yes*) Every now and then I go back and read Gibbons' *Decline and Fall of the
> Roman Empire*. And when I come and look at America, I say to myself, the
> parallels are frightening.[80]

In "The Drum Major Instinct" King was criticizing the war in Vietnam, which
made him unpopular in many people's eyes, even in the eyes of strong advocates of the Civil Rights Movement. Like Wright, King was critical of what he
saw as U.S. imperialism, and he warned of impending doom if the course of
foreign policy was not dramatically altered. Likewise, Wright's sermons point
to America's hypocrisy and warn of impending doom if the hypocrisy is not
reconciled. In his sermon immediately following 9/11 the warning was to call
the United States back from the impending "precipice" that would cause attacks
that would lead to more violence. In the second sermon the warning was that
God was not pleased with oppressive governments and that God would eventually damn them to show this displeasure.

These two sermons (out of perhaps hundreds that Wright had delivered
over the years) were used to caricature Wright and Trinity. For Obama, who
as I just mentioned was running a deracialized campaign—one that tried to
minimize issues of race in order to win white support—this obviously posed a
problem. Obama had tried to put some distance between himself and Wright.
They each had acknowledged the possible conflict of interests that might arise
in their relationship as Obama ran for president. When Obama announced
his candidacy, Wright was pulled from the program where he was to give the
invocation. Wright had anticipated that this might happen, saying, "If Barack
gets past the primary, he might have to publically distance himself from me."[81]
But when Wright's comments were aired over and over through the mainstream media, whose audience had rarely if ever been exposed to the black
church prophetic tradition, it had the inevitable effect of racializing Obama.
With each sound bite of the speeches, Barack Obama was becoming blacker
and blacker. Furthermore, he became more and more connected to a certain
type of blackness—sixties, civil rights, protest, sticking it to the man, left versus right blackness—which was opposite of his moving "beyond the lexicon of
the 60s," "turning the page," "[t]here is not a black America and a white America . . . there's a United States of America" candidacy.[82]

It was in this context that Obama took the bold step of confronting the issue of race in an address delivered at the National Constitution Center in Philadelphia titled "A More Perfect Union." In the speech, delivered during the campaign for the hotly contested Pennsylvania primary, he critically addressed the history of white racism in this country, making the point that the Constitution was "stained with the original sin of slavery." He made the argument that racism still existed and that furthermore slavery and the years of Jim Crow segregation had left a legacy that produced contemporary disparities between blacks and whites. However, Obama claimed that the nation had improved and grown steadily toward "a more perfect union" over time. Furthermore, he understood "white resentment" because "most working- and middle-class white Americans don't feel that they have been particularly privileged by their race." According to Obama, both sides are grounded in "legitimate concerns."[83]

Obama unequivocally denounced Wright's looped statements, calling them "wrong," "offensive," and "divisive." This, in a sense, continued the dominant frame that had been presented by the media. But Obama did not denounce Wright, as many called for him to do. Instead he said that Wright was "imperfect" but "like family," and he compared Wright to his maternal grandmother.

> I can no more disown him than I can disown the black community. I can no more disown him than I can my white grandmother—a woman who helped raise me, a woman who sacrificed again and again for me, a woman who loves me as much as she loves anything in this world, but a woman who once confessed her fear of black men who passed by her on the street, and who on more than one occasion has uttered racial or ethnic stereotypes that made me cringe.[84]

He said that he knew more about Wright than the caricatured image that had been presented and that he admired Wright for the things he had done in the community.

> The man I met more than twenty years ago is a man who helped introduce me to my Christian faith, a man who spoke to me about our obligations to love one another; to care for the sick and lift up the poor. He is a man who served his country as a U.S. Marine; who has studied and lectured at some of the finest universities and seminaries in the country, and who for over thirty years led a church that serves the community by doing God's work here on Earth— by housing the homeless, ministering to the needy, providing day care services and scholarships and prison ministries, and reaching out to those suffering from HIV/AIDS.[85]

According to Obama, Wright's problem was that "he had a distorted view of this country," one that "sees white racism as endemic, and that elevates what is wrong with America above all that we know is right with America." According to Obama, Wright had a stagnant view of America.

> It's that he spoke as if our society was static; as if no progress has been made; as if this country—a country that has made it possible for one of his own members to run for the highest office in the land and build a coalition of white and black; Latino and Asian, rich and poor, young and old—is still irrevocably bound to a tragic past. But what we know—what we have seen—is that America can change. That is the true genius of this nation. What we have already achieved gives us hope—the audacity to hope—for what we can and must achieve tomorrow.[86]

In this important speech Obama acknowledged the reality of racism and resulting racial disparities. He said that racism was not a fabrication of black people's imaginations but a historical and present-day reality. Ironically, though, he accused Wright of having no *hope* for the United States to redeem itself from a marred racial past.

The Philadelphia address went over well, and many said Obama did a good job handling the Wright incident. Polls indicated that the Philadelphia speech helped Obama to recover from the Wright controversy and regain his lead over Hillary Clinton.[87]

While Obama's speech was heralded by some as the most important speech delivered in recent history that dealt with the complicated issue of race in this country, it did not totally quell the Wright controversy. The loops kept spinning, and after Wright came back from Africa, where he had been spending a sabbatical, Wright set off on a mission to try to control his own image. Wright did an interview with Bill Moyers, gave a speech at the NAACP's annual Fight for Freedom Fund Dinner in Detroit, and gave a press conference at the National Press Club in Washington, D.C., defending himself and his church.

The Moyers interview can be contrasted to the National Press Club press conference to examine the impact Wright actually had on managing his image. At the Moyers interview Wright explained black liberation theology and the black prophetic tradition. He also provided background on Trinity UCC in particular and his years there as pastor and his relationship with Barack Obama. He explained the two sermons in question within the context of the black church prophetic tradition and black liberation theology. While everyone would not agree with every point that Wright made in the interview, he came across as a well-reasoned intellectual. The bombast did not exceed the content of what he was saying.

The National Press Club event probably had the opposite effect and is probably thought of to have hurt Wright's image and Obama's campaign the most. It was the third and last of the events, and Rev. Graylan Hagler called it a "public relations nightmare." Here Wright repeated some of the more controversial statements about AIDS, minister Louis Farrakhan, and U.S. imperialism. He did not show deference to the press, white America, or Barack Obama. And because of the way the media work, he could not control his image. "Obama's Crazy Minister" again surfaced as a headline as his bombastic style took precedence over what was actually being said. As Bill Moyers observed, Wright truly had "come to personify the black anger that so many whites fear."[88]

Denunciation and Deracialization

On April 29, 2008, the very next day after the event at the National Press Club, Obama finally did what so many had been calling for him to do—he "unequivocally" denounced Wright, saying this was "not the man [he] met 20 years ago." He said,

> I—we started this campaign with the idea that the problems that we face as a country are too great to continue to be divided; that, in fact, all across America people are hungry to get out of the old, divisive politics of the past. I have spoken and written about the need for us to all recognize each other as Americans, regardless of race or religion or region of the country; that the only way we can deal with critical issues like energy and health care and education and the war on terrorism is if we are joined together. And the reason our campaign has been so successful is because we had moved beyond these old arguments. What we saw yesterday out of Reverend Wright was a resurfacing and, I believe, an exploitation of those old divisions. Whatever his intentions, that was the result. It is antithetical to our campaign, it is antithetical to what I am about, it is not what I think America stands for, and I want to be very clear that moving forward Reverend Wright does not speak for me, he does not speak for our campaign. I cannot prevent him from continuing to make these outrageous remarks, but what I do want him to be very clear about, as well as all of you and the American people, is that when I say I find these comments appalling, I mean it. It contradicts everything that I'm about and who I am. And anybody who has worked with me, who knows my life, who has read my books, who has seen what this campaign's about, I think will understand that it is completely opposed to what I stand for and where I want to take this country.[89]

Graylan Hagler makes the astute observation that instead of hurting Obama's campaign, though, the National Press Club event actually ended up benefiting Obama because it moved him to break cleanly from Wright, Trinity, and subsequently the ideas that they had come to represent. Hagler writes,

> The separation of Obama and Wright signaled to White America that Obama was willing to sever relationships with aged concerns and suspicions harbored in the Black community. He therefore was able to declare in clear terms that he was not beholding [sic] to the Black community in his Presidency.[90]

While the public breakup was obviously terrible for Wright and Obama's relationship, for the re-deracialization of Obama's campaign it was probably even better than the Philadelphia address. As Hagler notes, Wright

> delivered to Obama a tremendous favor by allowing the candidate to separate himself and truly overcome race in the eyes of White America. Rev. Jeremiah A. Wright was unintentionally but certainly sacrificed on the altar of racial politics making space for Obama to state clearly and fervently "I am safe, and I am really one of you."[91]

The breakup had helped to re-deracialize Obama's candidacy. Moreover, he was able to do so without risking a decline in black support. Obama had given Jeremiah Wright a chance and did not disown him at first. In his Philadelphia speech he validated black concerns about the vestiges of slavery. He had already proven he was "black enough."

After white Chicago priest Father Pfleger mocked Hillary Clinton from Trinity's pulpit (claiming that Clinton cried after the New Hampshire primaries because she was accustomed to taking advantage of "white entitlement") the Obamas resigned from Trinity altogether—completing the disassociation from Trinity, Wright, and all who had come to symbolize "black radical thought" and thus furthering Obama's deracialization. The next church that Obama appeared in was Apostolic Church of God in Chicago (another black megachurch) on Father's Day, when Obama continued the disassociation from radical racial paradigms of the 1960s in his Father's Day address. In the Father's Day speech, Obama chastised black fathers and said they needed to "take responsibility" for the condition of black communities—yet another step from a political agenda that promotes the Great Society programs of the Johnson era and a healthy not laggard welfare state. This is not a distancing from "blackness" per se—because among black political thought there are very strong "self-help" and "personal responsibility" traditions—but from a certain kind of blackness.

Before Obama broke from Trinity and Wright, Bill Moyers (fellow UCC member and journalist) asked Rev. Wright "What blues are you singing?" due to the way he had been vilified. Wright responded that his blues song would be titled, "What man meant for evil, God meant for good." Wright explained that this is a quote from Joseph in the book of Genesis whose brothers had sold him into slavery. When Joseph and his brothers reunited, the brothers were worried that Joseph would not be able to forgive them for what they had done. Joseph told them not to worry because even though they had sold him into slavery, God used him to help his family to escape a famine. He would not have been able to do this had he not been sold away. Wright said that what while the loops of these excerpts of his sermons were taken out of context and used to vilify him and the church in order to hurt Obama, they actually helped the nation by prompting Obama to deliver a groundbreaking speech about race that moved race relations in the United States forward.

> Those sound bites, those snippets were taken for nefarious purposes but God can take that and do something very powerful with it. [I]n Philadelphia in response to the sound bites . . . Senator Obama made a very powerful speech in terms of our need as a nation to address the whole issue of race. That's something good that's already started because of you guys playing all these sound bites. . . . God can take what you do to try to hurt somebody to help a nation come to grips with truth, to help a nation come to grips with mis-education and to help a nation come to grips with things that we don't like to talk about.[92]

Wright was correct when he observed that the "Wright controversy," which had been used against Obama, would have unintended consequences. In fact, those looped excerpts set off a course of events that eventually allowed Obama to distance himself not only from Wright but also from certain ideas in black political thought that helped him to re-deracialize his campaign. The ultimate "Wright effect" therefore was not to harm Obama's successful run for the presidency of the United States and to make it less likely but to contribute to its success. Jeremiah Wright helped Obama by contributing to his political legitimacy locally in Chicago and among certain blacks nationwide. Wright also contributed to Obama's political campaign ideas about social justice, civil rights, Christianity, hope, efficacy, and collective action. Finally, while the caricaturing of Wright and Trinity and the exploitation of Wright and Obama's relationship was done to disparage Obama and hurt his candidacy by racializing Obama—in the end it allowed Obama to break with certain political ideas that are actually quite prevalent in black political thought in a very public way without experiencing any decline in support in response to his disassociation from these ideas. Obama's break from Wright and Trinity UCC allowed him to further utilize the strategy of deracialization, which was useful to attract white voters and which ultimately allowed him to win the Democratic nomination for the presidency.

The first three U.S. presidential elections of the twenty-first century provide us with valuable insight about the ways in which black megachurches are participating in debates about strategies and philosophies in black politics concerning the best ways to "answer the knock at midnight." In 2000, George W. Bush's campaign promise of faith-based initiatives took center stage, and a number of black megachurch pastors were the target of his message. This highlights the emphasis on cooperating with government that a number of black megachurches have incorporated into their community revitalization strategies. Cooperating with government can be productive. It is a way to harness resources and use them in communities that are resource poor. But cooperation also provides a challenge for black churches to maintain the independence that Mays and Nicholson said was the "genius of the Negro church."[93]

In 2004 moral values and the "culture wars" dominated political discourse, and black megachurches were again at the center of the discussion. This was most interesting, especially in that since the civil rights era politically active black churches have been distinguished by their participation in progressive politics. For students of the black church, we can no longer equate politically progressive with politically active.

Finally, in the 2008 U.S. presidential election we saw the election of the first black president. Black megachurches and their pastors contributed to his campaign in a number of ways—especially Rev. Jeremiah Wright and Trinity UCC (the church Obama attended for over twenty years). Wright and Trinity helped to legitimize Obama as a politician locally and to African Americans and also contributed to his political persona ideas about hope and faith. In the Democratic primary, though, their relationship racialized Obama (a problem for his deracialized campaign). For students of black churches, this begs the question of where black churches in general fit into deracialization campaign strategies.

Conclusion

Black megachurches remind one of the all-encompassing black churches of a bygone era that served as the social centers, political centers, education centers, and economic centers of black communities. Even as society has become more secular, many black megachurches have established their own schools and credit unions, built housing, provided leisure and recreational activities for children and adults, and engaged in the social and political issues of the day. They have helped to make "places of their own" for a number of mostly suburban and middle-class African Americans in post–civil rights America.[94] These churches are not necessarily tied to a geographically contingent community but are an imagined community of somewhat likeminded people drawn together by bundles of services and opportunities. Perhaps the most interesting characteristic of these churches is their diversity. They are particularistic communities with varied theological orientations that guide their public engagement.

While black megachurches are a product of post–civil rights prosperity and consequential social mobility, they also reflect some of the fissures in black politics that are evidenced by the roles that black megachurches played in the first three U.S. presidential elections of the twenty-first century. Their political participation reflects competing ideas about strategies for improving black communities and competing visions for a contemporary "black" political agenda. These churches also illustrate the central role in traditional electoral politics that some black churches still play by producing political candidates, mobilizing voters, and presenting ways of interpreting public policy issues to black communities.

In each of the first three elections of the twenty-first century black megachurches and black megachurch leaders played important roles and at the same time emphasized certain perspectives in the debate about how black politics should address post–civil rights challenges. In 2000 the story was cooperating with government. In 2004 the story was moral pathology—addressing the perceived decline in moral values as a way to address the challenges. And finally in 2008 the story was the reemergence of identity politics versus postracial politics, which is so popular of late.

Most of the research for this book was conducted during the 1990s and the early twenty-first century. Since then there have been dramatic changes in the context, for example, a severe economic downturn, the election of the first black president, and even more crystallized black class divisions. How does the social and political context affect the growth of black megachurches and their public engagement? How will cooperating with government, the prosperity gospel, and the moral pathology thesis (sets of ideas that have particularly taken hold in black megachurches) shift our understanding of the black activist churches in American politics? Likewise, the "Wright effect" on the 2008 election makes me question what role the small subset of churches like Trinity will play in preserving a strategy of "identity politics," especially in the face of talks about a "postracial" America.

This study, while comprehensive, barely scratches the surface of what needs to be understood about the black megachurch phenomenon. Black megachurches are an ever-expanding universe and reflect trends in the broader black church and broader black politics, yet what we have learned about black megachurches sparks a number of additional questions. For example, there needs to be a more in-depth comparison among black megachurches, white megachurches, and other black churches. Also, given the diversity of black megachurch political orientations there are remaining questions about who attends which black megachurches.

In sum, the analysis of the universe of black megachurches and their engagement in public life tells us a lot but also reveals many more questions about the role of black churches in politics. The answers to these questions will reveal more about African American religious life and yield important information about the broader realm of American religion and politics.

NOTES

Chapter 1

1   Martin Luther King Jr., "A Knock at Midnight," 1963, http://mlk-kpp01.stanford.edu/
    index.php/kingpapers/article/a_knock_at_midnight/ (accessed July 7, 2010).
2   King Jr., "A Knock at Midnight."
3   King Jr., "A Knock at Midnight."
4   King Jr., "A Knock at Midnight."
5   Shayne Lee, *T.D. Jakes: America's New Preacher* (New York: New York University Press,
    2005).
6   Jonathan Walton, *Watch This! The Ethics and Aesthetics of Black Televangelism* (New York:
    New York University Press, 2009).
7   Cheryl Gilkes, "Plenty Good Room: Adaptation in a Changing Black Church," *Annals of
    the American Academy of Political and Social Science* 558, no. 1 (1998): 101–21; Andrew Bill-
    ingsley, *Mighty Like a River: The Black Church and Social Reform* (Oxford: Oxford Univer-
    sity Press, 2003); Lawrence Mamiya, "River of Struggle, River of Freedom: Trends among
    Black Churches and Black Pastoral Leadership" (Durham, N.C.: Duke Divinity School,
    2006), http://www.ccts.uab.edu/pages/uploadfiles/Mamiya2006.pdf (accessed July 10,
    2010); Michael Leo Owens, *God and Government in the Ghetto* (Chicago: University of
    Chicago Press, 2007); Fredrick C. Harris, *Something Within: Religion in African Ameri-
    can Political Activism* (Oxford: Oxford University Press, 1999); Anthony Pinn, *The Black
    Church in the Post–Civil Rights Era* (Maryknoll, N.Y.: Orbis Books: 2002); Melissa Harris-
    Lacewell, "From Liberation to Mutual Fund: The Political Consequences of Differing
    Notions of Christ in the African American Church," in Wilson, *From Pews to Polling*

Places, 131–60; R. Drew Smith and Tamelyn Tucker-Worgs, "Megachurches: African-American Churches in Social and Political Context," in *The State of Black America 2000*, ed. Lee Daniels, 180–200 (New York: National Urban League, 2000); Tamelyn Tucker-Worgs, "'Get on Board Little Children, There's Room for Many More': Documenting the Megachurch Phenomenon," *Journal of the Interdenominational Theological Center: Project 2000 Special Edition* 29 (2002): 177–203; Cheryl Hall-Russell, "The African American Megachurch: Giving and Receiving," *New Directions for Philanthropic Fundraising* 48 (2005): 21–29.

8   Hamil Harris, "Growing in Glory," *Emerge Magazine*, April 6, 1997, 49–53. See, e.g., Nicole Maria Richardson, Krissah Williams, and Hamil R. Harris, "The Business of Faith: Black Megachurches Are Turning Pastors into CEOs of Multimillion-dollar Enterprises," *Black Enterprise Magazine*, May 2006, http://www.blackenterprise.com/2006/05/01/the-business-of-faith/ (accessed June 30, 2010); *Ebony Magazine*, "The New Black Spirituality," December 2004, 135–66, http://books.google.com/books?id=HssGvXb2xeMC&lpg=PA1&ots=FazraC8ytl&dq=ebony%20magazine%20megachurch&pg=PA1#v=onepage&q&f=false (accessed June 30, 2010).

9   See, e.g., Andrew Billingsley, "Twelve Gates to the City," in Billingsley, *Mighty Like a River*, 144–69; and C. Eric Lincoln and Lawrence Mamiya, *The Black Church in the African American Experience* (Durham, N.C.: Duke University Press, 1990), 385–88.

10   Gordon Jackson, "No Social Justice, No Spiritual Peace—Black Preachers Take a Stand," *Dallas Examiner*, July 13, 2006.

11   Julia Glick (Associated Press), "Black Leaders Blast Megachurches: Sharpton, Other Black Ministers, Say Black Conservative Churches Focus on the 'Bedroom Morality' of Gay Marriage and Prosperity Preaching," *Black Voices*, June 29, 2006, http://www.blackvoices.com/black_news/canvas_directory_headlines_features/_a/black-leaders-blast-megachurches/20060629094309990001 (accessed October 31, 2010).

12   Hans A. Baer and Merrill Singer, *African-American Religion in the Twentieth Century: Varieties of Protest and Accommodation* (Knoxville: University of Tennessee Press, 1992), 4.

13   C. Michelle Venable-Ridley, "Paul and the African American Community," in *Embracing the Spirit: Womanist Perspectives on Hope, Salvation and Transformation*, ed. Emilie Townes (Maryknoll, N.Y.: Orbis Books, 1997), 212–33.

14   Baer and Singer, *African-American Religion*, 6.

15   W.E.B. Du Bois, *The Souls of Black Folk* (Chicago: A.C. McClurg, 1907); Lincoln and Mamiya, *Black Church*, 199–204.

16   Gayraud Wilmore, *Black Religion and Black Radicalism: An Interpretation of the Religious History of Afro-American People*, 2nd ed. (Maryknoll, N.Y.: Orbis Books, 1983), 53–73; Lincoln and Mamiya, *Black Church*, 203; Baer and Singer, *African-American Religion*, 23.

17   Wilmore, *Black Religion*, 122–29.

18   Lincoln and Mamiya, *Black Church*, 51.

19   Lincoln and Mamiya, *Black Church*, 50–56; Carter G. Woodson, *The History of the Negro Church*, 2nd ed. (Washington, D.C.: Associated Publishers, 1921), 65. Morris Brown was run out of town for trying to start an AME church in the South, 67. As recently as 1989 the founding of African American Catholic Church by Bishop George Stallings occurred for the same purpose as the earlier "independent black church movement" churches—to protest racism. Rosemary D'Apolito, "The Activist Role of the Black Church," *Journal of Black Studies* 31, no. 1 (2000): 96–123.

20   Woodson, *History of the Negro Church*, 220–46.
21   See Evelyn Brooks Higginbotham, *Righteous Discontent: The Women's Movement in the Black Baptist Church, 1880–1920* (Cambridge, Mass.: Harvard University Press, 1992).
22   See Lincoln and Mamiya, *Black Church*, 207–12; also see Lewis Baldwin, "Revisiting the 'All Comprehending Institution,'" in Smith, *New Day Begun*, 15–38. Baldwin gives several possible explanations for the deradicalization of black churches: (1) the problems that black communities were facing overwhelmed black churches, (2) possibly the dominance of the leadership of Booker T. Washington, who emphasized accommodation and self-help, and (3) the death of radical nationalist AME bishop Henry McNeal Turner.
23   See Lewis Baldwin, "Revisiting the "All-Comprehending Institution," in Smith, *New Day Begun*, 15–38.
24   Benjamin E. Mays and Joseph W. Nicholson, "The Genius of the Negro Church," in Sernett, *African American Religious History*, 434.
25   Aldon Morris, *The Origins of the Civil Rights Movement: Black Communities Organizing for Change* (New York: Free Press, 1984). Allison Calhoun-Brown argues that the black church also provided the "nonviolence" ethos of the civil rights movement. Allison Calhoun-Brown, "Upon This Rock: The Black Church, Nonviolence and the Civil Rights Movement," *PS: Political Science & Politics* 33, no. 2 (2000): 168–74.
26   Charles Payne, "Men Led But Women Organized," in *Women in the Civil Rights Movement: Trailblazers and Torchbearers 1941–1965*, edited by Vicki L. Crawford, Jacqueline Anne Rouse, and Barbara Woods (Bloomington: Indiana University Press, 1993), 1–12.
27   Karl Marx, "Contribution to the Critique of Hegel's Philosophy of Right," in *Karl Marx: Early Writings*, ed. and trans. T. B. Baltimore, 43–59 (New York: McGraw-Hill, 1884/1963). See also Lincoln and Mamiya, *Black Church*, for an excellent description of the liberator/opiate debate.
28   Gary T. Marx, *Protest and Prejudice* (New York: Harper & Row, 1967), 94–105. Primarily Marx examines whether blacks who are more religious are more or less likely to participate in civil rights militancy. He finds that as religiosity increases, whether it is measured by attitudinal factors or organizational factors, militancy decreases. Furthermore, those who belong to churches in predominantly white denominations are more likely to be militant than those who belong to churches with historically black denominations. Moreover, those with "otherworldly religious orientations" are less likely than those with "temporal religious orientations" to take part in civil rights militancy.
29   Malcolm X, *The Autobiography of Malcolm X: As Told to Alex Haley* (1965; repr., New York: Ballantine, 1999), 246, 251 (emphasis in original).
30   E. Franklin Frazier, *The Negro Church in America* (New York: Schocken Books, 1964), 90.
31   Frazier, *Negro Church*. In another example of the opiate perspective, Gunnar Myrdal, in *American Dilemma: The Negro Problem and Modern Democracy* (New York: Harper, 1944), described the Negro church as having a great deal of potential power but actually serving as an opiate. He emphasized that black churches were too otherworldly and black preachers were too ignorant (having no formal theological training) to realize their potential power in society.
32   Adolph Reed, "Mythology of the Church in Contemporary Afro-American Politics," in *The Jesse Jackson Phenomenon: The Crisis of Purpose in Afro American Politics* (New Haven, Conn.: Yale University Press, 1986), 41–60.
33   See Wilmore, *Black Religion*; James Cone and G. Wilmore, eds., *Black Theology: A Documentary History Volume One: 1966–1979* (Maryknoll, N.Y.: Orbis Books, 1993).

34   Mary Sawyer traces the role of black religion in inspiring ministers and lay people in both electoral and protest politics. She argues that black politics was heavily influenced by the black church before and after the modern civil rights movement. "The Black Church and Black Politics: Models of Ministerial Activism," *Journal of Religious Thought* 52, no. 1 (1995): 45.

35   C. Eric Lincoln argued that the Negro church that Frazier wrote about changed to the black church after the civil rights movement in *The Negro Church since Frazier*. Lincoln and Mamiya argued that the civil rights movement had a profound impact on the black church and that black churches began to have a more prophetic orientation after the civil rights movement than they had before the movement.

36   James Cone, "Black Theology as Liberation Theology," in *The Westminster Dictionary of Christian Theology*, ed. Alan Richardson and John Bowden, 72–75 (Louisville, Ky.: Westminster, 1983), 74.

37   James Cone, "Black Spirituals: A Theological Interpretation," in *African American Religious Thought: An Anthology*, ed. Cornel West and Eddie S. Glaude, 775–89 (Louisville, Ky.: Westminster John Knox, 2003).

38   Albert J. Raboteau, "African Americans, Exodus and the American Israel," in Johnson, *African-American Christianity*, 1–17.

39   Fredrick C. Harris, "Something Within: Religion as a Mobilizer of African-American Political Activism," *Journal of Politics* 56, no. 1 (1994): 42–68.

40   These are priestly and prophetic, otherworldly and worldly, universalism and particularism, communal and privatistic, charismatic and bureaucratic, and resistance and accommodation.

41   Lincoln and Mamiya, *Black Church*, 10–16.

42   Baer and Singer, *African-American Religion*, ix.

43   Baer and Singer, *African-American Religion*.

44   Baer and Singer, *African-American Religion*, x.

45   Gayle Tate, "How Antebellum Communities Became Mobilized," *National Political Science Review* 4 (1994): 16–29.

46   Higginbotham, *Righteous Discontent*, 1–18.

47   See Harris, *Something Within*; R. Drew Smith, ed., *New Day Begun: African American Churches and Civic Culture in Post–Civil Rights America* (Durham, N.C.: Duke University Press, 2003); James Cavendish, "Church-Based Community Activism: A Comparison of Black and White Catholic Congregations," *Journal for the Scientific Study of Religion* 39, no. 3 (2000): 371–84.

48   Robert Putnam, with Robert Leonardi and Raffaella Nanetti, *Making Democracy Work: Civic Traditions in Modern Italy* (Princeton, N.J.: Princeton University Press, 1993); Robert Putnam, *Bowling Alone: The Collapse and Revival of American Community* (New York: Simon & Schuster, 2000); Theda Skocpol and Morris Fiorina, "Making Sense of the Civic Engagement Debate," in Skocpol and Fiorina, *Civic Engagement in American Democracy*, 1–26.

49   Putnam, *Bowling Alone*, 65.

50   David C. Leege, "Religion and Politics in Theoretical Perspective," in Leege and Kellstedt, *Rediscovering the Religious Factor in American Politics*, 3.

51   Putnam, *Bowling Alone*, 19. While many institutions that enhance social capital such as schools and civic associations favor elite groups that already are more likely to have access

to other political resources, Kay L. Schlozman, Sidney Verba, and Henry Brady found that this is not the case with churches. Churches especially provide access to social capital development to disadvantaged groups as well as advantaged groups. In a sense, churches provide more level playing fields and "bring to the table those who might not otherwise be involved." "Civic Participation and the Equality Problem," in Skocpol and Fiorina, *Civic Engagement in American Democracy*, 454.

52   Robert Wuthnow, "Mobilizing Civic Engagement: The Changing Impact of Religious Involvement," in Skocpol and Fiorina, *Civic Engagement in American Democracy*, 331–66.

53   Kraig Beyerlein and John R. Hipp, "From Pews to Participation: The Effect of Congregation Activity and Context on Bridging Social Capital," *Social Problems* 53, no. 1 (2006): 97–117.

54   Beyerlein and Hipp, "From Pews to Participation," 98.

55   Beyerlein and Hipp, "From Pews to Participation," 100.

56   Beyerlein and Hipp, "From Pews to Participation," 97–117.

57   Wuthnow, "Mobilizing Civic Engagement."

58   Calhoun-Brown, "What a Fellowship: Civil Society, African American Churches, and Public Life," in Smith, *New Day Begun*, 39–57.

59   Lincoln and Mamiya, in *Black Church*, point out that it is the large, mostly middle-class black churches that do the most economic development. Billingsley also points to size as a major determinant in outreach activity in a church in "12 Gates to the City" in *Mighty Like a River*. In their study of churches primarily in the Detroit area, L. Reese and G. Shields found the same. "Faith-Based Institutions and Community Economic Development" (paper, American Political Science Association annual meeting, Boston, September 1998). Walters and Brown also found this to be the case in a study of black churches in Washington, D.C. They also found that churches with financial holdings and larger weekly incomes participated more extensively in community outreach activities. Diane R. Brown and Ronald Walters, *Exploring the Role of the Black Church in the Community* (Washington, D.C.: Mental Health Research and Development Center and Institute for Urban Affairs and Research, Howard University, 1982).

60   R. Drew Smith and Corwin Smidt, "System Confidence, Congregational Characteristics and Black Church Civic Engagement," in Smith, *New Day Begun*, 58–88.

61   Calhoun-Brown, "What a Fellowship," 40.

62   Harris, *Something Within*, 9–10.

63   Harris, *Something Within*, 40.

64   Malcolm X, "The Ballot or the Bullet," April 6, 1964, Detroit, Michigan, before the Cleveland Chapter of the Congress of Racial Equality, http://www.hartford-hwp.com/archives/45a/065.html (accessed July 4, 2010).

65   Christian Smith, "Correcting a Curious Neglect, or Bringing Religion Back In," in *Disruptive Religion: The Force of Faith in Social Movement Activism*, ed. Christian Smith (New York: Routledge, 1996), 1–28, 6.

66   Owens, *God and Government*, 6.

67   Mark Chaves shows that black churches are more likely than white churches to participate in certain activities (education, mentoring, substance abuse prevention, and job training or employee assistance) and more likely to collaborate with secular organizations to provide these social services. *Congregations in America* (Cambridge, Mass.: Harvard University Press, 2004), 54, 69.

68   Lincoln and Mamiya, *Black Church*, xi (emphasis added).

Chapter 2

1   Interview with Rev. Jamal Harrison Bryant, June 15 2007.
2   Interview with Rev. Harold Carter Sr., June 16, 2007.
3   http://faithfulcentral.com/index.php (accessed June 1, 2010).
4   They often broadcast or "podcast" through Streamingfaith.com (an Internet community), which broadcasts radio stations and live events over the Internet.
5   In *Beyond Megachurch Myths: What We Can Learn from America's Largest Churches* (San Francisco: Jossey-Bass, 2007), xviii, Scott Thumma and Dave Travis explain that 2000 average weekend attendance is the number that is widely used in the literature on megachurches. They also explain that "average weekly attendance" is better to count than membership numbers. Membership is not as standardized because churches count membership in different ways.
6   Lincoln and Mamiya, *Black Church*, xii, write that these denominations "account for 80% of black religious affiliation."
7   Thumma and Travis, *Beyond Megachurch Myths*, 140.
8   Thumma and Travis, *Beyond Megachurch Myths*, 6.
9   Anne C. Loveland and Otis B. Wheeler, *From Meetinghouse to Megachurch: A Material and Cultural History* (Columbia: University of Missouri Press, 2003) 3–4.
10   Gilkes, "Plenty Good Room."
11   St. Clair Drake and Horace R. Cayton, *Black Metropolis: A Study of Negro Life in a Northern City* (Chicago: University of Chicago Press, 1993; repr. of 1945 text).
12   Clarence Taylor, *The Black Churches of Brooklyn* (New York: Columbia University Press, 1996).
13   Taylor, *Black Churches*.
14   Thumma and Travis, *Beyond Megachurch Myths*, 24.
15   ITC/Faith Communities Today Project 2000 Megachurch Survey (survey administered by the author). Survey respondents included pastors or assistant ministers of 31 black megachurches (randomly selected from a universe of 66 black megachurches identified in 2000). Project 2000 was a telephone-administered survey. This survey was part of a larger survey of black churches—ITC/Faith Communities Today Project 2000, whose results are reported in Lawrence Mamiya's "River of Struggle, River of Freedom."
16   Caryle Murphy and Hamil R. Harris, "Pastor Warns of Conflict; D.C. Gentrification Called Source of Racial Tension," *Washington Post*, April 8, 2000, Metro, B1.
17   Thumma and Travis, *Beyond Megachurch Myths*, 27.
18   Andrew Billingsley, *Climbing Jacob's Ladder: The Enduring Legacy of African American Families* (New York: Touchstone, 1992).
19   Scott Thumma, Dave Travis, and Warren Bird, "Megachurches Today Survey 2005," 2006, http://hirr.hartsem.edu/megachurch/megastoday2005detaileddata.pdf (accessed January 12, 2010).
20   Kenneth Wald and Allison Calhoun-Brown, *Religion and Politics in the United States* (Lanham, Md.: Rowman & Littlefield, 2007), 28; Walton, *Watch This!*
21   Thumma and Travis, *Beyond Megachurch Myths*, 27.
22   Thumma, "Exploring the Megachurch Phenomena: Their Characteristics and Cultural

Contexts," Hartford Institute for Religious Research, 1996, http://hirr.hartsem.edu/bookshelf/thumma_article2.html (accessed July 19, 2010); Scott Thumma, "The Kingdom, the Power and the Glory: Megachurches in Modern American Society" (Ph.D. diss., Emory University, 1996).

23 Gilkes, "Plenty Good Room," 112.

24 Thumma and Travis, *Beyond Megachurch Myths*, 59.

25 Mamiya, "River of Struggle," 4.

26 Gilkes, "Plenty Good Room," 103.

27 Thumma and Travis, *Beyond Megachurch Myths*, 60.

28 Lincoln and Mamiya, *Black Church*, 289–94.

29 Susie C. Stanley, "Shattering the Stained-Glass Ceiling" in *The Wisdom of the Daughters: Two Decades of the Voice of Christian Feminism*, ed. Rita Halteman Finger and Kari Sandhaas (Philadelphia: Innisfree Press, 2001), 83–86.

30 Smith and Smidt, "System Confidence."

31 See June Manning Thomas and Reynard N. Blake Jr., "Faith-Based Community Development and African American Neighborhoods," in *Revitalizing Urban Neighborhoods*, ed. W. Dennis Keating, Norman Krumholz, and Philip Star (Lawrence: University Press of Kansas, 1996), 131–44; Avis Vidal, *Rebuilding Communities: A National Study of Urban Community Development Corporations* (New York: Community Development Research Center, New School for Social Research, 1992); Reese and Shields, "Faith-Based Institutions."

32 Lincoln and Mamiya, *Black Church*, 256.

33 National Congress for Community Economic Development, "Reaching New Heights: Trends and Achievements of Community-Based Development Organizations," http://www.ncced.org/documents/NCCEDCensus2005FINALReport.pdf (accessed July 5, 2010).

34 Emily Barman and Mark Chaves, "All Creatures Great and Small: Megachurches in Context," *Review of Religious Research* 47 (2005): 329–46.

35 In *From Meetinghouse to Megachurch*, 122–23, Loveland and Wheeler give good and thorough examples of the seeker church services and also how the architecture of the churches serves the seeker strategy.

36 Barman and Chaves, "All Creatures," 338–39.

37 This is similar to what institutionalist scholars call "isomorphism." See, e.g., Paul J. DiMaggio and Walter W. Powell, "The Iron Cage Revisited: Institutional Isomorphism and Collective Rationality in Organizational Fields," *American Sociological Review* 48 (1983): 147–60; Heather Haveman, "Follow the Leader: Mimetic Isomorphism and Entry into New Markets," *Administrative Science Quarterly* 38 (1993): 593–627.

38 Robert L. Boyd, "The Storefront Church Ministry in African American Communities of the Urban North during the Great Migration: The Making of an Ethnic Niche," *Social Science Journal* 35, no. 3 (1998): 319–33.

39 Drake and Cayton, "Churches of Bronzeville," 437.

40 Boyd, "Storefront Church."

41 Bradford Grant, "The Sanctified Warehouse: An Architect Looks at Storefront Churches," *International Review of African American Art* 18, no. 3 (2002): 49–51.

42 Loveland and Wheeler, *From Meetinghouse to Megachurch*, 83.

43 http://www.kingdombuilders.com/templates/cuskingdombuilders/default.asp?id=23260 (accessed July 5, 2010).

44   Andrew Wiese, *Places of Their Own: African American Suburbanization in the Twentieth Century* (Chicago: University of Chicago Press, 2004), 253.

45   Wiese, *Places of Their Own.*

46   John R. Logan, "The New Ethnic Enclaves in America's Suburbs," Lewis Mumford Center for Comparative Urban and Regional Research, University of Albany, SUNY, July 9, 2001, http://mumford.albany.edu/census/suburban/SuburbanReport/page1.html (accessed November 15, 2010).

47   Wiese, *Places of Their Own*, 258.

48   Greenforest Community Baptist Church, http://www.greenforest.org/about_us/our_history.cfm (accessed May 15, 2002).

49   Project 2000.

50   Wiese, *Places of Their Own.* In *Places of Their Own*, Wiese describes black people's efforts to create suburban communities that reflected their aesthetic values and that provided material benefits in the twentieth century.

51   Interview with suburban migrant and megachurch member, March 14, 2008.

52   Gilkes, "Plenty Good Room," 112.

53   Gilkes, "Plenty Good Room," 102.

54   Lincoln and Mamiya, *Black Church.*

55   Interview with suburban migrant and megachurch member, March 14, 2008.

56   Omar McRoberts, *Streets of Glory: Church and Community in a Black Urban Neighborhood* (Chicago: University of Chicago Press, 2003), 59.

Chapter 3

1   "Communal versus privatistic" is taken from Lincoln and Mamiya, *Black Church*, who use these terms to describe one of the set of six dialectical tensions that contribute to their "dialectical model of black church."

2   Robert J. Schreiter, "Theology in the Congregation: Discovering and Doing," in *Studying Congregations: A New Handbook*, ed. Jackson Carroll, Carl Dudley, and William McKinney (Nashville: Abingdon, 1998), 23–39.

3   See, e.g., Kenneth D. Wald, Adam L. Silverman, and Kevin S. Fridy, "Making Sense of Religion in Political Life," *Annual Review of Political Science* 8 (2005): 121–43; Wald and Calhoun-Brown, "Mobilizing Religious Interests," in *Religion and Politics*, 109–42.

4   Wald and Calhoun-Brown, "Religion and Political Action," in *Religion and Politics*, 143–82.

5   Tamelyn Tucker, "Bringing the Church Back In: Black Megachurches and Community Development" (Ph.D. diss., University of Maryland, College Park, 2002); Owens, *God and Government.*

6   Wald, Silverman, and Fridy, "Making Sense of Religion," 132.

7   See, e.g., Aldon Morris, *Origins*; Calhoun-Brown, "What a Fellowship," 39–57; Harris, *Something Within.*

8   Richard Wood, "Religious Culture and Political Action," *Sociological Theory* 13, no. 3 (1999): 307–31, 307; McRoberts, *Streets of Glory*; Ronald Walters and Tamelyn Tucker-Worgs, "Black Churches and Electoral Engagement in the Nation's Capital," in Smith and Harris, *Black Churches and Local Politics*, 99–116.

9   Harris-Lacewell, "Liberation to Mutual Fund," 131.

10   Wald and Calhoun-Brown, *Religion and Politics*, 112.

11   See, e.g., Stephen T. Mockabee, "The Political Behavior of American Catholics: Change and Continuity," in Wilson, *From Pews to Polling Places*, 81–104; Clyde Wilcox and Carin Robinson, "Prayers, Parties and Preachers: The Evolving Nature of Political and Religious Mobilization," in Wilson, *From Pews to Polling Places*, 1–28; Kenneth Wald and Allison Calhoun-Brown, "Religion in the American Context," in *Religion and Politics*, 24–38.

12   Wald and Calhoun-Brown, *Religion and Politics*, 24–38.

13   Wald and Calhoun-Brown, *Religion and Politics*.

14   Wald and Calhoun-Brown, *Religion and Politics*, 30.

15   Wald and Calhoun-Brown, *Religion and Politics*, 32, 35.

16   Corwin Smidt, "Evangelical and Mainline Protestants at the Turn of the Millennium: Taking Stock and Looking Forward," in Wilson, *From Pews to Polling Places*, 34–35.

17   Wald and Calhoun-Brown, *Religion and Politics*.

18   Duke Helfand, "Megastar Pastor Straddles a Divide: Rick Warren Has the Pull to Draw McCain and Obama to the Same Stage. But the Far Right Is Far from Happy," *Los Angeles Times*, August 13, 2008, http://articles.latimes.com/2008/aug/13/local/me-warren13.

19   Lincoln and Mamiya, *Black Church*, 229.

20   Wald and Calhoun-Brown, *Religion and Politics*, 31.

21   Allison Calhoun-Brown, "The Politics of Black Evangelicals: What Hinders Diversity in the Christian Right," *American Politics Research* 26, no. 1 (1998): 81–109.

22   Lyman Kellstedt, "Religion, the Neglected Variable: An Agenda for Future Research on Religion and Political Behavior," in Leege and Kellstedt, *Rediscovering the Religious Factor in American Politics*, 277.

23   In *African-American Religion*, xv, Baer and Singer give three reasons that explain why scholars tend to paint African American religion with one broad brush. "First African Americans until recently received little significant notice in the mainstream media. . . . Second, most of the attention that has been given has been shaped by the tendency of whites and white institutions to project an image of the African American that blurs sharp differences. Finally, in responding to threat and slander from the dominant society, African-American intellectuals—most of whom until this century have been preachers—have been compelled to stress unity and commonality as rather than the celebration of diversity."

24   Elizabeth Cook and Clyde Wilcox, "Religious Orientations and Political Attitudes among Blacks in Washington, DC," *Polity* 22, no. 3 (1990): 527–43.

25   Allison Calhoun-Brown, "Politics of Black Evangelicals."

26   Lincoln and Mamiya, *Black Church*, 225–29, 292, 168.

27   Though the difference between an individual's theological orientation or religiosity and a church's theological orientation is significantly different, the attitudinal religiosity aspects overlap. Therefore, an examination of studies that look at individual religiosity as related to activity and attitudes is helpful to understanding the church's theological orientation and its relation to public engagement activity.

28   Tucker, "Bringing the Church Back In."

29   Results from the larger study are reported in Mamiya, "River of Struggle."

30   Dummy variables were created for twelve dichotomous variables that measured whether the churches took part in various public involvement activities. These activities include community development organizations, housing (affordable housing, senior housing, etc.), economic development (credit unions, employment services, commercial development), social service delivery (food delivery, clothing banks), and political development (standing

ministry concerning political or social activism, issue advocacy in the past twelve months, voter registration, or education in past twelve months).

31 One other variable, the social class level of the church, is also said to impact the public engagement activity of the church (Lincoln and Mamiya, *Black Church*; Jim Castelli and John McCarthy, "Religion-Sponsored Social Service Providers: The Not-So-Independent Sector" [Aspen Institute Nonprofit Sector Research Fund, 1988]). Two questions were asked of the Project 2000 subsample of thirty-one churches that addressed socioeconomic status. One addressed the education level of the church members. The other question addressed the income level of the church members. The ministers were clearly reluctant to answer questions about the education or economic status of their membership. Several of them responded that their membership departments do not account for the financial status or the education status of members. This may reflect some part of black church culture that promotes the idea that although in the secular world individuals may be classified by socioeconomic status, in church everyone has the same status.

32 The variables include whether the church is located in an urban or suburban area (Virginia Hodgkinson and Murray Weitzman, *From Belief to Commitment: The Community Service Activities and Finances of Religious Congregations in the United States* [Washington, D.C.: Independent Sector, 1993], the education level of the minister (Lincoln and Mamiya, *Black Church*), the size of the church (Lincoln and Mamiya, *Black Church*; Mark Chaves, "Religious Congregations and Welfare Reform: Who Will Take Advantage of Charitable Choice?" [Washington, D.C.: Aspen Institute, 1998]; Hodgkinson, et al., *From Belief to Commitment*), being located in the South (Mark Chaves and Lynn Higgins, "Comparing the Community Involvement of Black and White Congregations," *Journal for the Scientific Study of Religion* 31, no. 4 [1992]: 425–40), and the age of the church (Chaves and Higgins, "Comparing the Community Involvement").

33 Wilcox and Robinson, "Prayers, Parties and Preachers," 1–28.

34 Lincoln and Mamiya, *Black Church*; Hunt and Hunt, "Black Religion as Both Opiate and Inspiration of Civil Rights Militance: Putting Marx's Data to the Test," *Social Forces* 56, no. 1 (1977): 1–14; ; Lyman A. Kellstedt and John C. Green, "Knowing God's Many People: Denominational Preference and Political Behavior," in Leege and Kellstedt, *Rediscovering the Religious Factor in American Politics*, 53–71; John C. Green and James L. Guth, "From Lambs to Sheep: Denomination Change and Political Behavior," in Leege and Kellstedt, *Rediscovering the Religious Factor in American Politics*, 100–120; Lonna Rae Atkeson and Joseph Stewart Jr., "Dividing the Flock: Denomination and Political Participation" (paper, American Political Science Association annual meeting, Atlanta, September 1999); Darren E. Sherkat and Christopher G. Ellison, "The Politics of Black Religious Change: Disaffiliation from Back Mainline Denominations," *Social Forces* 70, no. 2 (1991): 431–54.

35 Walton, *Watch This!* 76–77.

36 Walton provides a nuanced description of neo-Pentecostalism and argues that churches that have been influenced by this movement actually fall into three different categories: neo-Pentecostal (those that have ties to traditional Pentecostal denominations), mainline charismatic (those that are mainline black churches, influenced by Pentecostal movements), and word of faith churches. Walton, *Watch This!*

37 Gilkes, "Plenty Good Room," 110.

38 Lincoln and Mamiya, *Black Church*, 386.

39 Walton, *Watch This!* 79–101.

40   Stephen Hunt, Malcolm Hamilton, and Tony Walker, "Tongues, Toronto and the Millennium," in *Charismatic Christianity: Sociological Perspectives* (New York: Palgrave Macmillan, 1997), 2.

41   Paul Morton, interview by Christopher Heron, http://gospelcity.com/artists/interviews/19 (accessed January 10, 2001).

42   Ever Increasing Faith Ministries, http://www.faithdome.org/ (accessed November 1, 2010).

43   This biographical sketch can be read in its entirety on the Crenshaw Christian Center, Los Angeles, Website, www.faithdome.org.

44   TWO was successful in stopping the expansion at that time, and since then it has participated in multiple programs with the University of Chicago, organized the community and built a jobs program, developed a community development corporation (CDC), and built housing. Art Golab, "Bishop Arthur Brazier Spent 48 Years behind Pulpit," *Chicago Sun Times*, November 5, 2010, http://www.suntimes.com/news/metro/2825858,bishop -arthur-brazier-obituary-102210.article (accessed November 5, 2010).

45   Smallwood Williams, *This Is My Story: A Significant Life Struggle: Autobiography of Smallwood Edmond Williams, D.D.* (Washington, D.C.: Willoughby, 1981).

46   Lincoln and Mamiya, *Black Church*, 76.

47   James Cone, "Black Theology and Black Liberation," 106.

48   Kelly Brown Douglas, *The Black Christ* (Maryknoll, N.Y.: Orbis Books, 1994), 4–5.

49   James Cone, "Black Theology and Black Liberation," in Cone and Wilmore, *Black Theology*, 106–13.

50   As quoted in Major Jones, *The Color of God: The Concept of God in Afro American Thought* (Macon, Ga.: Mercer University Press, 2000), 3.

51   James Cone and Gayraud Wilmore, "Introduction," in Cone and Wilmore, *Black Theology*, 89–91.

52   Joseph Washington Jr., "Are American Negro Churches Christian?" in Cone and Wilmore, *Black Theology*, 92–100, 100.

53   Cone and Wilmore, "Introduction," 89–91.

54   Lincoln and Mamiya, *Black Church*.

55   Wilmore, *Black Religion*.

56   Harris-Lacewell, "Liberation to Mutual Fund," 140.

57   Matthew 25:35-36 reads, "[F]or I was hungry and you gave me food, I was thirsty and you gave me something to drink, I was a stranger and you welcomed me, I was naked you gave me clothing, I was sick and you took care of me, I was in prison and you visited me." This indicates that this church also sees it as a part of their responsibility to engage in servicing people's everyday needs.

58   Cone, "Black Theology and Black Liberation," 106.

59   Douglas, *Black Christ*.

60   James Cone, "The White Church and Black Power," in Cone and Wilmore, *Black Theology*, 70–71.

61   Allison Calhoun-Brown, "The Image of God: Black Theology and Racial Empowerment in the African American Community," *Review of Religious Research* 40, no. 3 (1999): 197–213; Harris-Lacewell, "Liberation to Mutual Fund," 131–60.

62   Cone, "Black Theology and Black Liberation," 111.

63   Cone, "Black Theology and Black Liberation," 111.

64   Trinity United Church of Christ, Chicago, mission statement, http://www.tucc.org/.

65   St. Johns United Methodist Church, Houston, mission statement, http://stjohnsdown town.org/mission_.html.

66   Lincoln and Mamiya, *Black Church*, chap. 7.

67   Lincoln and Mamiya, *Black Church*, chaps. 7 and 8.

68   David Howard-Pitney, *The Afro-American Jeremiad: Appeals for Justice in America* (Philadelphia: Temple University Press, 2005).

69   Clayborne Carson, "Martin Luther King, Jr. and the African American Social Gospel," in Johnson, *African American Christianity*, 157–77.

70   Walton, *Watch This!*

71   Interview with Rev. Alice Davis, September 20, 1999.

72   Wald and Calhoun-Brown, *Religion and Politics*, 28; also see H. Beecher Hicks Jr., "Challenge to the African American Church: Problems and Perspectives for the Third Millennium," *Journal of Religious Thought* 51, no. 1 (1994): 81–97; Robert Marquand, "'User Friendly' Services Blur Denominational Distinctions," *Christian Science Monitor* 89, no. 95 (April 11, 1997), http://www.csmonitor.com/1997/0411/041197.us.us.3.html (accessed November 8, 2010).

73   Walton, *Watch This!*

74   http://www.fthcm.org/pages/page.asp?page_id=15019.

75   Thumma, "The Kingdom, the Power, and the Glory." Milmon Harrison's examination of the word of faith movement in African American churches also supports this finding. He finds that the nondenominational word of faith movement has influenced denominational black churches. Milmon Harrison, *Righteous Riches: The Word of Faith Movement in Contemporary African American Religion* (Oxford: Oxford University Press, 2005).

76   Robert Woodberry and Christian Smith, "Fundamentalism et al.: Conservative Protestants in America," *Annual Review of Sociology* 24 (1998): 25–56. Woodberry and Smith say that nondenominational churches belong in a "conservative Protestant" category.

77   See Hunt and Hunt, "Black Religion"; Lincoln and Mamiya, *Black Church*, 196–235; Kenneth Wald, Dennis E. Owen, and Samuel S. Hill Jr., "Political Cohesion in Churches," *Journal of Politics* 52, no. 1 (1990): 197–215.

78   Although there is a difference between the percentages of nondenominational and denominational churches that participate in various public engagement activities, when placing these variables into a logistic regression denominational status helps to explain only whether the church has a CDC. These regression models controlled for the pastors' education and whether the church is in an urban or suburban area.

79   Abundant Life Cathedral, Houston, http://www.alcchurch.org/.

80   Harrison, *Righteous Riches*. In the African American religious tradition the prosperity gospel movement is reminiscent of the new age thinking movement exemplified by the religious leader Father Jealous Divine. Divine taught that race was a social construction and that to say something was to make it reality. He preached celibacy, and the members of his church lived in communes that were segregated by sex. He believed in speaking away disease and poverty. Unlike the prosperity gospel churches, Father Divine's peace movement was political. He led a campaign against lynching, and he encouraged his mostly female church to study to pass the literacy test and to register to vote. Rev. Ike is another who comes to mind with the seed money. Beryl Satter, "Marcus Garvey, Father Divine and the

Gender Politics of Race Difference and Race Neutrality," *American Quarterly* 48, no. 1 (1996): 43–76.

81   E. W. Kenyon, *Two Kinds of Faith: Faith's Secret Revealed* (Lynnwood, Wash.: Kenyon's Gospel Publishing, 1969); Harrison, *Righteous Riches*; Walton, *Watch This!* 97.

82   Harrison, *Righteous Riches*; Walton, *Watch This!*

83   Jonathan Walton, *Watch This!*

84   Harrison, *Righteous Riches*, 134.

85   Lee, *T.D. Jakes*, 102; Harrison, *Righteous Riches*; Walton, *Watch This!* 99.

86   Harrison, *Righteous Riches*.

87   Harrison, *Righteous Riches*, 134.

88   Jonathan Walton discusses the popular culture images of "Daddy Rich" and others and says that they are all supposed to reflect Rev. Ike. Walton, *Watch This!*

89   Drake and Cayton, "Churches of Bronzeville," 354–55.

90   James Cone, panelist, "State of the Black Union 2003: The Black Church: Relevant, Repressive or Reborn," Detroit, February, 8, 2003.

91   Walton, *Watch This!*

92   Quoted in John Blake, "Not All at Seminary Welcome Bishop," *Atlanta Journal-Constitution*, May 11, 2006.

93   Harrison, *Righteous Riches*, 9 (emphasis in original).

94   John F. MacArthur, *Charismatic Chaos* (Grand Rapids: Zondervan, 1993), 286.

95   Ed Montgomery, *Breaking the Spirit of Poverty: Six Steps to Take You from Poverty to Prosperity* (Lake Mary, Fla.: Creation House, 1998), 10.

96   Montgomery, *Breaking the Spirit*, 34.

97   Montgomery, *Breaking the Spirit*, 51–59.

98   Harrison, *Righteous Riches*, 11.

99   New Light Christian Center Church, Houston, weekly bulletin, January 3, 1998.

100 Harrison, *Righteous Riches*, 11.

101 www.thepottershouse.org.

102 Lee, *T. D. Jakes*.

103 Lee, *T. D. Jakes*, 107.

104 Lee, *T. D. Jakes*, 110–11.

105 Walton, *Watch This!* 109.

106 Gilkes, "Plenty Good Room," 108.

107 Harris, *Something Within*, 181. Walton, *Watch This!* 95; Harris-Lacewell, "Liberation to Mutual Fund."

108 Lincoln and Mamiya, *Black Church*.

109 Lincoln and Mamiya, *Black Church*, 13.

110 Lincoln and Mamiya, *Black Church*, 13.

Chapter 4

1   Morris, *Origins*; Doug McAdam, *Political Process and the Development of Black Insurgency, 1930–1970* (Chicago: University of Chicago Press, 1999).

2   Lincoln and Mamiya, *Black Church*.

3   Interview with Rev. Dino Woodard, Abyssinian church historian, September 14, 1999.

4   Owens, *God and Government*.

5   Calvin Butts, interview by Calvin Simms, "'The Conversation' with Calvin Simms," *New York Times Magazine*, October 30, 2006, http://www.nytimes.com/ref/multimedia/conversation.html (accessed November 26, 2006).

6   This definition of community development organization (CDO) comes from Gittell et al., who wanted a broader definition of a community development nonprofit than the community development corporation (CDC). They wanted a term that went beyond housing and business development to include activities like "job training, child care, and community organizing." As I researched black megachurch community development nonprofits I saw that this definition that they developed was also appropriate for black megachurch community development nonprofits. Marilyn Gittell, Ortega Bustamante, and Tracy Steffy, *Women Creating Social Capital and Social Change: A Study of Women-Led Community Development Organizations* (New York: Howard Samuels State and Management and Policy Center, Graduate School and University Center of the City University of New York, 1999).

7   Ronald Ferguson and William Dickens, "Introduction," in Ferguson and Dickens, *Urban Problems and Community Development*, 5.

8   Sara Stoutland, "Community Development Corporations: Mission, Strategy and Accomplishments," in Ferguson and Dickens, *Urban Problems and Community Development*, 196.

9   This discussion of the history of CDCs relies on Sara Stoutland's description of the development of CDCs in three stages. Sara Stoutland, "Community Development Corporations: Mission, Strategy and Accomplishments," in Ferguson and Dickens, *Urban Problems and Community Development*, 196–97. Others, such as Neal Peirce and Carol Steinbach, *Corrective Capitalism: The Rise of America's Community Development Corporations* (New York: Ford Foundation, 1987), also provide a good discussion of the history of CDC development. See also Rachal Bratt, *Rebuilding a Low-Income Housing Policy* (Philadelphia: Temple University Press, 1989); Edward G. Goetz, *Shelter Burden: Local Politics and Progressive Housing Policy* (Philadelphia: Temple University Press, 1993); Vidal, *Rebuilding Communities*, and the National Congress for Community Economic Development, "Reaching New Heights" (2006) Census of CDCs. These authors especially describe the later CDCs (post-1980s) and their emphasis on and contribution to low-income housing development.

10   Peter Dreier and J. David Hulshanski, "The Limits of Localism: Progressive Housing Policies in Boston, 1984–89," *Urban Affairs Quarterly* 26, no. 2 (1990): 191–216.

11   National Congress for Community Economic Development, "Reaching New Heights: Trends and Achievements of Community-Based Organizations: 5th National Community Development Census," June 27, 2006, http://www.ncced.org/documents/NCCED Census2005FINALReport.pdf (accessed July 5, 2010).

12   Vidal, *Rebuilding Communities*.

13   Vidal, *Rebuilding Communities*; Stoutland, "Community Development Corporations," 198–200.

14   Avis Vidal and Ross Gittell, *Community Organizing: Building Social Capital as a Development Strategy* (Thousand Oaks, Calif.: Sage, 1998).

15   Edward Goetz, *Shelter Burden: Local Politics and Progressive Housing Policy* (Philadelphia: Temple University Press, 1993), 114, 116.

16   Vidal and Gittell, *Community Organizing*.

17   Vidal and Gittell, *Community Organizing*.

18 Rachal Bratt, "CDCs: Contributions Outweigh Contradictions, a Reply to Randy Stoeker," *Journal of Urban Affairs* 19, no. 1 (1997): 23–28.

19 Tony Robinson, "Inner-City Innovator: The Non-Profit Community Development Corporation," *Urban Studies* 33, no. 9 (1996): 1647–90, esp. 1649.

20 Vidal and Gittell, *Community Organizing.*

21 Peirce and Steinbach, *Corrective Capitalism.*

22 Randy Stoeker, "The CDC Model of Urban Redevelopment: A Critique and Alternative," *Journal of Urban Affairs* 19, no. 1 (1997): 1–22; Norman J. Glickman and Lisa J. Servon, "More Than Bricks and Sticks: Five Components of Community Development Corporation Capacity," *Housing Policy Debate* 9, no. 3 (1998): 497–539. See also Nancy Nye and Norman Glickman, "Working Together: Building Capacity for Community Development," *Housing Policy Debate* 11, no. 1 (2000): 163–98. They both examine ways to build the capacity of CDCs. They focus on organizations that encourage partnership between CDCs. These organizations pool funding and attempt to improve the management of CDCs. "Capacity" is operationalized as resources, organization, programs, networking, and political activity.

23 Stoutland, "Community Development Corporations," 197.

24 Morris, *Origins,* 77–100.

25 Gloria B. Frederick, "Organizing around Faith: The Roots and Organizational Dimensions of African American Faith-Based Community Development Corporations" (Ph.D. diss., Rutgers University, 2001), 271.

26 Frederick, "Organizing around Faith," 273.

27 Owens, *God and Government.*

28 Clemetson and Coates argue that black churches are predisposed to community development for three reasons: (1) the strong sense of cooperative economic fostered by the influence of west African culture, (2) the authenticating of the Judeo-Christian tradition, which calls for justice and righteousness, and (3) the creation of a religious system grounded in ministry to both the spiritual and social needs of the community. Robert Clemetson and Roger Coates, *Restoring Broken Places and Rebuilding Communities* (Washington, D.C.: National Congress for Community Economic Development, 1992) .

29 Frederick, "Organizing around Faith," 228–29; Owens, *God and Government.*

30 Owens, *God and Government.*

31 Owens, *God and Government,* 18, 155.

32 Owens, *God and Government,* 155.

33 Owens, *God and Government,* 9.

34 Michael Leo Owens, "Political Action and Black Church-Associated Community Development Corporations," paper presented on COMM-ORG: The On-Line Conference on Community Organizing and Development, May 3–6, 2000, http://comm-org.wisc.edu/papers2000/owensfront.htm (accessed November 4, 2010). Instead, the leaders of the CDCs may engage in these activities themselves, but they do not bring the resources of the CDC to bear on political development. There is also concern about co-optation of the ministers.

35 Vidal, *Rebuilding Communities.*

36 Dennis Judd and Todd Swanstrom, *City Politics: Private Power and Public Policy* (New York: Longman, 2002).

37 Chaves, *Congregations in America.*

38 A church may have more than one type of CDO.

39   Owens, *God and Government.*
40   Abyssinian Development Corporation, http://www.adc.org.
41   Abyssinian Development Corporation, http://www.adc.org (accessed uly 12, 2009).
42   Owens, *God and Government.* For a comprehensive look at black-church-affiliated CDCs, see Owens, "Political Action." In addition to Abyssinian, Owens details the public-private partnerships of other black-church-affiliated CDCs in New York, including several that are affiliated with black megachurches—Allen AME Church, Concord Baptist Church of Christ, and St. Paul Community Baptist Church.
43   Diane Winston, "Black Church Expands Communitarian Tradition," Occasional Report 5, no. 1, Lilly Endowment, Indianapolis, 16.
44   Abyssinian Development Corporation, http://www.adcorp.org/.
45   West Angeles CDC, http://www.westangelescdc.org/.
46   In 2005 the city of Houston erected a fence to stop people from seeking shelter under the Pierce Elevated. This displaced many people, and their whereabouts are really unknown. Some were given motel vouchers. This area is being gentrified. New housing in the area is for young urban professionals. Adjacent is a predominantly black and poor neighborhood that is also being gentrified.
47   According to St. John's website, http://breadoflifeinc.org/ (accessed October 30, 2010).
48   Lawrence H. Mamiya, "A Social History of the Bethel African Methodist Episcopal Church in Baltimore: The House of God and the Struggle for Freedom," in *American Congregations Volume 1: Portraits of Twelve Religious Communities,* ed. James P. Wind and James W. Lewis (Chicago: University of Chicago Press: 1994), 222.
49   Bethel AME history, www.Bethel1.org.
50   Tom Chalkley, "Black Baltimore Rising," *American Legacy,* Summer 2002, 61.
51   Bethel AME history, www.Bethel1.org.
52   Tom Chalkley, "Black Baltimore Rising," 62.
53   Bethel AME ministries, www.bethel1.org (accessed May 15, 2002).
54   Bethel AME is facing the problem that many inner-city black megachurches are facing, which is that it has outgrown its facilities. This over two-hundred-year-old church is planning to relocate to West Baltimore County, Maryland, where the leaders plan to build a three-thousand-seat church. They plan a complex that will include a cafeteria and banquet hall, auditorium, gymnasium, credit union, library, classrooms, family life center and broadcast station, and offices. The expansion of Bethel AME into West Baltimore County caused protest from residents who complained that it would bring too much traffic congestion and groundwater problems (Liz Atwood and Dennis O'Brien, "Engineers Find Site Suitable for Church," *Baltimore Sun,* March 30, 1999). The important question is what will become of the *much needed* CDOs and the efforts in which this church engages in Baltimore City. Will they continue to operate the Outreach Center and their other community development activities? How can they continue their two-hundred-year-old legacy in Baltimore City if they leave Baltimore City?
55   According to many scholars, increasing home ownership is an important component of urban community revitalization. Accordingly, through this "housing counseling" Grimes made the point that Union Temple tried to secure a place in the revitalization of D.C. for low- and moderate-income people and to make sure that they were not displaced. They wanted to "look out for the poor people" especially in the rapidly gentrifying areas of D.C. (interview with Rev. Fred Grimes, Union Temple Baptist Church, September 23, 1999).

56 Samuel Freedman, *Upon This Rock: The Miracles of a Black Church* (New York: Harper-Collins, 1993); Margaret Weir, "Power, Money, and Politics in Community Development," in Ferguson and Dickens, *Urban Problems and Community Development*, 186.

57 Timothy A. Ross, "The Impact of Community Organizing on East Brooklyn 1978–1995" (Ph.D. diss., University of Maryland, College Park, 1996), 191.

58 Freedman, *Upon This Rock*, 332.

59 Ross, "The Impact of Community Organizing."

60 Freedman, *Upon This Rock*. Also see Weir, "Power, Money, and Politics," who points out that the EBC's more overtly "political" activity was much less successful than their housing activity.

61 Scholars, such as Aldon Morris, argue that this is the reason that black ministers became the leaders of political movements. They were relatively free from economic reprisals by the white power structure in the South. In southern cities like Montgomery, Birmingham, and Baton Rouge, church members generally paid the minister a living salary. Morris, *Origins*; Woodson, *History of the Negro Church*.

62 Interview with Rev. Fred Grimes, Union Temple Baptist Church, September 23, 1999.

63 Weir, "Power, Money, and Politics," 185.

64 One of the goals of the Union Temple CDC was to combine this emphasis on housing with welfare-to-work training, in which at the completion of the welfare-to-work program the participants would also own a home. Another goal was to incorporate some of the other community development activities they already participated in and place them under the rubric of the CDC.

65 Rev. Fred Grimes, Union Temple Baptist Church, September 23, 1999.

66 Walters and Tucker-Worgs, "Black Churches."

67 Yolanda Woodlee, "Status Tags No License To Criticize; Attack on Williams Costs Pastor a Perk," *Washington Post*, April 4, 2001.

68 Owens, *God and Government*, 154.

69 Owens, *God and Government*, 188–89.

70 Lincoln and Mamiya, *Black Church*.

71 Harris, *Something Within*.

Chapter 5

1 Stanley, "Shattering the Stained Glass Ceiling," 83–86.

2 Lincoln and Mamiya, *Black Church*, 274.

3 Higginbotham, *Righteous Discontent*, 1.

4 See, e.g., Cheryl Townsend Gilkes, "The Politics of 'Silence': Dual-Sex Political Systems and Women's Traditions in African American Religion," in Gilkes, *If It Wasn't for the Women*, 92–117; Fredrick Harris, "In My Father's House: Religion and Gender in African American Political Life," in *Something Within*, 154–76.

5 Taylor, *Black Churches*, 169.

6 Gilkes, "Politics of 'Silence,'" 93.

7 Higginbotham, *Righteous Discontent*.

8 Maria W. Stewart, "Mrs. Stewart's Farewell Address to Her Friends in the City of Boston (1833)," in *Maria Stewart: America's First Black Woman Political Writer: Essays and Speeches*, ed. Marilyn Richardson (Bloomington: Indiana University Press, 1987), 68.

9   Mary Sawyer, "Black Religion and Social Change: Women in Leadership Roles," *Journal of Religious Thought* 47, no. 2 (1990–1991): 16.

10 Mark L. Chapman, *Christianity on Trial: African-American Religious Thought before and after Black Power* (Maryknoll, N.Y.: Orbis Books, 1996), 135–68.

11 Venable-Ridley, "Paul and the African American Community," 212.

12 Venable-Ridley, "Paul and the African American Community," 212–13.

13 Cheryl Sanders, "Black Women in Biblical Perspective: Resistance, Affirmation and Empowerment," in *Living the Intersection: Womanism and Afrocentrism in Theology*, ed. Cheryl Sanders (Minneapolis: Fortress, 1995), 130–31.

14 See, e.g., Sanders, "Black Women in Biblical Perspective," 121–46.

15 Sanders, "Black Women in Biblical Perspective," 131.

16 Sanders, "Black Women in Biblical Perspective," 131–40; see also Delores Williams, "Hagar's Story: A Route to Black Women's Issues," in *Sisters in the Wilderness: The Challenge of Womanist God-Talk* (Maryknoll, N.Y.: Orbis Books, 1993), 15–29.

17 Along with a handful of other black megachurches, this particular church was an advocate of the Promise Keepers, a primarily white evangelical group dedicated to restoring men to their "rightful" place as heads of households. The Promise Keepers is a gender-restrictive organization that insists that men should become more responsible for their households and should take back their natural role as heads of households from women, even if women do not want to relinquish these roles. It is a religious fundamentalist group very similar to Christian Right groups in rhetoric, except that the Promise Keepers promote racial reconciliation. They make very public efforts to reach out to racial minority groups, especially African Americans, although there are very few African Americans among their rank and file. Like other fundamentalist groups, they ascribe secondary roles to women. R. Lorraine Bernotksy, "Real Men Real Politics: Race and Gender in a Contemporary Men's Religious Movement" (paper, American Political Science Association annual meeting, Atlanta, September 1999).

18 Jualynne Dodson, "Power and Surrogate Leadership: Black Women and Organized Religion," *Sage* 5, no. 2 (1988): 37.

19 Dodson, "Power and Surrogate Leadership," 39.

20 Dodson, "Power and Surrogate Leadership." See also Bernice McNair Barnett, "Invisible Southern Black Women Leaders in the Civil Rights Movement: The Triple Constraints of Gender, Race and Class," *Gender & Society* 7, no. 2 (1993): 162–82. Here Barnett claims that it is primarily in their interaction with the larger white dominant community that black people utilize gender-specific roles that denote hierarchical power.

21 Gilkes traces aspects of the dual-sex system in black churches to more egalitarian west African societies and argues that this "dual-sex organization contrasts with the 'single-sex' system that exists in most of the Western world, where political status-bearing roles are predominantly the preserve of men. In the single-sex system, women can achieve distinction and recognition only by taking on the roles of men in public life and performing them well." Gilkes, "The Politics of 'Silence,'" 107.

22 Gilkes, "The Politics of 'Silence.'"

23 Cheryl Townsend Gilkes, "The Roles of Church and Community Mothers: Ambivalent American Sexism or Fragmented African Familyhood?" in *African-American Religion: Interpretive Essays in History and Culture*, ed. Timothy E. Fulop and Albert J. Raboteau

(New York: Routledge, 1997), 368. For an interesting commentary on Gilkes' "dual-sex system" concept, see Harris, *Something Within*.

24 Gilkes, "The Politics of 'Silence,'" 92–117.

25 See also Hans A. Baer, "The Limited Empowerment of Women in Black Spiritual Churches: An Alternative Vehicle to Religious Leadership," *Sociology of Religion* 65 (1993): 65–82. Baer makes the point that in the "Spiritualist churches," women exhibited more authority than in the Pentecostal churches or in the mainstream black churches. The tradition of ordaining women is older in the Spiritualist church than in the Pentecostal or mainstream black churches. Still, even though women were personally empowered through their church experience, their structural empowerment was limited. Though the church inspired "individual self-assertion, upward mobility, other psychological experience of feeling powerful," it did not lead to "mass mobilizations that change the basic power relations in our society." This is because this theology encourages "individualism" more than "group social change."

26 Taylor, *Black Churches*; Cheryl Sanders, *Saints in Exile: The Holiness-Pentecostal Experience in African American Religion and Culture* (Oxford: Oxford University Press, 1996).

27 Higginbotham, *Righteous Discontent*.

28 Harris, *Something Within*, 154–76.

29 Gilkes, "Politics of 'Silence.'"

30 Lincoln and Mamiya, *Black Church*, 300.

31 Drake and Cayton, "Churches of Bronzeville."

32 Taylor, *Black Churches*.

33 The term "stained-glass ceiling" was coined by feminist sociologist of religion Susie Stanley, "Shattering the Stained Glass Ceiling." She argues that the decline in female clergy in Pentecostal denominations that, early on, ordained women is a result of this "stained-glass ceiling."

34 Williams, *This Is My Story*, 65–66. Bishop Robert C. Lawson led the faction that broke from the Pentecostal Assemblies of the World and formed Church of Our Lord Jesus Christ of the Apostolic Faith. The main doctrinal differences were divorce and women in ministry. The Bible Way Church, led by the late Bishop Smallwood Williams, was established after breaking from the faction.

35 Caryle Murphy, "New Clergy Group Installs Its Leaders: Shiloh Baptist Pastor to Head Organization, Which Includes Women," *Washington Post*, February 9, 1998, Metro, D4. The ceremony was held at Israel Baptist Church, whose pastor, Rev. Morris Shearin, was one of the ministers expelled. Among the others expelled was Rev. Harkins of Nineteenth Street Baptist church, a social and politically active church in Washington, D.C.

36 Murphy, "New Clergy," D04.

37 Harris, "In My Father's House," in *Something Within*.

38 This is because of the differences in denominational traditions and practices. There was not representation from the two Church of God in Christ (COGIC) megachurches in this subsample (COGIC rules do not permit women pastors). But otherwise the subsample was representative of black megachurches.

39 Lincoln and Mamiya, *Black Church*, 287.

40 Not only is it difficult to compare the megachurch data and the black church data because of the significant passage of time in between data collection, but also Harris notes that it is difficult to compare the difference in the question wording of the National Black Politics

Study question and question wording from Lincoln and Mamiya's study. I would emphasize this difficulty in comparison. There is a key difference between Mamiya's (and the megachurch survey's) question, which read, "Now for each one, please say whether you strongly approve, somewhat approve, somewhat disapprove, or strongly disapprove: A woman as a pastor of a church," and the National Black Politics Study which read, "I am going to read some questions and please tell me if you strongly agree, somewhat agree, somewhat disagree: Black churches or places of worship should allow more women to become members of clergy." The difference is that "pastor" often refers to the senior pastor or minister of a church and "clergy" can refer to anyone in the ministry. Some may be opposed to women being the senior pastor of a church but not all women clergy.

41   Lincoln and Mamiya, *Black Church*, 292.

42   One way that women exerted religious leadership in the 1800s and 1900s was through the establishment of churches, many of which are prominent today. Clarence Taylor, *Black Churches*, 171, writes that many of the prominent churches in Brooklyn were originally established by groups of black women, and as they become institutionalized they took on male pastors. This is especially seen throughout the Church of God in Christ and many Spiritualist churches (Baer, "Limited Empowerment"). One black megachurch, First African Methodist Episcopal Church in Los Angeles, was founded by a woman, Biddy Mason, in 1872. FAME Church is the oldest black congregation in the city.

43   Mary Ellen Konieczny and Mark Chaves, "Resources, Race and Female-Headed Congregations in the U.S.," *Journal for the Scientific Study of Religion* 39, no. 3 (2000): 261–72, 261.

44   Gilkes, "Politics of 'Silence.'"

45   New Way Fellowship Church, http://www.newwayfellowship.com/ (accessed July 10, 2010).

46   St. John's United Methodist Church, Houston, mission statement, http://stjohns downtown.org/mission_.html (accessed July 5, 2010) (emphasis added).

47   Tate, "Antebellum Communities," 16-29.

48   Gilkes, "If It Wasn't for the Women: African American Women, Community Work and Social Change," in Zinn and Dill, *Women of Color in U.S. Society*, 231.

49   Gilkes, "If It Wasn't for the Women," 242.

50   Gittell, Bustamante, and Steffy, *Women Creating Social Capital*.

51   Gittell, Bustamante, and Steffy, *Women Creating Social Capital*. Gittell et al. examine 108 women-led CDCs in seven urban and two rural areas that had a *significant presence* of women-led community-based organizations.

52   Gittell, Bustamante, and Steffy, *Women Creating Social Capital*, 10.

53   Gittell, Bustamante, and Steffy, *Women Creating Social Capital*. Women who work in women-led CDCs are both professional women and community activists with knowledge of the history of the community. Sometimes there is a conflict between hiring women who have the technical skills for the job and may not be members of or have connections to the community and those who are community activists and have a standing in the community but may not have the technical skills. As for their staffs, women-led CDOs are more likely to invest in individuals who may not already have the technical skills suited for the job, and several report that they take into account women's family roles and domestic responsibilities in their families (especially considering that this community development work is often labor intensive and not a "nine to five" job).

54   Gittell, Bustamante, and Steffy, *Women Creating Social Capital*, 124.

55   Gittell, Bustamante, and Steffy, *Women Creating Social Capital*, 133.
56   Gittell, Bustamante, and Steffy, *Women Creating Social Capital*.

Chapter 6

1   Wiese, *Places of Their Own*.
2   Wiese, *Places of Their Own*, 255.
3   Ellen Berry, "Atlanta 'Legacy' March Troubles Rights Leaders: King's Daughter in Anti-Gay Marriage Protest," *Los Angeles Times*, December 11, 2004.
4   Berry, "Atlanta 'Legacy' March."
5   Ellen Berry, "March Clouded by Stand on Gay Unions," *Los Angeles Times*, December 11, 2004, http://articles.latimes.com/2004/dec/11/nation/na-march11 (accessed July 5, 2010).
6   Brentin Mock, "Bishop Eddie Long," Southern Poverty Law Center Intelligence Report, Spring 2007, http://www.splcenter.org/intel/intelreport/article.jsp?sid=409 (accessed July 5, 2010).
7   Andrew Wiese, "African American Suburban Development in Atlanta," *Southern Spaces*, September 29, 2006, http://www.southernspaces.org/2006/african-american-suburban-development-atlanta (accessed July 5, 2010).
8   Wiese, "African American Southern Development."
9   Bruce A. Dixon, "Black Mecca: Death of an Illusion: Atlanta Leads Nation in Child Poverty," *Black Commentator* 154 (October 13, 2005), http://www.blackcommentator.com/154/154_cover_dixon_black_mecca.pdf (accessed July 5, 2010).
10   Thomas Shapiro and Melvin Oliver, *Black Wealth, White Wealth: A New Perspective on Racial Inequality* (New York: Routledge, 1997); Linda Faye Williams, *The Constraint of Race: Legacies of White Skin Privilege in America* (University Park: Pennsylvania State University Press, 2003).
11   Robert C. Smith, *We Have No Leaders: African Americans in the Post–Civil Rights Era* (Albany: State University of New York Press, 1996), 279.
12   Katherine Tate, *From Protest to Politics: The New Black Voters in American Elections* (Cambridge, Mass.: Harvard University Press, 1998); Ralph C. Gomes and Linda Faye Williams, eds., *From Exclusion to Inclusion: The Long Struggle for African American Political Power* (Westport, Conn.: Greenwood Press, 1992). Both of these volumes explore the transition of African American politics from movement to electoral politics after the Civil Rights Movement.
13   Ralph Gomes and Linda Faye Williams, "Coalition Politics: Past, Present and Future," in Gomes and Williams, *From Exclusion to Inclusion*, 129–60; Rufus P. Browning, Dale Rogers Marshall, and David H. Tabb, *Racial Politics in American Cities* (New York: Longman Press, 2003).
14   Smith, *We Have No Leaders*; Ronald Walters, "The Challenge of Black Leadership: An Analysis of the Problem of Strategy Shift," *Urban League Review*, no. 5 (1980).
15   Cedric Johnson, *From Revolutionaries to Race Leaders: Black Power and the Making of African American Politics* (Minneapolis: University of Minnesota Press, 2007), xxxix.
16   Cedric Johnson, *From Revolutionaries to Race Leaders*.
17   Richard A. Oppel Jr. and Gustav Niebuhr, "The 43rd President; The Churches; Bush Meeting Focuses on the Role of Religion," *The New York Times*, December 21, 2000, A36.

18   R. Drew Smith, "Black Clergy and the Governmental Sector during George W. Bush's Presidency," in Smith and Harris, *Black Churches and Local Politics*, 187–99; Dana Milbank and Hamil R. Harris "Bush Religious Leaders Meet; President-Elect Begins Faith-Based Initiatives, Reaches for Blacks," *Washington Post*, December 21, 2000, A6, A12.

19   Smith, "Black Clergy."

20   Dana Milbank, "Bush to Host Black Ministers: Faith-Based Initiatives May Circumvent Civil Rights Leaders," *Washington Post*, December 19, 2000, A01.

21   Pearson was ousted from Higher Dimensions when he expressed his controversial views that there was no hell. In May 2009 he was appointed interim senior pastor at Christ Universal Temple, the new thought black megachurch in Chicago founded by Johnnie Coleman. There has been a bit of controversy with his appointment. A number of the members of Christ Universal Temple say that Pearson is not trained in new thought theology and should not be leading the church, even on an interim basis. Margaret Ramirez, "Some Christ Universal Temple Members Oppose Rev. Carton Pearson's Appointment," *Chicago Tribune*, May 11, 2009.

22   Milbank and Harris, "Bush Religious Leaders Meet."

23   Kirbyjon Caldwell, Sermon delivered to Windsor Village congregation, Windsor Village United Methodist Church, Houston, December 17, 2000.

24   Eva T. Thorne and Eugene F. Rivers, "Beyond the Civil Rights Industry: Why Black America Needs a New Politics—and How the Black Church Might Deliver One," *Boston Review* 1, no. 8 (2001), http://bostonreview.net/BR26.2/thorne.html (accessed November 4, 2010).

25   Owens, *God and Government*, 189; *New York Amsterdam News*, "Harlem Center Mall Sacrificed, Butts-Giuliani 'Racist' Feud at Core," February 10, 1999.

26   Owens, *God and Government*.

27   Owens, *God and Government*.

28   Chaves, *Congregations in America*.

29   Smith, "Black Clergy," 190.

30   CNN, "CNN National Exit Poll Data," 2004, http://www.cnn.com/ELECTION/2004/pages/results/states/US/P/00/epolls.0.html (accessed July 5, 2010).

31   CNN, "CNN Election Results, State Ballot Initiatives (2004 Elections)," 2004, http://www.cnn.com/ELECTION/2004/pages/results/ballot.measures/ (accessed July 5, 2010).

32   Morris Fiorina, *Culture Wars? The Myth of the Polarized America* (New York: Longman, 2004); Wald and Calhoun-Brown, *Religion and Politics*; CQ Weekly, "Effect of 'Moral Values' Voters Exaggerated, Say Analysts," November 13, 2004, http://library.cqpress.com.proxy-tu.researchport.umd.edu/cqweekly/weeklyreport108-000001419551 (accessed October 23, 2009).

33   Wald and Calhoun-Brown, *Religion and Politics*, 125.

34   Walton, *Watch This!* 138–39.

35   Adrienne Gaines, "The Political Power of Pentecostals," *Charisma Magazine*, January 31, 2006, http://www.charismamag.com/index.php/component/content/article/260-cover-story/12393-the-bishops-campaign (accessed October 28, 2009).

36   High Impact Leadership Coalition, "About the HILC," http://www.thetruthinblackandwhite.com/About_HILC/ (accessed October 28, 2009).

37   Neela Banerjee, "Black Churches Struggle over Their Role in Politics," *The New York Times*, March 6, 2005, 23.

38   Hamil R. Harris, "Using Politics to Amplify a Message, Bishop Harry Jackson Forges
     Ties with GOP in a Mission to 'Restore America to Its Moral Compass,'" *Washington Post*,
     August 13, 2005.

39   Kelly Brown Douglas, *Sexuality and the Black Church: A Womanist Perspective* (Maryknoll,
     N.Y.: Orbis Books, 1999).

40   Cathy Cohen, *The Boundaries of Blackness: AIDS and the Breakdown of Black Politics* (Chi-
     cago: University of Chicago Press, 1999), 19.

41   Cohen, *Boundaries of Blackness*.

42   Joseph Lowery, "Sermon at Rankin Chapel," Howard University, Rankin Chapel, Wash-
     ington, D.C., April 12, 2008.

43   Tamelyn Tucker-Worgs and Aziza Jones, "Black Megachurches and the 2004 Elections"
     (paper, National Conference of Black Political Scientists meeting, Washington, D.C.,
     March 2005).

44   A. R. Williams, "The Marital Skit: How To Keep Your Husband So the Ho Don't Get
     Him," World Overcomers Christian Church, Memphis, December 9, 2007.

45   A. R. Williams, "The Case against Same Sex Marriage in America," World Overcom-
     ers Christian Church, Memphis, November 30, 2008.; A. R. Williams, "Can a Gay Per-
     son Be a Christian?" World Overcomers Christian Church, Memphis, 2009, http://www
     .worldovercomers.org/video (accessed October 15, 2009).

46   A. R. Williams, "Can a Gay Person Be a Christian?"

47   It is unusual for a black church to explicitly rest its theological orientation on the "founding
     fathers," probably because of the nation's "original sin"—enslavement of African people.
     Still, it is Williams' philosophy that African Americans should be patriotic and even revere
     the "founding fathers." In the supporting documents for this philosophy, World Overcom-
     ers attempts to address the slavery issue by claiming that the "founding fathers" opposed
     slavery and that the broken chain on the original Statue of Liberty symbolizes the freedom
     of enslaved Africans. www.worldovercomers.org (accessed August 5, 2010).

48   E.g., Lincoln and Mamiya's, *Black Church*, study of black churches.

49   Mary Mitchell, "Obama's Better Off Not Playing Pulpit Politics with South Carolina
     Pastor," *Chicago Sun-Times*, February 20, 2007, http://www.suntimes.com/news/politics/
     obamacommentary/264185,CST-NWS-mitch20.stng (accessed July 5, 2010).

50   Laurie Goodstein, "Without a Pastor of His Own, Obama Turns to Five," *The New York
     Times*, March 14, 2009, http://www.nytimes.com/2009/03/15/us/politics/15pastor
     .html?_r=1 (accessed November 7, 2009).

51   Graylan Hagler, "Wright Does Obama a Favor: Wright the Sacrificial Lamb," *BMoreNews*,
     http://www.opednews.com/articles/2/opedne_michael__080502_african_american
     _per.htm (accessed December 14, 2009).

52   Barack Obama, *Dreams from My Father: A Story of Race and Inheritance* (New York: Three
     Rivers Press, 2004), 274.

53   Obama, *Dreams from My Father*, 279.

54   Barack Obama, "Barack Obama Election Night Speech U.S. Senate Race (2004)," Novem-
     ber 2004, http://en.wikisource.org/wiki/Obama_election_night_speech_in_Illinois,
     _2004 (accessed August 5, 2010).

55   Melissa Harris-Lacewell and Jan Junn, "Old Friends, New Alliances: How the 2004 Illi-
     nois Senate Race Complicates the Study of Race and Religion," *Journal of Black Studies* 38,

no. 1 (2007): 30–50; Barack Obama, *The Audacity of Hope: Thoughts on Reclaiming the American Dream* (New York: Vintage, 2008), 249.

56 Rachel L. Swarns, "So Far Obama Can't Take Black Vote for Granted," *The New York Times*, February 2, 2007, http://www.nytimes.com/2007/02/02/us/politics/02obama .html (accessed December 9, 2009).

57 Ta-Nehisi Paul Coates, "Is Obama Black Enough?" *Time*, February 1, 2007, http://www .time.com/time/nation/article/0,8599,1584736,00.html#ixzz0Z1tZoGLA (accessed July 5, 2010).

58 Jeremiah Wright, "Martin Luther King Jr. Celebration Sermon," Howard University, Rankin Chapel, Washington, D.C., January 2007.

59 Obama, *Audacity of Hope*, 244.

60 Obama, *Dreams from My Father*, 246.

61 Obama, *Dreams from My Father*, 245.

62 Obama, *Dreams from My Father*, 286.

63 Obama, *Dreams from My Father*, 282.

64 Jeremiah Wright, "The Audacity of Hope," *Preaching Today*, http://www.preaching today.com/sermons/sermons/audacityofhope.html (accessed July 5, 2010).

65 Obama, *Dreams from My Father*, 294.

66 Obama, *Dreams from My Father*.

67 Obama, *Dreams from My Father*, 452.

68 Barack Obama, "2004 Democratic National Convention Keynote Address: The Audacity of Hope," July 27, 2004, http://www.americanrhetoric.com/speeches/convention2004/ barackobama2004dnc.htm (accessed August 5, 2010).

69 Obama, "2004 Democratic National Convention Keynote."

70 Byron D. Orey and Boris E. Ricks, "A Systematic Analysis of the Deracialization Concept," Faculty Publications, University of Nebraska at Lincoln, Department of Political Science, 2007; Robert C. Smith, "Recent Elections and Black Politics: The Maturation or Death of Black Politics?" *PS: Political Science & Politics* 23, no. 2 (1990): 160–62, http:// www.jstor.org/stable/420059 (accessed June 14, 2010); Carol K. Sigelman, Lee Sigelman, Barbara J. Walkosz, and Michael Nitz, "Black Candidates, White Voters: Understanding Racial Bias in Political Perceptions," *American Journal of Political Science* 39, no. 1 (1995): 243–65, http://www.jstor.org/stable/2111765 (accessed June 14, 2010).

71 Joseph McCormick and Charles Jones, "The Conceptualization of Deracialization," in *Dilemmas of Black Politics*, ed. Georgia Persons (New York: HarperCollins, 1993), 66–84; Orey and Ricks, "A Systematic Analysis," 326.

72 Organizing for America, http://www.barackobama.com/issues/ (accessed June 23, 2010).

73 Edward Herman and David Peterson, "Jeremiah Wright in the Propaganda System," *Monthly Review*, September 2008, http://monthlyreview.org/080901herman-peterson. php (accessed August 5, 2010).

74 Mike Wereschagin, David Brown, and Salena Zito, "Clinton: Wright Would Not Have Been My Pastor," *Pittsburgh Tribune-Review*, March 25, 2008, http://www.pittsburghlive .com/x/pittsburghtrib/news/breaking/s_558930.html (accessed December 8, 2009).

75 Jeremiah Wright, "The Day of Jerusalem's Fall," AC360, September 16, 2001, http:// ac360.blogs.cnn.com/2008/03/21/the-full-story-behind-rev-jeremiah-wrights-911 -sermon/ (accessed August 3, 2010).

76 Wright, "Day of Jerusalem's Fall."

77   Wright, "Day of Jerusalem's Fall."

78   Wright, "Day of Jerusalem's Fall."

79   Jeremiah Wright, "Confusing God and Government," *AC360*, April 13, 2003, http://ac360.blogs.cnn.com/2008/03/21/the-full-story-behind-wright%E2%80%99s-%E2%80%9Cgod-damn-america%E2%80%9D-sermon/ (accessed August 3, 2010).

80   Martin Luther King Jr., "The Drum Major Instinct," February 4, 1968, Martin Luther King, Jr. and the Global Freedom Struggle, http://mlk-kpp01.stanford.edu/index.php/encyclopedia/documentsentry/doc_the_drum_major_instinct/ (accessed November 13, 2009).

81   Jodi Cantor, "A Candidate, His Minister and the Search for Faith," *The New York Times*, April 30, 2007, http://www.nytimes.com/2007/04/30/us/politics/30obama.html?_r=2&pagewanted=all&oref=login (accessed August 5, 2010).

82   Obama, *Audacity of Hope*, 273, 274.

83   Barack Obama, "A More Perfect Union," March 18, 2008, http://my.barackobama.com/page/content/hisownwords (accessed August 3, 2010).

84   Obama, "More Perfect Union."

85   Obama, "More Perfect Union."

86   Obama, "More Perfect Union."

87   "Gallup Daily: Obama Edges Ahead of Clinton," *Gallup Daily Polls*, March 22, 2008, http://www.gallup.com/poll/105529/Gallup-Daily-Obama-Edges-Ahead-Clinton.aspx (accessed June 21, 2010).

88   Jeremiah Wright, interview by Bill Moyers, in *Bill Moyers Journal: Jeremiah Wright Guest*, April 25, 2008. http://www.pbs.org/moyers/journal/04252008/profile.html (accessed July 9, 2010).

89   "Obama Denounces Wright Press Conference April 29, 2008 Transcript," April 29, 2008, http://blogs.suntimes.com/sweet/2008/04/obama_denounces_wright_press_c.html (accessed June 21, 2010).

90   Hagler, "Wright Does Obama a Favor."

91   Hagler, "Wright Does Obama a Favor."

92   Wright, interview by Moyers.

93   Mays and Nicholson, "Genius of the Negro Church."

94   Wiese, *Places of their Own.*

BIBLIOGRAPHY

Atkeson, Lonna Rae, and Joseph Stewart Jr. "Dividing the Flock: Denomination and Political Participation." Paper, American Political Science Association annual meeting, Atlanta, September 1999.

Baer, Hans A. "The Limited Empowerment of Women in Black Spiritual Churches: An Alternative Vehicle to Religious Leadership." *Sociology of Religion* 65 (1993): 65–82.

Baer, Hans A., and Merrill Singer. *African-American Religion in the Twentieth Century: Varieties of Protest and Accommodation.* Knoxville: University of Tennessee Press, 1992.

Baldwin, Lewis. "Revisiting the 'All Comprehending Institution.'" In Smith, *New Day Begun,* 15–38.

Banerjee, Neela. "Black Churches Struggle over Their Role in Politics." *The New York Times,* March 6, 2005.

Barman, Emily, and Mark Chaves. "All Creatures Great and Small: Megachurches in Context." *Review of Religious Research* 47 (2005): 329–46.

Barnett, Bernice McNair. "Invisible Southern Black Women Leaders in the Civil Rights Movement: The Triple Constraints of Gender, Race and Class." *Gender & Society* 7, no. 2 (1993): 162–82.

Bernotksy, R. Lorraine. "Real Men Real Politics: Race and Gender in a Contemporary Men's Religious Movement." Paper, American Political Science Association annual meeting, Atlanta, September 1999.

Berry, Ellen. "Atlanta 'Legacy' March Troubles Rights Leaders: King's Daughter in Anti-Gay Marriage Protest." Los Angeles Times, December 11, 2004.

———. "March Clouded by Stand on Gay Unions." Los Angeles Times, December 11, 2004.

"Bethel AME History." Bethel AME Church (Baltimore). www.Bethel1.org (accessed June 25, 2010).

Beyerlein, Kraig, and John R. Hipp. "From Pews to Participation: The Effect of Congregation Activity and Context on Bridging Social Capital." Social Problems 53, no. 1 (2006): 97–117.

Billingsley, Andrew. Climbing Jacob's Ladder: The Enduring Legacy of African American Families. New York: Touchstone, 1992.

———. Mighty Like a River: The Black Church and Social Reform. Oxford: Oxford University Press, 2003.

Blake, John. "Not All at Seminary Welcome Bishop." Atlanta Journal-Constitution, May 11, 2006.

Boyd, Robert L. "The Storefront Church Ministry in African American Communities of the Urban North during the Great Migration: The Making of an Ethnic Niche." Social Science Journal 35, no. 3 (1998): 319–33.

Bratt, Rachel. Rebuilding a Low-Income Housing Policy. Philadelphia: Temple University Press, 1989.

———. "CDCs: Contributions Outweigh Contradictions, a Reply to Randy Stoeker." Journal of Urban Affairs 19, no. 1 (1997): 23–28.

Brown, Dianne R., and Ronald Walters. Exploring the Role of the Black Church in the Community. Washington, D.C.: Mental Health Research and Development Center and Institute for Urban Affairs and Research, Howard University, 1982.

Browning, Rufus P., Dale Rogers Marshall, and David H. Tabb. Racial Politics in American Cities. New York: Longman Press, 2003.

Bryant, Jamal Harrison. Interview by Tamelyn Tucker-Worgs. June 15, 2007.

Butts, Calvin. Interview by Calvin Simms. "'The Conversation' with Calvin Simms." New York Times Magazine, October 30, 2006. http://www.nytimes.com/ref/multimedia/conversation.html (accessed November 26, 2006).

Calhoun-Brown, Allison. "The Image of God: Black Theology and Racial Empowerment in the African American Community." Review of Religious Research 40, no. 3 (1999): 197–213.

———. "The Politics of Black Evangelicals: What Hinders Diversity in the Christian Right?" American Politics Research 26, no. 1 (1998): 81–109.

———. "Upon This Rock: The Black Church, Nonviolence and the Civil Rights Movement." PS: Political Science & Politics 33, no. 2 (2000): 168–74.

———. "What a Fellowship: Civil Society, African American Churches, and Public Life." In Smith, *New Day Begun*, 39–57.

Cantor, Jodi. "A Candidate, His Minister and the Search for Faith." *The New York Times*, April 30, 2007.

Carson, Clayborne. "Martin Luther King, Jr. and the African American Social Gospel." In Johnson, *African American Christianity*, 157–77.

Carter Sr., Harold. Interview by Tamelyn Tucker-Worgs. June 16, 2007.

Castelli, Jim, and John McCarthy. "Religion-Sponsored Social Service Providers: The Not-So-Independent Sector." Washington, D.C.: Aspen Institute Nonprofit Sector Research Fund, 1988.

Cavendish, James. "Church-Based Community Activism: A Comparison of Black and White Catholic Congregations." *Journal for the Scientific Study of Religion* 39, no. 3 (2000): 371–84.

Chalkley, Tom. "Black Baltimore Rising." *American Legacy*, Summer 2002, 54–56, 58, 61–62, 64, 69.

Chapman, Mark L. *Christianity on Trial: African-American Religious Thought before and after Black Power.* Maryknoll, N.Y.: Orbis Books, 1996.

Chaves, Mark. *Congregations in America.* Cambridge, Mass.: Harvard University Press, 2004.

———. "Religious Congregations and Welfare Reform: Who Will Take Advantage of Charitable Choice?" Washington, D.C.: Aspen Institute, 1998.

Chaves, Mark, and Lynn Higgins. "Comparing the Community Involvement of Black and White Congregations." *Journal for the Scientific Study of Religion* 31, no. 4 (1992): 425–40.

Clemetson, Robert, and Roger Coates. *Restoring Broken Places and Rebuilding Communities.* Washington, D.C.: National Congress for Community Economic Development, 1992.

CNN. "CNN Election Results, State Ballot Initiatives (2004 Elections)." 2004. http://www.cnn.com/ELECTION/2004/pages/results/ballot.measures/ (accessed July 5, 2010).

———. "CNN National Exit Poll Data." 2004. http://www.cnn.com/ELECTION/2004/pages/results/states/US/P/00/epolls.0.html (accessed July 5, 2010).

Coates, Ta-Nehisi Paul. "Is Obama Black Enough?" *Time*, February 1, 2007.

Cohen, Cathy. *The Boundaries of Blackness: AIDS and the Breakdown of Black Politics.* Chicago: University of Chicago Press, 1999.

Cone, James. "Black Spirituals: A Theological Interpretation." In *African American Religious Thought: An Anthology*, edited by Cornel West and Eddie S. Glaude, 775–89. Louisville, Ky.: Westminster John Knox, 2003.

———. "Black Theology and Black Liberation." In Cone and Wilmore, *Black Theology*, 106–13.

————. "Black Theology as Liberation Theology." In *Westminster Dictionary of Christian Theology*, edited by Alan Richardson and John Bowden, 72–75. Louisville, Ky.: Westminster, 1983.

————, panelist. "State of the Black Union 2003: The Black Church: Relevant, Repressive or Reborn." Detroit, February 8, 2003.

————. "The White Church and Black Power." In Cone and Wilmore, *Black Theology*, 66–85.

Cone, James, and Gayraud Wilmore, eds. *Black Theology: A Documentary History Volume One: 1966–1979*. Maryknoll, N.Y.: Orbis Books, 1993.

————. "Introduction." In Cone and Wilmore, *Black Theology*, 89–91.

Cook, Elizabeth, and Clyde Wilcox. "Religious Orientations and Political Attitudes among Blacks in Washington, DC." *Polity* 22, no. 3 (1990): 527–43.

CQ Weekly. "Effect of 'Moral Values' Voters Exaggerated, Say Analysts." November 13, 2004. http://library.cqpress.com.proxy-tu.researchport.umd.edu/cqweekly/weeklyreport108-000001419551 (accessed October 23, 2009).

Crenshaw Christian Center. "Biography of Frederick K. Price." www.faithdome.org (accessed January 10, 2001).

D'Apolito, Rosemary. "The Activist Role of the Black Church." *Journal of Black Studies* 31, no. 1 (2000): 96–123.

Davis, Alice. Interview by Tamelyn Tucker-Worgs. September 20, 1999.

DiMaggio, Paul J., and Walter W. Powell. "The Iron Cage Revisited: Institutional Isomorphism and Collective Rationality in Organizational Fields." *American Sociological Review* 48 (1983): 147–60.

Dixon, Bruce. "Black Mecca: Death of an Illusion: Atlanta Leads Nation in Child Poverty." *Black Commentator* 154 (October 13, 2005). http://www.blackcommentator.com/154/154_cover_dixon_black_mecca.pdf (accessed July 5, 2010).

Dodson, Jualynne. "Power and Surrogate Leadership: Black Women and Organized Religion." *Sage* 5, no. 2 (1988): 37–41.

Douglas, Kelly Brown. *The Black Christ*. Maryknoll, N.Y.: Orbis Books, 1994.

————. *Sexuality and the Black Church: A Womanist Perspective*. Maryknoll, N.Y.: Orbis Books, 1999.

Drake, St. Claire, and Horace R. Cayton. "The Churches of Bronzeville." In Sernett, *African American Religious History*, 435–52.

Dreier, Peter, and J. David Hulshanski. "The Limits of Localism: Progressive Housing Policies in Boston, 1984–89." *Urban Affairs Quarterly* 26, no. 2 (1990): 191–216.

Du Bois, W.E.B. *The Souls of Black Folk*. Chicago: A.C. McClurg, 1907.

Ebony Magazine. "The New Black Spirituality." December 2004, 135–66. http://books.google.com/books?id=HssGvXb2xeMC&lpg=PA1&ots=FazraC8ytl&dq=ebony%20magazine%20megachurch&pg=PA1#v=onepage&q&f=false (accessed June 30, 2010).

Ferguson, Ronald, and William Dickens. "Introduction." In Ferguson and Dickens, *Urban Problems and Community Development*, 1–32.

———, eds. *Urban Problems and Community Development*. Washington, D.C.: Brookings Institution, 1999.

Fiorina, Morris. *Culture Wars? The Myth of the Polarized America*. New York: Longman, 2004.

Frederick, Gloria B. "Organizing around Faith: The Roots and Organizational Dimensions of African American Faith-Based Community Development Corporations." Ph.D. diss., Rutgers University, 2001.

Freedman, Samuel G. *Upon This Rock: The Miracles of a Black Church*. New York: HarperCollins, 1993.

Gaines, Adrienne S. "The Political Power of Pentecostals." *Charisma Magazine*, January 31, 2006. http://www.charismamag.com/index.php/covers/260-cover-story/12393-the-bishops-campaign (accessed October 23, 2009).

"Gallup Daily: Obama Edges Ahead of Clinton." *Gallup Daily Polls*. March 22, 2008. http://www.gallup.com/poll/105529/Gallup-Daily-Obama-Edges-Ahead-Clinton.aspx (accessed June 21, 2010).

Gilkes, Cheryl Townsend. "If It Wasn't for the Women: African American Women, Community Work and Social Change." In *Women of Color in U.S. Society*, edited by Maxine Baca Zinn and Bonnie Thornton Dill, 229–46. Philadelphia: Temple University Press, 1994.

———. *If It Wasn't for the Women: Black Women's Experience and Womanist Culture in Church and Community*. Maryknoll, N.Y.: Orbis Books, 2001.

———. "Plenty Good Room: Adaptation in a Changing Black Church." *Annals of the American Academy of Political and Social Science* 558, no. 1 (1998): 101–21.

———. "The Politics of 'Silence': Dual-Sex Political Systems and Women's Traditions in African American Religion." In Gilkes, *If It Wasn't for the Women*, 92–117.

———. "The Roles of Church and Community Mothers: Ambivalent American Sexism or Fragmented African Familyhood?" In *African-American Religion: Interpretive Essays in History and Culture*, edited by Timothy Fulop and Albert Raboteau, 365–88. New York: Routledge, 1997.

Gittell, Marilyn, Ortega Bustamante, and Tracy Steffy. *Women Creating Social Capital and Social Change: A Study of Women-Led Community Development Organizations*. New York: Howard Samuels State and Management and Policy Center, Graduate School and University Center of the City University of New York, 1999.

Glickman, Norman J., and Lisa J. Servon. "More Than Bricks and Sticks: Five Components of Community Development Corporation Capacity." *Housing Policy Debate* 9, no. 3 (1998): 497–539.

Goetz, Edward G. *Shelter Burden: Local Politics and Progressive Housing Policy*. Philadelphia: Temple University Press, 1993.

Gomes, Ralph, and Linda Faye Williams. "Coalition Politics: Past, Present and Future." In Gomes and Williams, *From Exclusion to Inclusion*, 129–60.

———, eds. *From Exclusion to Inclusion: The Long Struggle for African American Political Power.* Westport, Conn.: Greenwood Press, 1992.

Goodstein, Laurie. "Without a Pastor of His Own, Obama Turns to Five." *The New York Times*, March 14, 2009.

Grant, Bradford. "The Sanctified Warehouse: An Architect Looks at Storefront Churches." *International Review of African American Art* 18, no. 3 (2002): 49–51.

Green, John C, and James L. Guth. "From Lambs to Sheep: Denomination Change and Political Behavior." In Leege and Kellstedt, *Rediscovering the Religious Factor in American Politics*, 100–120.

Grimes, Fred. Interview by Tamelyn Tucker-Worgs. September 23, 1999.

Hagler, Graylan. "Wright Does Obama a Favor: Wright the Sacrificial Lamb." *BMore-News.* http://www.opednews.com/articles/2/opedne_michael_080502_african _american_per.htm (accessed December 14, 2009).

Hall-Russell, Cheryl. "The African American Megachurch: Giving and Receiving." *New Directions for Philanthropic Fundraising* 48 (2005): 21–29.

Harris, Fredrick C. "Something Within: Religion as a Mobilizer of African-American Political Activism." *Journal of Politics* 56, no. 1 (1994): 42–68.

———. *Something Within: Religion in African American Political Activism.* Oxford: Oxford University Press, 1999.

Harris, Hamil R. "Growing in Glory: The Generation of the Megachurch." *Emerge Magazine*, April 6, 1997, 49–53.

———. "Using Politics to Amplify a Message, Bishop Harry Jackson Forges Ties with GOP in a Mission to 'Restore America to Its Moral Compass.'" *Washington Post*, August 13, 2005.

Harris-Lacewell, Melissa. "From Liberation to Mutual Fund: The Political Consequences of Differing Notions of Christ in the African American Church." In Wilson, *From Pews to Polling Places*, 131–60.

Harris-Lacewell, Melissa, and Jan Junn. "Old Friends, New Alliances: How the 2004 Illinois Senate Race Complicates the Study of Race and Religion." *Journal of Black Studies* 38, no. 1 (2007): 30–50.

Harrison, Milmon. *Righteous Riches: The Word of Faith Movement in Contemporary African American Religion.* Oxford: Oxford University Press, 2005.

Haveman, Heather A. "Follow the Leader: Mimetic Isomorphism and Entry into New Markets." *Administrative Science Quarterly* 38 (1993): 593–627.

Helfand, Duke. "Megastar Pastor Straddles a Divide: Rick Warren Has the Pull to Draw McCain and Obama to the Same Stage. But the Far Right Is Far from Happy." *Los Angeles Times*, August 13, 2008.

Herman, Edward, and David Peterson. "Jeremiah Wright in the Propaganda System." *Monthly Review*, September 2008. http://monthlyreview.org/080901herman -peterson.php (accessed August 5, 2010).

Hicks, H. Beecher. "Challenge to the African American Church: Problems and Perspectives for the Third Millennium." *Journal of Religious Thought* 51, no. 1 (1994): 81–97.

Higginbotham, Evelyn Brooks. *Righteous Discontent: The Women's Movement in the Black Baptist Church, 1880–1920.* Cambridge, Mass.: Harvard University Press, 1992.

High Impact Leadership Coalition. "About the HILC." http://www.thetruth inblackandwhite.com/About_HILC/ (accessed October 28, 2009).

Hodgkinson, Virginia, and Mary Weitzman, eds. *From Belief to Commitment: The Community Service Activities and Finances of Religious Congregations in the United States.* Washington, D.C.: Independent Sector, 1993.

Howard-Pitney, David. *The Afro-American Jeremiad: Appeals for Justice in America.* Philadelphia: Temple University Press, 2005.

Hunt, Larry L., and Janet G. Hunt. "Black Religion as Both Opiate and Inspiration of Civil Rights Militance: Putting Marx's Data to the Test." *Social Forces* 56, no. 1 (1977): 1–14.

Hunt, Stephen, Malcolm Hamilton, and Tony Walter. "Tongues, Toronto and the Millennium." In *Charismatic Christianity: Sociological Perspectives*, edited by Hunt, Hamilton, and Walter, 1–16. New York: Palgrave Macmillan, 1997.

Jackson, Gordon. "No Social Justice, No Spiritual Peace—Black Preachers Take a Stand." *Dallas Examiner*, July 13, 2006.

Johnson, Cedric. *From Revolutionaries to Race Leaders: Black Power and the Making of African American Politics.* Minneapolis: University of Minnesota Press, 2007.

Johnson, Paul E., ed. *African-American Christianity: Essays in History.* Berkeley: University of California Press, 1994.

Jones, Major. *The Color of God: The Concept of God in Afro American Thought.* Macon, Ga.: Mercer University Press, 2000.

Judd, Dennis, and Todd Swanstrom. *City Politics: Private Power and Public Policy.* New York: Longman, 2002.

Kellstedt, Lyman. "Religion, the Neglected Variable: An Agenda for Future Research on Religion and Political Behavior." In Leege and Kellstedt, *Rediscovering the Religious Factor in American Politics*, 273–304.

Kellstedt, Lyman A., and John C. Green. "Knowing God's Many People: Denominational Preference and Political Behavior." In Leege and Kellstedt, *Rediscovering the Religious Factor in American Politics*, 53–71.

Kenyon, E. W. *Two Kinds of Faith: Faith's Secret Revealed.* Lynnwood, Wash.: Kenyon's Gospel Publishing, 1969.

King Jr., Martin Luther. "The Drum Major Instinct" (sermon). February 4, 1968. Martin Luther King, Jr. and the Global Freedom Struggle. http://mlk-kpp01.stanford.edu/index.php/encyclopedia/documentsentry/doc_the_drum_major_instinct/ (accessed November 13, 2009).

———. "A Knock at Midnight." 1963. Martin Luther King Jr. Research and Education Institute. http://mlk-kpp01.stanford.edu/index.php/kingpapers/article/a_knock_at_midnight/ (accessed July 26, 2010).

Konieczny, Mary Ellen, and Mark Chaves. "Resources, Race and Female-Headed Congregations in the U.S." Journal for the Scientific Study of Religion 39, no. 3 (2000): 261–72.

Lee, Shayne. T.D. Jakes: America's New Preacher. New York: New York University Press, 2005.

Leege, David C. "Religion and Politics in Theoretical Perspective." In Leege and Kellstedt, Rediscovering the Religious Factor in American Politics, 3–25.

Leege, David C., and Lyman A. Kellstedt, eds. Rediscovering the Religious Factor in American Politics. Armonk, N.Y.: M. E. Sharpe, 1993.

Lincoln, C. Eric, and Lawrence Mamiya. The Black Church in the African American Experience. Durham, N.C.: Duke University Press, 1990.

Logan, John R. "The New Ethnic Enclaves in America's Suburbs," Lewis Mumford Center for Comparative Urban and Regional Research, University of Albany, SUNY, July 9, 2001. http://mumford.albany.edu/census/suburban/SuburbanReport/page1.html (accessed November 15, 2010).

Loveland, Anne C., and Otis B. Wheeler. From Meetinghouse to Megachurch: A Material and Cultural History. Columbia: University of Missouri Press, 2003.

Lowery, Joseph. "Sermon at Rankin Chapel." Howard University, Rankin Chapel, Washington, D.C., April 12, 2008.

MacArthur, John F. Charismatic Chaos. Grand Rapids: Zondervan, 1993.

Mamiya, Lawrence. "River of Struggle, River of Freedom: Trends among Black Churches and Black Pastoral Leadership." Duke Divinity School, Durham, N.C., 2006. http://www.ccts.uab.edu/pages/uploadfiles/Mamiya2006.pdf (accessed July 10, 2010).

———. "A Social History of the Bethel African Methodist Episcopal Church in Baltimore: The House of God and the Struggle for Freedom." In American Congregations Volume 1: Portraits of Twelve Religious Communities, edited by James P. Wind and James W. Lewis, 221–92. Chicago: University of Chicago Press: 1994.

Manning Thomas, June, and Reynard N. Blake Jr. "Faith-Based Community Development and African American Neighborhoods." In Revitalizing Urban Neighborhoods, edited by W. Dennis Keating, Norman Krumholz, and Philip Star, 131–44. Lawrence: University Press of Kansas, 1996.

Marquand, Robert. "'User Friendly' Services Blur Denominational Distinctions."

Christian Science Monitor 89, no. 95 (April 11, 1997). http://www.csmonitor
.com/1997/0411/041197.us.us.3.html (accessed November 8, 2010).

Marx, Gary T. *Protest and Prejudice*. New York: Harper & Row, 1967.

Marx, Karl. "Contribution to the Critique of Hegel's Philosophy of Right." In *Karl Marx: Early Writings*, edited and translated by T. B. Bottomore, 43–59. New York: McGraw-Hill, 1884/1963.

Mays, Benjamin E., and Joseph W. Nicholson. "The Genius of the Negro Church." In Sernett, *African American Religious History*, 423–34.

McAdam, Doug. *Political Process and the Development of Black Insurgency, 1930–1970*. Chicago: University of Chicago Press, 1999.

McCormick, Joseph, and Charles Jones. "The Conceptualization of Deracialization." In *Dilemmas of Black Politics*, edited by Georgia Persons, 66–84. New York: Harper-Collins, 1993.

McRoberts, Omar. *Streets of Glory: Church and Community in a Black Urban Neighborhood*. Chicago: University of Chicago Press, 2003.

Megachurch Member 1. Interview by Tamelyn Tucker-Worgs. March 14, 2008.

Megachurch Member 2. Interview by Tamelyn Tucker-Worgs. March 14, 2008.

Milbank, Dana. "Bush to Host Black Ministers: Faith-Based Initiatives May Circumvent Civil Rights Leaders." *Washington Post*, December 19, 2000, A01.

Milbank, Dana, and Hamil R. Harris. "Bush Religious Leaders Meet; President-Elect Begins Faith-Based Initiatives, Reaches for Blacks." *Washington Post*, December 21, 2000, A6, A12.

Mitchell, Mary. "Obama's Better Off Not Playing Pulpit Politics with South Carolina Pastor." *Chicago Sun-Times*, February 20, 2007.

Mock, Brentin. "Bishop Eddie Long." Southern Poverty Law Center Intelligence Report, Spring 2007. http://www.splcenter.org/intel/intelreport/article.jsp?sid=409 (accessed July 5, 2010).

Mockabee, Stephen T. "The Political Behavior of American Catholics: Change and Continuity." In Wilson, *From Pews to Polling Places*, 81–104.

Montgomery, Ed. *Breaking the Spirit of Poverty: Six Steps to Take You from Poverty to Prosperity*. Lake Mary, Fla.: Creation House, 1998.

Morris, Aldon. *The Origins of the Civil Rights Movement: Black Communities Organizing for Change*. New York: Free Press, 1984.

Morton, Paul. Interview by Christopher Heron. http://gospelcity.com/artists/interviews/19 (accessed January 10, 2001).

Murphy, Caryle. "New Clergy Group Installs Its Leaders: Shiloh Baptist Pastor to Head Organization, Which Includes Women." *Washington Post*, February 9, 1998, Metro, D4.

Murphy, Caryle, and Hamil R. Harris. "Pastor Warns of Conflict, D.C. Gentrification Called Source of Racial Tension." *Washington Post*, April 8, 2000, B1.

Myrdal, Gunnar. *American Dilemma: The Negro Problem and Modern Democracy*. New York: Harper, 1944.

National Congress for Community Economic Development. *Coming of Age: Trends and Achievements of Community-Based Development Organizations*. Washington, D.C.: NCCED, 1998.

———. "Reaching New Heights: Trends and Achievements of Community-Based Organizations: 5th National Community Development Census." June 27, 2006. http://www.ncced.org/documents/NCCEDCensus2005FINALReport.pdf (accessed July 5, 2010).

"New Light Christian Center Church Weekly Bulletin." Houston, Tex.: New Light Christian Center Church, January 3, 1998.

New York Amsterdam News. "Harlem Center Mall Sacrificed, Butts-Giuliani 'Racist' Feud at Core." February 10, 1999.

Nye, Norman, and Norman Glickman. "Working Together: Building Capacity for Community Development." *Housing Policy Debate* 11, no. 1 (2000): 163–98.

Obama, Barack. *The Audacity of Hope: Thoughts on Reclaiming the American Dream*. New York: Vintage, 2008.

———. "Barack Obama Election Night Speech U.S. Senate Race (2004)." November 2004. http://en.wikisource.org/wiki/Obama_election_night_speech_in_Illinois _2004 (accessed August 5, 2010).

———. "2004 Democratic National Convention Keynote Address: The Audacity of Hope." July 27, 2004. http://www.americanrhetoric.com/speeches/convention2004/barackobama2004dnc.htm (accessed August 5, 2010).

———. *Dreams from My Father: A Story of Race and Inheritance*. New York: Three Rivers Press, 2004.

———. "A More Perfect Union." March 18, 2008. http://my.barackobama.com/page/content/hisownwords (accessed August 3, 2010).

———. "Obama Denounces Wright Press Conference April 29, 2008 Transcript." April 29, 2008. http://blogs.suntimes.com/sweet/2008/04/obama_denounces _wright_press_c.html (accessed June 21, 2010).

Oppel Jr., Richard A., with Gustav Niebuhr. "The 43rd President: The Churches; Bush Meeting Focuses on the Role of Religion." *The New York Times*, December 21, 2000, A36.

Orey, Byron D., and Boris E. Ricks. "A Systematic Analysis of the Deracialization Concept." Faculty Publications, University of Nebraska at Lincoln, Department of Political Science, 2007.

Owens, Michael Leo. *God and Government in the Ghetto*. Chicago: University of Chicago Press, 2007.

———. "Policy and Pulpits: Devolution, Urban Microregimes and Black Churches." Paper, American Political Science Association annual meeting, San Francisco, August 29–September 2, 2001.

————. "Political Action and Black Church-Associated Community Development Corporations." Paper presented on COMM-ORG: The On-Line Conference on Community Organizing and Development, May 3–6, 2000. http://comm-org .wisc.edu/papers2000/owensfront.htm (accessed November 4, 2010).

Payne, Charles. "Men Led But Women Organized." In *Women in the Civil Rights Movement: Trailblazers and Torchbearers 1941–1965*, edited by Vicki L. Crawford, Jacqueline Anne Rouse, and Barbara Woods, 1–12. Bloomington: Indiana University Press, 1993.

Peirce, Neal, and Carol Steinbach. *Corrective Capitalism: The Rise of America's Community Development Corporations*. New York: Ford Foundation, 1987.

Pinn, Anthony. *The Black Church in the Post–Civil Rights Era*. Maryknoll, N.Y.: Orbis Books, 2002.

Putnam, Robert. *Bowling Alone: The Collapse and Revival of American Community*. New York: Simon & Schuster, 2000.

Putnam, Robert, with Robert Leonardi and Raffaella Nanetti. *Making Democracy Work: Civic Traditions in Modern Italy*. Princeton, N.J.: Princeton University Press, 1993.

Raboteau, Albert. "African Americans, Exodus and the American Israel." In Johnson, *African-American Christianity*, 1–17.

Ramirez, Margaret. "Some Christ Universal Temple Members Oppose Rev. Carton Pearson's Appointment." *Chicago Tribune*, May 11, 2009.

Reed, Adolph. *The Jesse Jackson Phenomenon: The Crisis of Purpose in Afro American Politics*. New Haven, Conn.: Yale University Press, 1986.

Reese, Laura, and Gary Shields. "Faith-Based Institutions and Community Economic Development." Paper, American Political Science Association annual meeting, Boston, September 1998.

Richardson, Nicole Maria, Krissah Williams, and Hamil Harris. "The Business of Faith: Black Megachurches Are Turning Pastors into CEOs of Multimillion-Dollar Enterprises." *Black Enterprise Magazine*, May 2006. http://www.blackenterprise. com/2006/05/01/the-business-of-faith/.

Robinson, Tony. "Inner-City Innovator: The Non-Profit Community Development Corporation." *Urban Studies* 33, no. 9 (1996): 1647–90.

Ross, Timothy A. "The Impact of Community Organizing on East Brooklyn 1978–1995." Ph.D. diss., University of Maryland, College Park.

Sanders, Cheryl. "Black Women in Biblical Perspective: Resistance, Affirmation and Empowerment." In *Living the Intersection: Womanism and Afrocentrism in Theology*, edited by Cheryl Sanders, 121–46. Minneapolis: Fortress, 1995.

————. *Saints in Exile: The Holiness-Pentecostal Experience in African American Religion and Culture*. Oxford: Oxford University Press, 1996.

Satter, Beryl. "Marcus Garvey, Father Divine and the Gender Politics of Race Difference and Race Neutrality." *American Quarterly* 48, no. 1 (1996): 43–76.

Sawyer, Mary. "The Black Church and Black Politics: Models of Ministerial Activism." *Journal of Religious Thought* 52, no. 1 (1995): 45–62.

———. "Black Religion and Social Change: Women in Leadership Roles." *Journal of Religious Thought* 47, no. 2 (1990–1991): 16–21.

Schlozman, Kay, Sidney Verba, and Henry Brady. "Civic Participation and the Equality Problem." In Skocpol and Fiorina, *Civic Engagement in American Democracy*, 427–59.

Schreiter, Robert J. "Theology in the Congregation: Discovering and Doing." In *Studying Congregations: A New Handbook*, edited by Jackson Carroll, Carl Dudley, and William McKinney, 23–39. Nashville: Abingdon, 1998.

Sernett, Milton C., ed. *African American Religious History: A Documentary Witness.* Durham, N.C.: Duke University Press, 1999.

Shapiro, Thomas, and Melvin Oliver. *Black Wealth, White Wealth: A New Perspective on Racial Inequality.* New York: Routledge, 1997.

Sherkat, Darren E., and Christopher G. Ellison. "The Politics of Black Religious Change: Disaffiliation from Black Mainline Denominations." *Social Forces* 70, no. 2 (1991): 431–54.

Sigelman, Carol, Lee Sigelman, Barbara J. Walkosz, and Michael Nitz. "Black Candidates, White Voters: Understanding Racial Bias in Political Perceptions." *American Journal of Political Science* 39, no. 1 (1995): 243–65.

Skocpol, Theda, and Morris Fiorina, eds. *Civic Engagement in American Democracy.* Washington, D.C.: Brookings Institution, 1999.

———. "Making Sense of the Civic Engagement Debate." In Skocpol and Fiorina, *Civic Engagement in American Democracy*, 1–26.

Smidt, Corwin. "Evangelical and Mainline Protestants at the Turn of the Millennium: Taking Stock and Looking Forward." In Wilson, *From Pews to Polling Places*, 29–51.

Smith, Christian. "Correcting a Curious Neglect, or Bringing Religion Back In." In *Disruptive Religion: The Force of Faith in Social Movement Activism*, edited by Christian Smith, 1–28. New York: Routledge, 1996.

Smith, R. Drew. "Black Clergy and the Governmental Sector during George W. Bush's Presidency." In Smith and Harris, *Black Churches and Local Politics*, 187–99.

———, ed. *New Day Begun: African American Churches and Civic Culture in Post–Civil Rights America*, 58–88. Durham, N.C.: Duke University Press, 2003.

Smith, R. Drew, and Fredrick Harris, eds. *Black Churches and Local Politics: Clergy Influence, Organizational Partnerships and Civic Empowerment.* Lanham, Md.: Rowman & Littlefield, 2005.

Smith, R. Drew, and Corwin Smidt. "System Confidence, Congregational Characteristics and Black Church Civic Engagement." In Smith, *New Day Begun*, 58–88.

Smith, R. Drew, and Tamelyn Tucker-Worgs. "Megachurches: African-American Churches in Social and Political Context." In *The State of Black America 2000*, edited by Lee Daniels, 180–200. New York: National Urban League, 2000.

Smith, Robert C. "Recent Elections and Black Politics: The Maturation or Death of Black Politics?" *PS: Political Science & Politics* 23, no. 2 (1990): 160–62.

———. *We Have No Leaders: African Americans in the Post–Civil Rights Era.* Albany: State University of New York Press, 1996.

Stanley, Susie C. "Shattering the Stained Glass Ceiling." In *The Wisdom of the Daughters: Two Decades of the Voice of Christian Feminism,* edited by Rita Halteman Finger and Kari Sandhaas, 83–86. Philadelphia: Innisfree Press, 2001.

Stewart, Maria. "Mrs. Stewart's Farewell Address to Her Friends in the City of Boston (1833)." In *Maria Stewart: America's First Black Woman Political Writer: Essays and Speeches,* edited by Marilyn Richardson, 65–74. Bloomington: Indiana University Press, 1987.

Stoeker, Randy. "The CDC Model of Urban Redevelopment: A Critique and Alternative." *Journal of Urban Affairs* 19, no. 1 (1997): 1–22.

Stoutland, Sara. "Community Development Corporations: Mission, Strategy and Accomplishments." In Ferguson and Dickens, *Urban Problems and Community Development,* 193–240.

Swarns, Rachel L. "So Far Obama Can't Take Black Vote for Granted." *The New York Times,* February 2, 2007.

Tate, Gayle. "How Antebellum Communities Became Mobilized." *National Political Science Review* 4 (1994): 16–29.

Tate, Katherine. *From Protest to Politics: The New Black Voters in American Elections.* Cambridge, Mass.: Harvard University Press, 1998.

Taylor, Clarence. *The Black Churches of Brooklyn.* New York: Columbia University Press, 1996.

Thorne, Eva T., and Eugene F. Rivers. "Beyond the Civil Rights Industry: Why Black America Needs a New Politics—and How the Black Church Might Deliver One." *Boston Review* 1, no. 8 (2001). http://bostonreview.net/BR26.2/thorne.html (accessed November 4, 2010).

Thumma, Scott. "Exploring the Megachurch Phenomena: Their Characteristics and Cultural Contexts." Hartford Institute for Religious Research, 1996. http://hirr.hartsem.edu/bookshelf/thumma_article2.html (accessed June 19, 2010).

———. "The Kingdom, the Power and the Glory: Megachurches in Modern American Society." Ph.D. diss., Emory University, 1996.

Thumma, Scott, and Dave Travis. *Beyond Megachurch Myths: What We Can Learn from America's Largest Churches.* San Francisco: Jossey-Bass, 2007.

Thumma, Scott, Dave Travis, and Warren Bird. "Megachurches Today Survey 2005." Hartford Institute for Religion Research, 2006. http://hirr.hartsem.edu/megachurch/megastoday2005detaileddata.pdf (accessed January 12, 2010).

Tucker, Tamelyn. "Bringing the Church Back In: Black Megachurches and Community Development." Ph.D. diss., University of Maryland, College Park, 2002.

Tucker-Worgs, Tamelyn. "'Get on Board Little Children, There's Room for Many More': Documenting the Megachurch Phenomenon." *Journal of the Interdenominational Theological Center: Project 2000 Special Edition* 29 (2002): 177–203.

Tucker-Worgs, Tamelyn, and Aziza Jones. "Black Megachurches and the 2004 Elections." Paper, National Conference of Black Political Scientists meeting, Washington, D.C., March 2005.

Venable-Ridley, C. Michelle. "Paul and the African American Community." In *Embracing the Spirit: Womanist Perspectives on Hope, Salvation and Transformation*, edited by Emilie Townes, 212–33. Maryknoll, N.Y.: Orbis Books, 1997.

Vidal, Avis. *Rebuilding Communities: A National Study of Urban Community Development Corporations.* New York: Community Development Research Center, New School for Social Research, 1992.

Vidal, Avis, and Ross Gittell. *Community Organizing: Building Social Capital as a Development Strategy.* Thousand Oaks, Calif.: Sage, 1998.

Wald, Kenneth, and Allison Calhoun-Brown. *Religion and Politics in the United States.* Lanham, Md.: Rowman & Littlefield, 2007.

Wald, Kenneth, Dennis E. Owen, and Samuel S. Hill Jr. "Political Cohesion in Churches." *Journal of Politics* 52, no. 1 (1990): 197–215.

Wald, Kenneth D., Adam L. Silverman, and Kevin S. Fridy. "Making Sense of Religion in Political Life." *Annual Review of Political Science* 8 (2005): 121–43.

Walters, Ronald. "The Challenge of Black Leadership: An Analysis of the Problem of Strategy Shift." *Urban League Review*, no. 5 (1980): 77–88.

Walters, Ronald, and Tamelyn Tucker-Worgs. "Black Churches and Electoral Engagement in the Nation's Capital." In Smith and Harris, *Black Churches and Local Politics*, 99–116.

Walton, Jonathan. *Watch This! The Ethics and Aesthetics of Black Televangelism.* New York: New York University Press, 2009.

Washington Jr., Joseph. "Are American Negro Churches Christian?" In Cone and Wilmore, *Black Theology*, 92–100.

Weir, Margaret. "Power, Money, and Politics in Community Development." In Ferguson and Dickens, *Urban Problems and Community Development*, 139–92.

Wereschagin, Mike, David Brown, and Salena Zito. "Clinton: Wright Would Not Have Been My Pastor." *Pittsburgh Tribune-Review*, March 25, 2008.

Wiese, Andrew. "African American Suburban Development in Atlanta." *Southern Spaces*, September 29, 2006. http://www.southernspaces.org/2006/african-american-suburban-development-atlanta (accessed July 5, 2010).

———. *Places of Their Own: African American Suburbanization in the Twentieth Century.* Chicago: University of Chicago Press, 2004.

Wilcox, Clyde, and Carin Robinson. "Prayers, Parties and Preachers: The Evolving Nature of Political and Religious Mobilization." In Wilson, *From Pews to Polling Places*, 1–28.

Williams, A. R. "Can a Gay Person Be a Christian?" World Overcomers Christian Church, Memphis, 2009.

———. "The Case against Same Sex Marriage in America." World Overcomers Christian Church, Memphis, November 30, 2008.

———. "The Marital Skit: How To Keep Your Husband So the Hoe Don't Get Him." World Overcomers Christian Church, Memphis, December 9, 2007.

Williams, Delores. Sisters in the Wilderness: The Challenge of Womanist God-Talk. Maryknoll, N.Y.: Orbis Books, 1993.

Williams, Linda Faye. The Constraint of Race: Legacies of White Skin Privilege in America. University Park: Pennsylvania State University Press, 2003.

Williams, Smallwood. This Is My Story: A Significant Life Struggle: Autobiography of Smallwood Edmond Williams. Washington, D.C.: Willoughby, 1981.

Wilmore, Gayraud. Black Religion and Black Radicalism: An Interpretation of the Religious History of Afro-American People. 2nd ed. Maryknoll, N.Y.: Orbis Books, 1983.

Wilson, J. Matthew, ed. From Pews to Polling Places: Faith and Politics in the American Religious Mosaic. Washington, D.C.: Georgetown University Press, 2007.

Winston, Dianne. "Black Church Expands Communitarian Tradition." Occasional Report 5, no. 16, Lilly Endowment, Indianapolis.

Wood, Richard. "Religious Culture and Political Action." Sociological Theory 13, no. 3 (1999): 307–31.

Woodard, Dino. Interview by Tamelyn Tucker-Worgs. September 14, 1999.

Woodberry, Robert, and Christian Smith. "Fundamentalism et al.: Conservative Protestants in America." Annual Review of Sociology 24 (1998): 25–56.

Woodlee, Yolanda. "Status Tags No License to Criticize; Attack on Williams Costs Pastor a Perk." Washington Post, April 4, 2001.

Woodson, Carter G. The History of the Negro Church. 2nd ed. Washington, D.C.: Associated Publishers, 1921.

———. "The Negro Church, an All-Comprehending Institution." Negro History Bulletin 3, no. 1 (1939).

Wright, Jeremiah. "The Audacity to Hope." Preaching Today. http://www.preaching today.com/sermons/sermons/audacityofhope.html (accessed July 5, 2010).

———. "Confusing God and Government." AC360, April 13, 2003. http://ac360 .blogs.cnn.com/2008/03/21/the-full-story-behind-wright%E2%80%99s -%E2%80%9Cgod-damn-america%E2%80%9D-sermon/ (accessed August 3, 2010).

———. "The Day of Jerusalem's Fall." AC360, September 16, 2001. http://ac360.blogs. cnn.com/2008/03/21/the-full-story-behind-rev-jeremiah-wrights-911-sermon/ (accessed August 3, 2010).

———. Interview by Bill Moyers. In Bill Moyers Journal: Jeremiah Wright Guest. April 25, 2008. http://www.pbs.org/moyers/journal/04252008/profile.html (accessed July 9, 2010).

————. "Martin Luther King Jr. Celebration Sermon." Howard University, Rankin Chapel, Washington, D.C., January 2007.

Wuthnow, Robert. "Mobilizing Civic Engagement: The Changing Impact of Religious Involvement." In Skocpol and Fiorina, *Civic Engagement in American Democracy*, 331–66.

X, Malcolm. *The Autobiography of Malcolm X: As Told to Alex Haley*. 1965. Repr., New York: Ballantine, 1999.

————. "The Ballot or the Bullet." April 6, 1964. http://www.hartford-hwp.com/archives/45a/065.html (accessed July 4, 2010).

INDEX

239